SALMON P. CHASE.

BENCH AND BAR:

A COMPLETE DIGEST OF THE

WIT, HUMOR, ASPERITIES, AND AMENITIES OF THE LAW.

BY L. J. BIGELOW,

COUNSELLOR-AT-LAW.

With Portraits and Illustrations.

NEW YORK:

HARPER & BROTHERS, PUBLISHERS,

FRANKLIN SQUARE.

1867.

DEDICATION.

TO

HON. ROSCOE CONKLING,

THE ACCOMPLISHED LAWYER,

FINISHED ORATOR, AND SAGACIOUS STATESMAN,

THIS VOLUME

IS RESPECTFULLY DEDICATED BY

THE AUTHOR.

PREFACE.

"WELL planned and well written, the story of the Great Seal would be a rare story," says John Cordy Jeaffreson in his delightful "Book about Lawyers." Thoroughly collected and well arranged, thought I, the anecdotes of the Bench and Bar would make a popular book, not only with lawyers but the general reader; and this volume is the result of that idea. The field was a much wider one than I supposed when I began the work of collection, but it has been faithfully gleaned; and while some may have been overlooked which were well worthy of preservation, I trust that the best specimens of legal wit, humor, and incidents have been gathered in the following pages.

L. J. B.

New York, 1867.

CONTENTS.

LIST OF ILLUSTRATIONS.

1.

The Chancellors of England.

THE BENCH AND THE BAR.

CHAPTER I.

ANECDOTES OF THE LORD CHANCELLORS OF ENGLAND.

THE *Great Seal of England* is the signet of the lord chancellor, who is the first officer of state, being President of the House of Lords, and the head of the judicial system of the kingdom. Although English monarchs have usually had but one great seal at a time, it has from time immemorial been customary to speak of the lord chancellor or lord keeper as holding "*the seals.*" Ambitious lawyers are commonly said to be candidates for "the seals;" and when the House of Lords receives a new president, the fortunate man is applauded for having won "the seals." The term has often created in uninquiring minds a misapprehension that the chancellor is invariably the keeper of at least two seals; and it has even led legal writers into mistake. In the introduction to his "Lives of the Chancellors," Lord Campbell says: "In early times the king used occasionally to deliver to the chancellor several seals of different materials, as one of gold and one of silver, but with the same impression, to be used for the same purpose; and hence we still talk of 'the seals being in commission,' or of a particular individual being 'a candidate for the seals,' meaning the office of lord chancellor; although, with the exception of the rival great seals used by the king and the Parliament during the civil war in the time of Charles I., there has not

SEAL OF WILLIAM THE CONQUEROR.

been for many centuries more than one great seal in existence at the same time." The "great seal" was often mentioned in the plural number as "the seals" because it was made in two parts—the obverse and the reverse of the seal being indeed separate and distinct seals. But few English sovereigns are known to have had two or more contemporaneous great seals; and it is improbable that the monarchs who were thus rich in seals made it a rule to intrust them both or all at the same time to one officer. Kings who had occasion to travel in foreign lands not unfrequently had two different great seals, or a great seal and a fac-simile—one for the use of royalty on his travels, the other for the use of the chancellor intrusted with the conduct of affairs at home; one being in the custody of the keeper in attendance on his liege lord, the other being left with the chief of the High Court of Chancery. But in cases where the two seals have different designs, common prudence would dictate that they should be kept from the grasp of one man; and it can not be doubted that in most instances prudence controlled the action of the crown with regard to this matter, as kings are continually found destroying their discarded seals for the sake of avoiding the confusion and troubles that might ensue if, without an especial reason, they retained in use, or even in existence, seals of diverse patterns. From remote days the destruction of discarded great seals has been accomplished with due ceremony, and, until recent times, with great completeness. It is matter of record that Edward III.'s first seal was broken "in minutas pecias" on October 5, 1327. At that early date the pieces of a destroyed seal were a perquisite of the chancellor, and his perquisite they have remained to this day. In modern times chancellors have jealously preserved the damasked seats that have fallen to them as perquisites of office, regarding them as trophies to be handed down among most

B

precious heir-looms by their descendants to their descendants.

Prior to the fourteenth century the great seal was so perpetually on its travels that a more obstinate vagabond could not have been found in the kingdom. Whithersoever the king went it did its best to dance attendance on the royal person; and, in order that it might the more easily achieve its courtly purpose, special arrangements were made for its entertainment and convenience. In whatever city the monarch tarried, an hospitium or inn was set apart for the residence of the chancellor, his masters, and his clerks. A stout horse was always in readiness, on which the rolls could be packed, and wheresoever the chancellor rested, the rude sofa of the period, a woolsack, gave solace to his aching limbs.

The adventures of the great seal on its travels would of themselves make an amusing book. When Richard I. started for Palestine, he left the government of his realm to Chancellor Longchamp, and took with him the great seal, under the custody of Vice-chancellor or Keeper Malchien. Proud of his office, and obeying the usage of the time, Keeper Malchien always bore the great seal round his neck, to the great admiration of the vagrant and chivalric courtiers. Off Cyprus the good man had the ill luck to topple overboard into the sea and to be drowned, together with the bawble under his charge. Whether Malchien could swim, and whether the weight of the seal and its chain rendered vain his efforts for self-preservation, the record sayeth not. It is enough to know that the great seal and its keeper "went under," as we Americans express it, and were no more seen. Charles II.'s first great seal also found a watery grave in the Severn, having been thrown into that river, so that it might not fall into the hands of Cromwell's soldiers. James II. made away with his great seal

SEAL OF THE COMMONWEALTH.

in 1688. When the foolish, fallen king, disguised and full of fears, stole from Whitehall on the night of December 10 and entered a hackney-coach, the great seal was in his pocket. Clattering over uneven ways, the humble carriage passed through dark and dangerous streets to the horse-ferry, Westminster. At that point the fugitive dismissed the driver, and made the transit of the river in a boat rowed by a single sculler. Half the passage was accomplished, when the sovereign drew forth the seal, and dropped it beneath the gloomy surface of the water. But the grave surrendered its victim. William of Orange used this same seal in the first business of his reign. The exact day of its recovery is unknown; but a fortunate fisherman caught it in his net, and, after his first surprise had subsided, bore it in triumph to the Lords of the Council, who in due course placed it in the hands of the Deliverer. It was used until 1680, when a new great seal, adorned with likenesses of William and Mary, was substituted for the late king's device. On Mary's death William III. had another great seal engraven, from which his consort's image and name were omitted.

One of the strangest accidents that befell George III.'s third great seal occurred at Encombe, in the autumn of 1812. Eldon was then lord chancellor, and was residing at his country seat, when part of the house was destroyed by a fire that broke out at night. With admirable expedition the fire-engine was at work, and Lady Eldon's maid-servants were helping to supply it with water. "It was," wrote Lord Eldon, "really a very pretty sight; for all the maids turned out of their beds, and they formed a line from the water to the fire-engine, handing the buckets; they looked very pretty, all in their shifts." (From all of which it is evident that Eldon, with all his stupidity and gruffness, had an eye for beauty.) But, ere the chancellor found time

SEAL OF WILLIAM AND MARY.

to survey the maid-servants with approval, he had provided for the safety of the great seal, which he was accustomed to keep in his bedchamber. At the first alarm of fire the chancellor hastened out of doors with the great seal, and burying it in a flower-bed, confided it to the care of mother earth. That prudent act accomplished, he ran to the aid of his maid-servants. But when morning came, and the sun looked down on a mansion damaged, not destroyed, by fire, it occurred to Eldon that it was time for him to recover the seal from its undignified concealment. With that intention he bustled off to the long terrace where he had buried the treasure; but, on arriving there, to his lively chagrin and alarm, he found that he had omitted to mark the exact spot of its interment. Whether the grave had been dug in this bed or in that—whether on the right or the left of the gravel walk—whether above or below the fish-tank—he could not say. In his perplexity he sought counsel of Lady Eldon, and by her advice the same maid-servants who had figured so picturesquely by firelight, together with the entire staff of gardeners, were provided with spades, shovels, trowels, pokers, tongs, curling-irons, old umbrellas, and other suitable implements, and were ordered to probe old mother earth in the region of the long terrace, until she delivered up the "pestiferous metal" which had been committed to her in trust. "You never saw any thing so ridiculous," observed his lordship, "as seeing the whole family down that walk probing and digging till we found it." A burden of anxious care must have fallen from the chancellor's mind when the cry of "Found, my lord!" reached his ears.

Another curious danger once befell the great seal. King John, in 1206, in order to raise money for his necessities, put up the great seal at auction, and it was purchased by Walter de Lacy, who paid five thousand marks for it during the term of his natural life, and a grant was made out to him in due form. He held the office six years.

The Lord Chancellor, in the English popular mind, represents all that is most elevated in dignity and power. Besides living at the head of the House of Lords and the judges of the realm, he is the "keeper of the king's conscience," the nominator of all the inferior judges, and by far the largest dispenser of church patronage. The first keeper of the seals who was endowed with the title of lord chancellor was Maurice, who received the great seal in 1067. The incumbents of the office were for a long period ecclesiastics; and they usually enjoyed episcopal or archiepiscopal rank, and lived in the London palaces attached to their sees or provinces. The first keeper of the seals of England was Fitzgilbert, appointed by Queen Matilda soon after her coronation, and there was no other layman appointed till the reign of Edward III. The practice of appointing bishops, however, was soon resumed, and continued without interruption till the fall of Wolsey. After Wolsey came Sir Thomas More and a succession of lawyers, who, with two exceptions, continued to fill the office till Lord Bacon was convicted of corruption, when lawyers being, as a consequence, in bad odor, James I. appointed Bishop Williams, the only Protestant divine who ever held the great seal. Nearly all the lay commoners who have been honored with this high position have been ennobled; and Campbell, in his Lives of the Chancellors, informs us that in his time there were sitting in the House of Lords sixteen peers descended from chancellors in the direct male line. These are known to English law as the "law lords." The same author also tells us that during the last three hundred years six lord chancellors have been impeached—Cardinal Wolsey, Lord Bacon, Lord Keeper Finch, Lord Clarendon, Lord Somers, and Lord Macclesfield, and of these Lord Somers was alone acquitted.

In this connection we must also mention Lord Westbury, who had to resign in 1865, in obedience to the popular will, and under circumstances which indicate pretty clearly that the judicial ermine of England is not entirely free from stain.

THE WIT OF SIR THOMAS MORE.

Sir Thomas More, the most celebrated of the lord chancellors, by reason of his learning, piety, brilliant mind, and tragic death, has left behind him a reputation as the first wit of his rank and age. No lawyer has given better witticisms to the jest-books; and the wide and lasting popularity of his pleasantries is a weighty proof that the multitude can appreciate humor that is free from coarseness, and gayety that has no taint of buffoonery. Like all legal wits, he enjoyed a pun. But though he would condescend to play with words as a child plays with shells on a sea-beach, he could at will command the laughter of his readers without having recourse to mere verbal antics. Much of his humor was of the sort that is ordinarily called *quiet* humor, because its effect does not pass off in shouts of merriment. His wit was not less ready than brilliant, and on one occasion its readiness saved him from a sudden and horrible death. Sitting on the roof of his high gate-house at Chelsea, he was enjoying the beauties of the Thames and the sunny richness of the landscape, when his solitude was broken by the unlooked-for arrival of a wandering maniac. Wearing the horn and badge of a Bedlamite, the unfortunate creature showed the signs of his malady in his equipment as well as his countenance. Having cast his eye downward from the parapet to the foot of the tower, he conceived a mad desire to hurl the chancellor from the flat roof. "Leap, Tom, leap!" screamed the athletic fellow, laying a firm hand on More's shoulder. Fixing his attention with a steady look, More said, coolly, "Let us first throw my little dog down, and see what sport that will be." In a trice the dog was thrown into the air. "Good!" said More, feigning delight at the experiment; "now run down, fetch the dog, and we'll throw him off again." Obeying the command, the dangerous intruder left More free to secure himself by a bar, and to summon assistance with his voice.

Sir Thomas Manners, with whom More had been very familiar when a boy, was created Earl of Rutland about the same time that More was made lord chancellor; and being much puffed up by his elevation, the former treated with much superciliousness his old school-fellow, who still remained a simple knight.

"*Honores mutant mores*," cried the upstart earl, meeting More one day.

"The proper translation of which," said the imperturbable chancellor, "is, 'Honors change manners.'"

More's most exquisite saying was that observation which will ever be among familiar quotations—"To aim at honor in this world is to set a coat of arms over a prison gate."

When Sir William Kingston was conducting him to the scaffold, More had some difficulty in mounting it, and said to him playfully, "Master Lieutenant, I pray you see me safe up; and as for my coming down, let me shift for myself."

He said to the executioner, "Pluck up thy spirit, man, and be not afraid to do thy duty; my neck is very short: take heed, therefore, that thou strike not awry."

When he had laid his head on the block, he desired the executioner "to wait till he had removed his beard, for that had never offended his highness."

ANECDOTES OF LORD BACON.

Sir Nicholas Bacon, lord chancellor under Queen Elizabeth, by the urbane placidity which marked the utterance of his happiest speeches, often recalled to his hearers the courteous easiness of More's repartees. Neither satire nor importunity could ruffle or confuse him. When Queen Elizabeth, looking disdainfully at his modest country mansion, told him that the place was too small, he answered with the flattery of gratitude, "Not so, madam; your highness has made me too great for my house." Liecester having suddenly asked him his opinion of two aspirants for court favor, he responded on the spur of the moment, "By my troth, my lord, the one is a grave councillor; the other is a proper young man, and so he will be as long as he lives." But notwithstanding his deliberation and the stutter that hindered his utterances, he could be quicker than the quickest, and sharper than the most acrid, as the loquacious barrister discovered who was suddenly checked in a course of pert talkativeness by this tart remark from the stammering lord keeper: "There is a difference between you and me—for me it is a pain to s-speak; for you a pain to hold your tongue." Some of the stories of his facetiousness on the bench are so unworthy of his powers that their badness inclines the critic to question their authenticity. Among these doubtful anecdotes may be placed the story of the convicted felon named Hog, who implored Sir Nicholas not to pass sentence of death upon him because hog and bacon were near akin to each other; to which piece of improbable sauciness Sir Nicholas, then acting as a judge on the Northern Circuit, is said to have answered, with brutal jocularity, "Nay, my friend, you and I can not be kindred except you be hanged, for hog is not bacon until it be hanged; so the sentence of the court is, etc., etc." More appropriate to the dignity of his office than this outburst of savage pleasantry was the silence which he maintained when a rogue in the dock, pointing to him, exclaimed, "I charge you, in the queen's name, to seize and take away that man in the red gown there, for I go in danger of my life because of him!" But though he refrained from laughing at the interruption in court, he often laughed over the recollection of it at his dinner-table. That the familiar story of his fatal attack of cold is altogether true one can not well believe, for it seems highly improbable that the lord keeper, in his seventieth year, would have sat down to be shaved near an open window in the month of February. But though the anecdote may not be historically exact, it may be accepted as a faithful portraiture of his more stately and severely courteous humor.

"Why did you suffer me to sleep thus exposed?" asked

the lord keeper, waking in a fit of shivering from slumber into which his servant had allowed him to drop as he sat to be shaved in a place where there was a sharp current of air.

"Sir, I durst not disturb you," answered the punctilious valet, with a lowly obeisance. Having eyed him for a few seconds, Sir Nicholas rose and said, "By your civility I lose my life." Whereupon the lord keeper retired to the bed from which he never rose.

AN HONEST CHANCELLOR.

"Simon the Norman" is celebrated among the few chancellors who have lost the office by refusing to comply with the royal will, and to do an unconstitutional act. He was a great favorite at court, and seemed likely to have a long official career, but was suddenly removed because he had incurred the displeasure of Henry III. (more probably of Queen Eleanor) because he would not put the great seal to a grant of fourpence on every sack of wool owned by the Earl of Flanders, the queen's uncle.

A LADY KEEPER OF THE SEALS.

The Queen Eleanor referred to in the foregoing incident once held the seals, and is known as the "lady keeper." Legend and chronicle preserve the memory of her singular grace and lively humor, the brightness of her jewels and the splendor of her state, her unjust acts and evil fame. Having occasion to cross the sea and visit Gascony, A.D. 1253, Henry III. made her keeper of the seal during his absence, and in that character she in her own person presided in the *Aula Regia*, hearing causes, and, it is to be feared, forming her decisions less in accordance with justice

QUEEN ELEANOR.

than her own private interests. Never did judge set law and equity more fearfully at naught. Not content with the exorbitant sums which she wrung from the merchants whom she compelled to unload their ships at her royal hythe, the lady keeper required the city to pay her a large sum—due to her, as she pretended, from arrears of "queen gold;" and when Richard Picard and John de Northampton, sheriffs of London, had the presumption to resist this claim, she very promptly packed them off to the Marshalsea. Having thus disposed of the sheriffs, she, on equally unlawful grounds, subjected the lord mayor to like treatment. But the great event during her tenure of the seals was the birth of her daughter Catharine, on St. Catharine's Day, 1253. The keeper of the seals was not actually delivered on the bed of justice, but, with only a slight departure from literal truth, the historian may affirm that the little princess was born upon the woolsack.

A GALLANT AND WITTY CHANCELLOR.

Few chancellors have borne the seals more lightly than Anthony Ashley Cooper, Earl of Shaftesbury, the wit of whom Charles II. said, "My chancellor knows more law than all my judges, and more divinity than all my bishops;" and the partisan who was placed on the woolsack solely in order that he might violate the law, and who, after he had fulfilled the infamous purpose of his elevation, was extolled by Dryden's venal muse as a miracle of judicial purity. He clutched the seals, well knowing that they would draw upon him the indignation of honest men and the contempt of competent lawyers; but the reckless politician held cheap the opinions of honest men, and the courtier who was never even called to the bar had neither respect for the learning, nor belief in the integrity of lawyers. He began his judicial career with characteristic cleverness and levity. Knowing that the legal dignitaries were laughing in their sleeves at his advancement, he resolved to render them ridiculous in the eyes of the London mob, and for that purpose he required the judges, in accordance with an old custom revived at the Restoration, and discontinued since 1665, to attend him from his residence in the Strand to Westminster Hall, not in their carriages, but on horseback. Never had London witnessed a more ludicrous spectacle than this procession of mounted lawyers, many of whom had not for years been in the saddle, some of whom had never had a riding-lesson. Shaftesbury, a perfect horseman, won the applause of the crowd, unable to doubt the competence of a chancellor whose seat was perfect in the saddle; but he fared less to his own satisfaction when he was required to deliver decisions before the dismounted bar. King's counsel, sergeants, and other barristers perplexed him with mischievous questions and unintelligible motions, and day after day they forced him to contradict his own judgments. But though, after rough lessons, he had the prudence to hold his peace, and interfere as little as possible with matters that were beyond his comprehension, he continued to preside in his court with undiminished good-humor, if not with undiminished effrontery, looking "more like a rakish young nobleman at the university than a lord high chancellor," and attired "in an ash-colored gown, silver-laced, and full-ribboned pantaloons displayed, without any black at all in his garb, unless it were his hat." Another witticism, currently attributed to various recent celebrities, but usually fathered upon Richard Brinsley Sheridan—on whose reputation have been heaped the brilliant *mots* of many a speaker whom he never heard, and the indiscretions of many a sinner whom he never knew—is certainly as old as Shaftesbury's bright and unprincipled career. When Charles II. exclaimed, "Shaftesbury, you are the most profligate man in my dominions," the reckless chancellor answered, "Of a subject, sir, I believe I am."

But the best fun of Shaftesbury's chancellorship did not appear till the very moment when his rivals at court ousted him from the judicial seat which he occupied for nearly thirteen months. It was arranged that his degradation should be consummated on Sunday, November 9, 1673, when in the ordinary discharge of official duty he came to Whitehall to attend on the king at chapel. The triumph of his enemies was no secret to him; and when he saw an unusually dense throng of gallants and beauties assembled in the galleries and on the stairs of the palace, he needed no assurance that they had come to witness his dismissal. For a minute there was a hush of busy tongues as he passed through the crowd to the king's closet. He was still lord chancellor, and showing the respect due to his office, the loungers drew aside, and made a passage for him with suitable obeisance. But he would in another minute be an *ex*-chancellor; and as he passed on with firm, light step, bearing the purse of state in his right hand, the courtly mob closed in upon his heels, and exchanged mischievous smiles and curious glances.

Soon the chancellor was on his knee in the royal closet kissing the king's hand.

"Sire," he said, "I know you intend to give the seals to the attorney general, but I am sure your majesty never designed to dismiss me with contempt."

"God's fish, my lord," answered Charles, who could be cruel to his friends when their backs were turned, but found it difficult to be uncivil to his enemies when they looked him in the face, "I will not do it with any circumstance as may look like an affront."

"Then, sire," entreated the earl, "I desire your majesty will permit me to carry the seals before you to chapel, and will send for them afterward to my house."

Of course the request was granted.

Till the time arrived for the congregation to enter the chapel Shaftesbury kept his sovereign merry with good stories; and when the Protestant king passed from his closet to chapel through two rows of courtiers, with amazement they saw him in friendly conversation with the keeper of his conscience, and Heneage Finch, who aspired to succeed him, turned white with apprehension as his eyes fell on the purse of state, which the foppish chancellor still swung jauntily to and fro as he laughed gayly at one of Charles's jokes.

AN INGENIOUS AND WITTY CONSTRUCTION.

William de Wickham, one of the lord chancellors in the reign of Edward III., was the designer of Windsor Castle nearly in the form in which it exists to the present day. The architect gave deep offense to his royal master by placing on one of the gates the inscription "*This made Wickham,*" which was construed into an arrogant appropriation to himself of all the glory of the edifice. But he insisted that the words were to be read as a translation of " Wichamum fecit hoc"—not of "Hoc fecit Wichamus;" that, according to the usual idiom of the English language, "Wickham" was here the accusative case instead of the nominative, and that he only wished posterity to know that his superintendence of the work had gained him the royal favor, and thus had raised him from low degree to exalted fortune; in other words, "This castle was the making of Wickham." Edward was appeased, and ever afterward delighted to honor him.

AN ARTFUL ARGUMENT.

That "circumstances alter cases," especially with lawyers, is not a fact of modern origin. Sir John Fortescue, when lord chancellor during the War of the Roses, wrote a treatise to support, on principles of constitutional law, the claim of the House of Lancaster to the crown. But when Edward was firmly established on the throne, Sir John expressed his willingness to submit himself to the reigning monarch. Edward, with some malice, required that, as a condition of his pardon, he must write another treatise upon the disputed question of the succession in support of the claim of the House of York against the House of Lancaster. The old lawyer complied, showing that he could support either side with equal ability.

LORD ELLESMERE'S POOR WIT.

Lord Francis Bacon, the profound scholar, philosopher, and corrupt judge, who has been defined as

"The wisest, brightest, meanest of mankind,"

was the author of a "Collection of Apophthegms" which Macaulay in one of his essays considers "the best jest-book in the world." In it he has recorded two of Ellesmere's (Lord Egerton) feeble attempts at punning. He was asked, during his tenure of the mastership of the rolls, to *commit* a cause, *i. e.*, to refer it to a master in chancery; he used to answer, "What has the cause done that it should be committed?" It is also recorded of him that, when he was asked for his signature to a petition of which he disapproved, he would tear it in pieces with both hands, saying, "You want my hand to this? You shall have it; ay, and both my hands too." Such exhibitions of sportive temper were applauded by the by-standers, who, respecting his wit as judicial wit ought to be respected, were charmed by the old man's venerable aspect. Of Egerton's student days a story is extant, which has merits, independent of its truth. The hostess of a Smithfield tavern had received a sum of money from three graziers in trust for them, and on engagement to restore it to them on their joint demand. Soon after this transfer, one of the co-depositors, fraudulently representing himself to be acting as the agent of the other two, induced the old lady to give him possession of the whole of the money, and thereupon absconded. Forthwith the other two depositors brought an action against the landlady, and were on the point of gaining a decision in their favor, when young Egerton, who had been taking notes of the trial, rose as *amicus curiæ*, and argued, "This money, by the contract, was to be returned to *three*, but *two* only sue; where is the *third?* let him appear with the others;

till then the money can not be demanded from her." Non-suit for the plaintiffs—for the young student a hum of commendation.

GRIM WIT OF JEFFREYS.

The name of Chancellor Jeffreys is the most infamous and hated one in the history of the judiciary of England, or any country in the civilized world. As a criminal judge he probably pronounced the death-penalty more times than any justice who ever presided over any court, and he seemed to take a fiendish delight in the imposition of cruel and extreme sentences. Among the thousands of his victims, he sentenced the noble Sydney to death and mutilation corruptly and unjustly, with insufficient evidence to establish the charge of high treason.

As some explanation for the inhuman barbarity and malicious cruelty which characterized his administration as a criminal justice, it should be stated that he was grossly intemperate, suffered severely from attacks of gravel and rheumatism, which necessarily gave him an irate temper.

As a reward for his infamy and persecution of the king's enemies, James II. made him lord chancellor, but he died miserably, at last, in the Tower of London, on the 18th of April, 1689. Lord Jeffreys, near the close of his career, barely escaped being torn to pieces by the enraged populace. While a prisoner in the Tower, he received a barrel marked "Colchester oysters," of which he was known to be very fond. Seeing it, he exclaimed, "Well, I have some friends left still;" but, on opening it, the gift was—a halter. During his last sickness the press turned with the vindictive virulence and opprobrium toward himself which his judicial butcheries had excited in the public mind. Among other things, his pretended will was published, of which the following was the concluding legacy: "*Item*, I order an ell and a half of fine cambric to be cut into handkerchiefs for drying up all the wet eyes at my funeral, together with half a pint of burnt claret for all the mourners in the kingdom."

This judge, whose crimes were greater than those of the most hardened felon who ever received a judicial sentence, died at the early age of forty-one, and left a name which will be immortal in the annals of historic infamy and official corruption.

Perhaps of all the anecdotes of Jeffreys's cruelty the most thoroughly sickening is that which describes his conduct when, as recorder of London, he passed sentence of death on his old and familiar friend, Richard Langhorn, the Catholic barrister, one of the victims of the Popish Plot phrensy. It is recorded that Jeffreys, not content with consigning his friend to a traitor's doom, malignantly reminded him of their former intercourse, and with devilish ridicule admonished him to prepare his soul for the next world. However much the reader may feel inclined to question the truthfulness of the popular portraits of Jeffreys; however much he may assign to party rage when he endeavors to separate the actual badness of the man from the exaggerations of his political enemies, and however much he may regard the judge's violent speeches as indications of the prevailing tone of the bar and of society, rather than of the speaker's individual peculiarities of temper, he still feels a genuine delight whenever apocryphal biography represents the bloody chief justice as worsted in a wordy conflict which he had provoked by overbearing speech. If he actually, as he is said to have done, interrupted the venerable Maynard by saying, "You have lost your knowledge of law; your memory, I tell you, is failing through old age," how must every hearer of the speech have exulted when Maynard quietly answered, "Yes, Sir George,

I have forgotten more law than you ever learned; but allow me to say, I have not forgotten much."

ANECDOTES OF LORD THURLOW.

This chancellor, who seems to have attained great notoriety in the reign of George III., was certainly no ornament to the bench, and gives no credit to the bar. He had a certain mental vigor and erratic judgment which were often neutralized by his passion, haste, and caprice. His manners were coarse and brutal, his habits immoral in the extreme, and, on the whole, he was, notwithstanding his great reputation, a disgrace to the English ermine. He drank freely, and indulged in the most shocking profanity. A solicitor once had to prove a death before him, and being told upon every statement he made, "Sir, that is no proof," at last exclaimed, much vexed, "My lord, it is very hard that you will not believe me. I knew him well to his last hour; I saw him dead and in his coffin, my lord. My lord, he was my client." "Good heavens, sir!" exclaimed the rude and insulting lord chancellor, "why did you not tell me that before? I should not have doubted the fact one moment, for I think nothing can be more likely to kill a man than to have you for an attorney."

Lord Thurlow's rudeness occasionally drew down upon him sarcasm as bitter as his own. Of good legal *ana* connected with parliamentary discussions, relative to George III.'s attacks of madness, perhaps the best is that which preserves the pithy criticism on Lord Thurlow uttered by Wilkes, best known as "Liberty Wilkes." Thurlow could shed tears and be wondrous pathetic whenever tears could aid his eloquence. After dexterously coquetting between the queen's and the prince's parties in 1788, he delivered in the House of Lords his memorable declaration of gratitude to, and affection for, the afflicted king. Having broken this harangue with several distinct fits of nervous agitation, and at one point having wept copiously, he resumed the clearest melody of his sonorous voice, and concluded with these words: "A noble viscount has, in an eloquent and energetic manner, expressed his feelings on the present melancholy situation of his majesty — feelings rendered more poignant from the noble viscount's having been in the habit of personally receiving marks of indulgence and kindness from his suffering sovereign. My own sorrow, my lords, is aggravated by the same cause. My debt of gratitude is indeed ample for the many favors which have been graciously conferred upon me by his majesty; *and when I forget my sovereign, may my God forget me!*" As Thurlow sat down the sensation among his brother peers was profound; but Wilkes, who had been an auditor of the speech, was less deeply affected. A vicious light burned brightly in his squinting eyes, and as a more than usually diabolical sneer played upon his hideous face, the people's friend hissed out, "God forget you! He'll see you d—d first."

Thurlow, a thorough partisan, was not by any means a narrow one. Sympathizing with success, he always meant to fight on the winning side; but, more daring or more shameless than most time-serving politicians, he took but small pains to conceal his true character. At the time of King George III.'s first madness the Tory chancellor showed himself quite ready to serve the Whigs, if they should ever need his assistance; and at a later period, as a purely official upholder of church and state, he frankly told a deputation of Nonconformists that he would join them, and cordially adopt their religious opinions as soon as their sect had made itself the Established Church. And when his political life met a premature and violent end, he gave the following characteristic counsel to Sir John Scott: "Stick by Pitt;

he has tripped up my heels, and I would have tripped up his if I could. I confess I never thought the king would have parted with me so easily. My course is run, and for the future I shall remain neutral. But you must on no account resign; I will not listen for a moment to such an idea. We should be looked on as a couple of fools. Your promotion is certain, and it shall not be balked by any such whimsical proceedings." Though this friendly and generous speech contains little to which the moralist can take exception, it must be admitted that its tone leaves no room for doubt that the speaker regarded politics as a game in which clever men sought personal advancement, and stuck to those who could help them.

Yet this despicable nature was for many years the leader of the nobility of England, and the despot of the House of Lords. Every school-boy will remember his crushing reply to the Duke of Grafton, who had taunted him with his plebeian origin. The story, as usually told, omits to describe Thurlow's manner on the occasion, and this is done so splendidly in Jeaffreson's "Book about Lawyers" that I am tempted to give the extract in full:

"The insult," says Jeaffreson, "by the Duke of Grafton was offered during the inquiry into the Earl of SANDWICH'S administration of Greenwich Hospital, and was promptly answered. Leaving the woolsack, the chancellor walked slowly to a spot near the top of the Duke of Grafton's bench—from which place he ordinarily addressed the House—and having deliberately taken up his position, he surveyed the offender with those terrible black eyes, the wrathful light of which few antagonists could face without flinching. Before the country clergyman's son had spoken a word, the Duchess of Cleveland's descendant felt the despicable nature of his misconduct, and saw the magnitude of his blunder. Soon the stillness of the House was broken by Thurlow's grand voice saying, 'I am amazed.' Another pause; and then, in a louder tone, the vindicator of his personal honor continued: 'Yes, my lords, I am amazed at his grace's speech. The noble duke can not look before him, behind him, or on either side of him, without seeing some noble peer who owes his seat in this House to successful exertions in the profession to which I belong. Does he not feel that it is as honorable to owe it to these, as to being the accident of an accident? To all these noble lords the language of the noble duke is as applicable and as insulting as it is to myself. But I don't fear to meet it single and alone. No one venerates the peerage more than I do; but, my lords, I must say that the peerage solicited me, not I the peerage. Nay, more, I can say, and will say, that as a peer of Parliament, as speaker of this right honorable House, as keeper of the great seal, as guardian of his majesty's conscience, as Lord High Chancellor of England, nay, even in that character alone in which the noble duke would think it an affront to be considered—as a man—I am at this moment as respectable—I beg leave to add, I am at this moment as much respected—as the proudest peer I now look down upon.'"

From the date of that speech until his final retirement from office Thurlow was the tyrant of the Upper House, ruling its members with a haughty arrogance such as no subsequent chancellor has ventured to display. Nor was the speech less effectual beyond the circle of its actual hearers. Redounding to the honor of the law and the respectability of the grade from which he had risen, it delighted the speaker's profession, and inspired the middle classes with a sense of their worth and dignity; and thus, while the proudest nobles of the land had enough generosity to applaud the chancellor's spirit, the multitude found pleasure in repeating his words.

Anecdotes illustrating Lord Thurlow's wit are not so numerous as those recounting his baseness, but enough have been preserved to show that he possessed a vein of genuine humor, though the best of these also contain evidences of his rudeness and lack of principle. In his undergraduate days at Cambridge he is said to have worried the tutors with a series of disorderly pranks and impudent *escapades*, but on one occasion he unquestionably displayed at the university the quick wit that in after life rescued him from many an embarrassing position:

"Sir," observed a tutor, giving the unruly undergraduate a look of disapproval, "I never come to the window without seeing you idling in the court."

"Sir," replied young Thurlow, imitating the tutor's tone, "I never come into the court without seeing you idling at the window."

The manner in which he once procured a horse to convey him about his circuit shows his wit and tricky nature. When he first began practice—when he was, as Jeaffreson describes him, "lazy, keen-eyed, loquacious Ned Thurlow"—he was sorely perplexed, in his poverty, as to the means of procuring a horse on which to ride the rounds of his courts. In his trouble he called on a horse-dealer, and in the confident tone of a man who, without inconvenience, could at his own cost put a cavalry regiment in the field, intimated that he stood in need of a very superior roadster. As to price, money was an affair of total indifference to him, so long as he could get a really desirable article. "Show me a horse that you can recommend, and if I like him *after trial*, I'll have him at your own price." What could mortal dealer do but assent to this proposal, coming from the well-looking, imperious young man, who subsequently ruled English hereditary legislators with insolent despotism, and whose aspect was so imposing that a shrewd observer said, "It is impossible for any one to *be* so wise as Thurlow looks." Forthwith a strong and serviceable hackney was saddled, and forthwith the young barrister mounted. The trial lasted longer than the dealer thought fair. Instead of returning to the stables in the course of the afternoon, Thurlow rode off to Winchester; and when the owner of the steed again looked upon his property, the creature had visited every town on the circuit. Together with the horse, the dealer received a note from Thurlow, intimating that "the animal, notwithstanding some good points, did not altogether suit him."

LABOR IS PLEASURE.

Lord Chancellor King, who held office in the reigns of George I. and II., was, like Lord Thurlow, proud of his plebeian descent. His father was a retail grocer and salter at Exeter. The chancellor ascribed all his success in life to his love of labor, and chose for his motto, "*Labor ipse voluptas.*" An admirer has paraphrased this sentiment as follows, in a sketch in the Biographia Britannica:

" 'Tis not the splendor of the place,
The gilded coach, the purse, the mace,
Nor all the pompous strains of state,
With crowds that at your levee wait,
That make you happy, make you great;
But while mankind you strive to bless,
With all the talents you possess,
While the chief joy that you receive
Arises from the joy you give,
Duty and taste in you unite
To make the heavy burden light;
For pleasure rightly understood
Is only labor to be good."

PECULIARITIES OF LORD CHANCELLOR ELDON.

It is very easy to conceive that John Scott (Lord Eldon) and Lord Thurlow were bosom friends, for they had all the bad qualities of nature in common. Eldon was equally treacherous and uncouth with Thurlow, and more penurious, as well as much wittier. Under his supremacy, the chancellor's private carriage was a miserable, battered, jingling, ramshackle coach, drawn by two lean, luckless brutes, that roused the derision of the street-boys. Frequently the chancellor, purse in hand, drove from Bedford Square or Hamilton Place to Westminster in a hackney-coach; and on one occasion he actually left in a common hackney-carriage some state papers of high importance. Fortunately, the driver was either honest or drunk, and promptly restored the documents. When Lord Eldon and Sir Arthur Pigott each made a stand in court for his favorite pronunciation of the word "lien"--Lord Eldon calling the word *lion*, and Sir Arthur maintaining that it was to be pronounced like *lean* — Jekyll, who was at the same time the brightest wit and most shameless punster of Westminster Hall, with an allusion to the parsimonious arrangements of the chancellor's kitchen, perpetrated the following *jeu d'esprit:*

"Sir Arthur, Sir Arthur, why what do you mean
By saying the chancellor's *lion* is *lean*?
D'ye think that his kitchen's so bad as all that,
That nothing within it can ever get fat?"

The anecdotes illustrating Lord Eldon's humor are not more numerous than those told of Thurlow; but he was frequently the occasion of wit in others, and it is notable that he very sensibly took all repartees with great good grace. He was noted for his indecision of character and manner, and many of his judgments were apparently influenced by the last arguments which he heard. Sir

George Rose, whose court witticisms form a chapter of themselves, alluding to this characteristic weakness of the chancellor, once wrote the following lines:

> "Mr. Leech made a speech,
> Pithy, clear, and strong;
> Mr. Hart, on the other part,
> Was prosy, dull, and long;
> Mr. Parker made that darker
> Which was dark enough without;
> Mr. Bell spoke so well
> That the chancellor said, 'I doubt.'"

Far from being offended by this allusion to his notorious mental infirmity, Lord Eldon, shortly after the verses had floated into circulation, concluded one of his decisions by saying, with a significant smile, "And here, Mr. Rose, *the chancellor does not doubt.*"

Like his friend Thurlow, Lord Eldon could weep when art required it, and on one occasion, by practicing that theatrical artifice, drew down upon himself the bitter sarcasm of Horne Tooke. It was at the trial of Tooke that this occurred. Erskine had made some reflection on Eldon's character, and he, in reply, said, "I can endure any thing but an attack on my good name. My good name is the little patrimony I have to leave my children, and, with God's help, gentlemen of the jury, I will leave it to them unimpaired." As he uttered these words tears suffused his eyes. For a moment Horne Tooke, who persisted in regarding all the circumstances of his perilous position as farcical, smiled at the lawyer's outburst with silent amusement; but as soon as he saw a sympathetic brightness in the eyes of one of the jury, the dexterous demagogue, with characteristic humor and effrontery, accused Sir John Mitford, the solicitor general, of needless sympathy with the sentimental disturbance of his colleague. "Do you know what Sir John Mitford is crying about?" the prisoner inquired of the jury. "He is thinking of the destitute condition of Lord Eldon's children, and the *little patrimony* they are likely to divide among them." The jury and all present were not more tickled by the satire upon the attorney general than by the indignant surprise which enlivened the face of Sir John Mitford, who was not at all prone to tears, and had certainly manifested no pity for Lord Eldon's forlorn condition.

One of the best stories pinned upon Lord Eldon relates to a challenge which an indignant suitor is said to have sent to him, demanding reparation for insults offered by him to the challenger. In a trial at York that had arisen from a horse-race, it was stated in evidence that one of the conditions of the race required that "each horse should be ridden by a gentleman." The race having been run, the holders refused to pay the stakes to the winner on the ground that he was not a gentleman; whereupon the equestrian whose gentility was thus called in question brought an action for the money. After a very humorous inquiry, which terminated in a verdict for the defendants, the plaintiff challenged the defendant's counsel, Lord Eldon, for maintaining that he was no gentleman; to which invitation reply was made that the challenged "could not think of fighting one who had been found *no gentleman* by the solemn verdict of twelve of his countrymen."

James Boswell—Sam Johnson's Boswell—was one of Eldon's aversions; and one of the chancellor's smartest speeches was his reply to Boswell's importunate entreaties for a definition of the word "taste."

"Well, then, Boswell," he said, "we must have an end of this. 'Taste,' according to my definition, is the judgment you manifested when you determined to quit Scotland, and come to the south."

Eldon was equally noted for his gallantry and vanity.

"What a lovely woman!" was his exclamation, upon passing a beauty when pacing up and down Westminster Hall previous to the opening of the court.

"What an excellent judge!" said the lady, when her sensitive ear caught the flattering decree of the Lord High Chancellor of England.

Singular enough, both Thurlow and Eldon displayed great good sense, liberality, and humanity in the dispersal of the ecclesiastical patronage which belonged to the office which each held, and many are the good stories told of interviews between them and the clergymen suing for places and preferment.

"Who sent you, sir?" Thurlow asked savagely of a country curate, who had boldly forced his way into the chancellor's library in Great Ormond Street in the hope of winning the presentation to a vacant living. "In whose name do you come that you venture to pester me about your private affairs? I say, sir, what great lord sent you to bother me in my house?"

"My lord," answered the applicant, with a happy combination of dignity and humor, "no great man supports my entreaty; but I may say with honesty that I come to you in the name of the Lord of Hosts."

Pleased by the spirit and wit of the reply, Thurlow exclaimed, "The Lord of Hosts! the Lord of Hosts! You are the first person that ever applied to me in that lord's name; and though his title can't be found in the peerage, by —— you shall have the living."

On another occasion the same chancellor was less benign, but not less just, to a clerical applicant. Sustained by Queen Charlotte's personal favor and intercession with Thurlow, the clergyman in question felt so sure of obtaining the valuable living which was the object of his ambition, that he regarded his interview with the chancellor as a purely formal affair.

"I have, sir," observed Lord Thurlow, "received a letter from the curate of the parish to which it is my intention to prefer you, and, on inquiry, I find him to be a very worthy man. The father of a large family, and a priest who has labored zealously in the parish for many years, he has written to me, not asking for the living, but modestly entreating me to ask the new rector to retain him as curate. Now, sir, you would oblige me by promising me to employ the poor man in that capacity."

"My lord," replied Queen Charlotte's *protégé*, "it would give me great pleasure to oblige your lordship in this matter, but, unfortunately, I have arranged to take a personal friend for my curate."

His eyes flashing angrily, Thurlow answered, "Sir, I can not force you to take this worthy man for your curate, but I can make him the rector; and by —— he shall have the living, and be in a position to offer you the curacy."

And forthwith, to the applicant's inexpressible surprise and chagrin, the chancellor's words were carried out.

Dating the letter from No. 2 Charlotte Street, Pimlico, Lord Eldon's eldest son sent his father the following anonymous epistle:

"Hear, generous lawyer! hear my prayer,
Nor let my freedom make you stare,
In hailing you Jack Scott!
Tho' now upon the woolsack placed,
With wealth, with power, with title graced,
Once nearer was our lot.

"Say by what name the hapless bard
May best attract your kind regard—
Plain Jack? Sir John? or Eldon?
Give, from your ample store of giving,
A starving priest some little living—
The world will cry 'Well done.'

"In vain, without a patron's aid,
I've prayed and preached, and preached and prayed—
Applauded, but *ill fed*.

Such vain *eclat* let others share;
Alas, I can not feed on *air*—
I ask not *praise*, but *bread*."

Satisfactorily hoaxed by the rhymer, the chancellor went to Pimlico in search of the clerical poetaster, and found him not.

Prettier, though less comic, is the story of Miss Bridge's morning call upon Lord Eldon. The chancellor was sitting in his study over a table of papers, when a young and lovely girl—slightly rustic in her attire, slightly embarrassed by the novelty of her position, but thoroughly in command of her wits—entered the room and walked up to the lawyer's chair.

"My dear," said the chancellor, rising and bowing with Old-world courtesy, "who *are* you?"

"Lord Eldon," answered the blushing maiden, "I am Bessie Bridge, of Weobly, the daughter of the Vicar of Weobly, and papa has sent me to remind you of a promise which you made him when I was a little baby, and you were a guest in his house on the occasion of your first election as member of Parliament for Weobly."

"A promise, my dear young lady?" interposed the chancellor, trying to recall how he had pledged himself.

"Yes, Lord Eldon, a promise. You were standing over my cradle when papa said to you, 'Mr. Scott, promise me that if ever you are lord chancellor when my little girl is a poor clergyman's wife, you will give her husband a living;' and you answered, 'Mr. Bridge, my promise is not worth half a crown, but I give it to you, wishing it were worth more.'"

Enthusiastically the chancellor exclaimed,

"You are quite right. I admit the obligation. I remember all about it;" and then, after a pause, archly surveying the damsel, whose graces were the reverse of matronly, he added, "But surely the time for keeping my promise has not yet arrived? You can not be any one's wife at present?"

For a few seconds Bessie hesitated for an answer, and then, with a blush and a ripple of silver laughter, she replied,

"No, but I do so wish to be *somebody's* wife. I am engaged to a young clergyman; and there's a living in Herefordshire near my old home that has recently fallen vacant, and if you'll give it to Alfred, why then, Lord Eldon, we shall marry before the end of the year."

Is there need to say that the chancellor forthwith summoned his secretary, that the secretary forthwith made out the presentation to Bessie's lover, and that, having given the chancellor a kiss of gratitude, Bessie made good speed back to Herefordshire, hugging the precious document the whole way home?

A bad but eager sportsman, Lord Eldon used to blaze away at his partridges and pheasants with such uniform want of success, that his younger brother, Lord Stowell, had truth as well as humor on his side when he observed, "My brother has done much execution this shooting-season; with his gun he has *killed a great deal of time.*" Having ineffectually discharged two barrels at a covey of partridges, the chancellor was slowly walking to the gate of one of his Encombe turnip-fields when a stranger of clerical garb and aspect hailed him from a distance, asking, "Where is Lord Eldon?" Not anxious to declare himself to the witness of his ludicrously bad shot, the chancellor answered evasively, and with scant courtesy, "Not far off." Displeased with the tone of this curt reply, the clergyman rejoined, "I wish you'd use your tongue to better purpose than you do your gun, and tell me civilly where I can find the chancellor." "Well," responded the sportsman, when he had slowly approached his questioner, "here you see the chancellor—I am Lord Eldon." It was an untoward introduction to the chancellor for the strange clergyman, who had traveled from the north of Lancashire to ask for the presentation to a vacant living. Partly out of humorous compassion for the applicant, who had offered rudeness, if not insult, to the person whom he was most anxious to propitiate, partly because, on inquiry, he ascertained the respectability of the applicant, and partly because he wished to seal by kindness the lips of a man who could report on the authority of his own eyes that the best lawyer was also the worst shot in all England, Eldon gave the petitioner the desired preferment. "But now," the old chancellor used to add in conclusion, whenever he told the story, "see the ingratitude of mankind. It was not long before a large present of game reached me, with a letter from my new-made rector, purporting that he had sent it me because, *from what he had seen of my shooting*, he supposed I must be badly off for game. Think of turning upon me in this way, and wounding me in my tenderest point."

Among Eldon's humorous answers to applications for preferment should be remembered his letter to Dr. Fisher, of the Charter-house: On one side of a sheet of paper, "Dear Fisher, I can not to-day give you the preferment for which you ask.—I remain your sincere friend, ELDON. —*Turn over*;" and on the other side, "I gave it to you yesterday."

AN ENGLISH "APPLE-SASS CASE."

Every American has either seen or heard of Owens's comical representation of the old farmer who is involved in a suit for the recovery of a "barrell of apple-sass." Many of them will be surprised that there is an English foundation for that humorous idea, and that no less a dignitary than

Lord Chancellor Eldon was the judge in the case, which became familiarly known as the "apple-pie case." In the early months of Eldon's married life, while playing the part of an Oxford don, he was required to decide in an important action brought by two undergraduates against the cook of University College. The plaintiffs declared that the cook had "sent to their rooms an apple-pie *that could not be eaten.*" The defendant pleaded that he had a remarkably fine fillet of veal in the kitchen. Having set aside this plea on grounds obvious to the legal mind, and not otherwise than manifest to unlearned laymen, Eldon ordered the apple-pie to be brought in court; but the messenger dispatched to do the judge's bidding returned with the astounding intelligence that during the progress of the litigation a party of undergraduates had actually devoured the pie—fruit and crust. Nothing but the pan was left. Judgment: "The charge here is, that the cook has sent up an apple-pie that can not be eaten. Now that can not be said to have been uneatable which has been eaten; and as this apple-pie has been eaten, it was eatable. Let the cook be absolved."

THE WIT AND HUMOR OF LORD ERSKINE.

Lord Chancellor Erskine's character, as preserved, is not much better than that of his rival Eldon, though he was not so coarse. His high place among political barristers is rendered all the more remarkable by his comparative failure as a parliamentary debater. Extreme in his political views, he made his place, and, to a great degree, kept it, at the bar, by acting the part of the forensic champion of Liberal opinions; but though his services to the popular party were almost inestimable, and though his more inflammatory orations raised in the middle and lower classes of the country a spirit of generous intolerance of oppression, he was never a really effective speaker in either House of Parliament, and as a senator in either assembly he had scarcely any more weight than an ordinary member. His first speech in the House of Commons was a humiliating miscarriage; and, unlike Sheridan, Disraeli, and other brilliant debaters who commenced parliamentary life with an oratorical *fiasco*, he never obliterated the unfavorable impression of his maiden effort.

He never altogether overcame the effects of his unfortunate *début* in the Commons, where Pitt, having worsted him at the outset, treated him with undeserved disrespect and contemptuous hostility to the last; and in the Upper House he never did justice to his powers, though he was upon the whole a personally popular and, at times, a loquacious rather than eloquent member. But though his parliamentary career was at best one of inferior distinction, he was emphatically a political barrister. In private life, as well as in public, he was at all times a keen, though never an acrimonious politician, displaying the strength of his convictions in modes that were usually forcible, and sometimes whimsical. Thus his fantastic motto, "Trial by Jury," was an avowal of political feeling rather than a professional sentiment. Nor was his political fervor more remarkable than his political disinterestedness and consistency. Eldon was equally firm and thorough, but his disinterestedness was never fairly put to trial. Erskine's public virtue, on the other hand, was tested by temptation.

The prevailing amiability of Erskine's disposition may be seen in the good-nature of his *jeux d'esprit.* Known as a wit far more than as an orator, and fully conscious of the power which his light satiric faculty gave him over juries, he was perpetually winning men's opinions by tickling their sense of humor; but though a volume might be made up of his bright sayings and inimitable drolleries, the occasions when he wounded the susceptibilities of a fellow-creature merely for the sake of a jest could be counted on ten fingers. Experiencing no mercy from his opponents, he never repaid coarseness with cruelty. In moments of the most intense excitement he was saved by thorough gentlemanliness rather than by caution from those indiscretions of speech which nervous talkers so frequently commit at the suggestion of fancy and under the spur of irritation.

When Thelwall, instead of regarding his advocate with grateful silence, insisted on interrupting him with vexatious remarks and impertinent criticisms, Erskine neither threw up his brief nor lost his temper, but retorted with an innocent flash of merriment. To a slip of paper on which the prisoner had written, "I'll be hanged if I don't plead my own cause," he contented himself with returning answer, "You'll be hanged if you do." Some of his puns would have been bad had they come from the lips of any other man; but he uttered them with such spirit and with such an appearance of irrepressible gayety of heart that they were irresistible to hearers accustomed to hear good things—to hearers, moreover, who would gladly have persuaded themselves that the people's advocate, instead of being a man of genius, was a compound of buffoon and demagogue. His *mots* were often excellent, but it was the tone and joyous animation of the speaker that gave them their charm.

Counselor Lamb, an old man when Lord Erskine was at the height of his reputation, was a man of timid manners and nervous temperament, and usually prefaced his plea with an apology to that effect. On one occasion, when opposed to Erskine, he happened to remark that he felt himself growing more and more timid as he grew older. "No wonder," replied the witty barrister, good-naturedly, "every one knows that the older a lamb grows the more sheepish he becomes."

Erskine's humanity toward animals is perpetuated in his bill "For the Prevention of Cruelty to Animals," in one of his speeches upon which measure he passionately observed, "As to the tendency of barbarous sports of any description whatsoever, to nourish the natural characteristic of manliness and courage—the only shadow of argument I ever heard on such occasions—all I can say is this, that from the mercenary battles of the lowest of beasts—human boxers—up to those of the highest and noblest that are tormented by man for his degrading pastime, I enter this public protest against such reasoning. I never knew a man remarkable for heroic bearing whose very aspect was not lighted up by gentleness and humanity; nor a *kill-and-eat-him* countenance that did not cover the heart of a bully or a poltroon." Of many quaint stories illustrating his fine tenderness for the mute creation, one may be inserted in this paragraph. Having expostulated with a ruffian for violently beating a feeble and emaciated horse, he was asked by the rascal, "Why! it is my own, mayn't I use it as I please?" The man's tone heightened the insolence of his words, and, having uttered them, he renewed his attack on the poor brute. In a trice Erskine, who was armed with a stout cane, gave the offender a sound thrashing. "What right have you to strike me?" roared the fellow, beside himself with rage and pain. "Pooh, man!" replied the executioner, "my stick is my own, mayn't I use it as I please?" Erskine's reply to Sir John Sinclair's solicitation for a subscription to the testimonial which Sir John invited the nation to present to himself is his neatest joke. On the one side of a sheet of paper the letter ran, "My dear Sir John, I am certain there are few in this kingdom who set a higher value on your services than myself, and I have the honor to subscribe," on the other side it concluded, "myself your obedient faithful servant, ERSKINE."

JUDICIAL INCOMPETENCY OF VARIOUS LORD CHANCELLORS.

Ignorant lord chancellors were more numerous than witty ones; and some who are generally received at the present time as of superior judgment were really men of great ignorance. From the days of Wriothesley, who may be regarded as the most conspicuous and unquestionable instance of judicial incompetency in the annals of English lawyers, the multitudes have always delighted in stories that illustrate the ignorance and incapacity of men who are presumed to possess, by right of their office, an extraordinary share of knowledge and wisdom. What law student does not rub his hands as he reads of Lord St. John's trouble during term while he held the seals, and of the impatience with which he looked forward to the long vacation, when he would not be required to look wise and speak authoritatively about matters concerning which he was totally ignorant. Delicious are the stories of Francis Bacon's clerical successor, who endeavored to get up a *quantum suff.* of chancery law by falling on his knees and asking enlightenment of Heaven.

Lord Campbell is looked upon by the general public as one of the ablest of the lord chancellors of England—an erroneous idea, based chiefly on the fact that he rose from a reporter in Parliament to be lord chancellor. His judicial and literary merits have been ridiculously overrated. His "Chancellors" and "Chief Justices," the volumes on which is based his literary reputation, are conspicuous for their many inaccuracies, and for the total absence of original thought and inquiry. Written without due deliberation and without adequate research, at a period when the successful lawyer had neither sufficient political excitement, nor enough professional employment, these biographies are hasty compilations, combining new mistakes with the blunders of inadvertence or prejudice, or sheer ignorance of former writers; though, taken with all their faults, the volumes have good qualities and purposes. As a painter of the social history of his profession, Campbell is still without an equal; and by keeping him in the memory of ordinary readers, when his judgments shall be forgotten by all save lawyers, his books will undoubtedly accomplish the hope of their author.

Chancellor Henry Bathurst was also held in low esteem by the bar on account of his ignorance; and little pains was taken by his contemporaries to conceal their contempt. Such was the rage for attributing foolish speeches to him that he could scarcely open his lips in public without becoming the victim of malicious misrepresentation. Again and again has the story been told, that at the close of the trial of the Duchess of Kingston for bigamy, he gravely addressed her grace in the following terms: "Madam, the lords have considered the charge, and evidence brought against, and have likewise considered of every thing which you have alleged in your defense; and upon the whole matter their lordships have found you not guilty of the felony wherewith you stand charged; but, on dismissing you, their lordships earnestly exhort you not to commit the same crime a second time."

A good story is told of Lord Keeper Williams, the successor of Francis Bacon, whose incompetence for his legal office (though he had been thoroughly educated for the pulpit) was a jest with lawyers of every grade. Seizing an opportunity when sudden illness had deprived the lord keeper of the *saving* presence of his master of the rolls, a malapert counselor rose and made a motion which, Williams's biographer assures us, was "crammed like a grenade with obsolete words, coins of far-fetched antiquity, which had long been disused. With these misty and recondite phrases he thought to leave Williams groping about in the dark." But on this occasion impudence met with signal discomfiture; for with equal readiness and good temper the lord keeper completely turned the tables on his adversary. With a serious face the lord keeper answered him in a cluster of most crabbed motions picked out of metaphysics and logic, as "categorematical" and "syncategorematical," and a deal of such drumming stuff, that the motioner, being foiled at his own weapon, and well laughed at in the court, went home with a new lesson—that he that tempts a wise man in jest shall make a fool of himself in earnest.

A good story is told of Lord Keeper Kenyon, in which he is represented as at once guilty of bombast in his style, and of perpetrating a very ludicrous Irish bull. He was passing sentence on a dishonest butler, who had been convicted of stealing large quantities of wine from his master's cellar. "Prisoner at the bar," the judge is reported to have said, "you stand convicted on the most conclusive evidence of a crime of inexpressible atrocity—a crime that defiles the sacred springs of domestic confidence, and is calculated to strike alarm into the breast of every Englishman who invests largely in the choicer vintages of Southern Europe. Like the serpent of old, you have stung the hand of your protector. Fortunate in having a generous employer, you might, without dishonesty, have continued to supply your wretched wife and children with the comforts of sufficient prosperity, and even with some of the luxuries of affluence; but dead to every claim of natural affection, and blind to your own real interests, you burst through all the restraints of religion and morality, and have for many years been *feathering your nest with your master's bottles.*"

Kenyon was really ignorant, and this Hibernicism was owing to his stupidity. The best illustration of his imbecility, and his singular mistakes in using metaphorical language, is his "great" oration made at the trial of Williams for publishing Tom Paine's "Age of Reason," when the learned judge, in his summing up, observed, "Christianity, from its earliest institution, met with its opposers. The professors were very soon called upon to publish their 'Apologies' for the doctrines they had embraced. In what manner they did that, and whether they had the advantage of their adversaries, or sunk under the superiority of their arguments, mankind for near two thousand years have had the opportunity of judging. They have seen what *Julian*, Justin Martyr, and other apologists have written, and have been of opinion that the argument was in favor of those publications." Telling this story in his own way, and improving it—as he was fully justified in doing—Coleridge in the "Table Talk" assures his readers that Lord Kenyon, in his address to the jury in a trial for blasphemy, said, "Above all, gentlemen, need I name to you the Emperor Julian, who was so celebrated for the practice of every Christian virtue that he was called *Julian the Apostle?*"

LORD KENYON'S PENURIOUSNESS.

Penurious lawyers were as numerous as witty ones at the English bar in the past ages. Lord Kenyon was noted for his sordid attire. While he was a leading advocate within the bar, his ordinary costume would have disgraced a copying-clerk; and, during his later years, it was a question among barristers whether his breeches were made of velvet or leather. The wits maintained that, when he kissed hands upon his elevation to the attorney's place, he went to court in a second-hand suit purchased from Lord Stormont's *valet*. In the letter attributed to him by a clever writer in the "Rolliad" he is made to say, "My income has been cruelly estimated at seven, or, as some will have it, eight thousand pounds per annum. I shall save myself the mortification of denying that I am rich, and refer you to the constant habits and whole tenor of my life. The proof to my friends is easy. My tailor's bill for the last fifteen years is a record of the most indisputable authority. Malicious souls may direct you, perhaps, to Lord Stormont's *valet de chambre*, and can vouch the anecdote that, on the day when I kissed hands for my appointment to the office of attorney general, I appeared in a laced waistcoat that once belonged to his master. I bought the waistcoat, but despise the insinuation; nor is this the only instance in which I am obliged to diminish my wants and apportion them to my very limited means. Lady K—— will be my witness that, until my last appointment, I was an utter stranger to the luxury of a pocket-handkerchief." The pocket-handkerchief which then came into his possession was supposed to have been found in the pocket of the second-hand waistcoat; and Jekyll always maintained that, as it was not considered in the purchase, it remained the valet's property, and did not pass into the lawyer's rightful possession. This was the only handkerchief which Lord Kenyon is said to have ever possessed, and Lord Ellenborough alluded to it when, in a conversation that turned upon the economy which the income-tax would necessitate in all ranks of life, he observed, "Lord Kenyon, who is not very nice, intends to meet the crisis by laying down his handkerchief."

Of his two wigs (one considerably less worn than the other) and of his two hats (the better of which would not have greatly disfigured an old-clothes man, while the worse would have been of service to a professional scarecrow) Lord Kenyon took jealous care. The inferior wig was always worn with the better hat, and the more dilapidated hat with the superior wig; and it was noticed that when he appeared in court with the shabbier wig he never removed his *chapeau;* whereas, on the days when he sat in his more decent wig, he pushed his old cocked hat out of sight. In the privacy of his house, and in his carriage whenever he traveled beyond the limits of town, he used to lay aside wig and hat, and cover his head with an old red night-cap. Concerning his great-coat, the original blackness of which had been tempered by long usage into a fuscous green, capital tales were fabricated. The wits could not spare even his shoes. "Once," Dr. Dibdin gravely narrated, "in the case of an action brought for the non-fulfillment of a contract on a large scale for shoes, the question mainly was, whether or not they were well and soundly made, and with the best materials. A number of witnesses were called, one of them, a first-rate character in the gentle craft, being closely questioned, returned contradictory answers, when the chief justice observed, pointing to his own shoes, which were regularly bestridden by the broad silver buckle of the day, 'Were the shoes any thing like these?' 'No, my lord,' replied the evidence, 'they were a good deal better, and more genteeler.'" Dr. Dibdin is at needless pains to assure his readers that the shoemaker's answer was followed by uproarious laughter.

Under the steadily strengthening spell of avarice, he ceased to invite even old friends to his table; and it was rumored that, in course of time, his domestic servants complained with reason that they were required to consume the same fare as their master deemed sufficient for himself. "In Lord Kenyon's house," a wit exclaimed, "all the year through it is Lent in the kitchen, and Passion Week in the parlor." Another caustic quidnunc remarked, "In his lordship's kitchen the fire is dull, but the spits are always bright;" whereupon Jekyll interposed, with an assumption of testiness, "Spits! in the name of common sense I order you not to talk about his spits, for nothing turns upon them."

ANECDOTES OF ELLENBOROUGH.

Many are the good stories told of "judicial wigs," and among the best of them is the anecdote which Samuel Rogers delighted to tell at the expense of Edward Law (Lord Ellenborough). "He was once about to go on circuit, when Lady Ellenborough said that she should like to accompany him. He replied that he had no objection, provided she did not encumber the carriage with bandboxes, which were his utter abhorrence. During the first day's journey Lord Ellenborough, happening to stretch his legs, struck his foot against something below the seat; he discovered that it was a bandbox. Up went the window, and out went the bandbox. The coachman stopped, and the footman, thinking that the bandbox had tumbled out of the window by some extraordinary chance, was going to pick it up, when Lord Ellenborough furiously called out, 'Drive on!' The bandbox, accordingly, was left by the ditch-side. Having reached the county town where he was to officiate as judge, Lord Ellenborough proceeded to array himself for his appearance in the court-house. 'Now,' said he, 'where's my wig—where *is* my wig?' 'My lord,' replied his attendant, 'it was thrown out of the carriage window!'"

Lord Ellenborough, great wit as he was, as frequently appears as the cause of wit in others as in the character itself. One of the most amusing stories related of him is that relative to his action on finding himself mimicked by Charles Mathews, the comedian. In personating Counselor Flexible, in the farce entitled "Love, Law, and Physic," the actor greatly delighted his house by imitations of Erskine and Garrow, and drew a tempest of applause by his account of the judge's summing up in the case of *Litigant* vs. *Camphor*. "When he came," says Mrs. Mathews, in her biography of the actor, "to the judge's summing up, the effect was quite astounding to him, for he had no idea of its being so received. The shout of recognition and enjoyment indeed was so alarming to his nerves, so unlike all former receptions of such efforts, that he repented the attempt in proportion as it was well taken, and a call for it a second time fairly upset him, albeit not unused to loud applause and approbation. The next morning every paper informed Lord Ellenborough how he had been made the laugh of a densely crowded theatre, and filled him with reasonable fear that for many a term he would not be able to raise his voice in his own court without throwing counsel and clients, solicitors and suitors, into convulsions of merriment. Enraged by the indignity, he wrote for protection to the lord chamberlain, who, with equal prudence and tact, soothed the anger in the judicial breast, and obtained from the actor a ready promise not to renew his misconduct. "Love, Law, and Physic" was not withdrawn; but Counselor Flexible never again entertained the public with the "judge's charge," although it was vociferously demanded at each succeeding presentation of the farce. To a select party at Carlton House the comedian, however, was induced to repeat the imitation, on which occasion the prince-regent and his brother of York were infinitely amused. "The prince was in raptures," the wifely biographer assures her readers, "and declared himself astonished at the closeness of the imitation, shutting his eyes while he listened to it with excessive enjoyment, and many exclamations of wonder and delight, such as 'Excellent!' 'Perfect!' 'It is himself!' The Duke of York manifested his approval by peals of laughter."

Among legal wits, Lord Ellenborough enjoys a high place; and though in dealing out satire upon barristers and witnesses, and even on his judicial coadjutors, he was often needlessly severe, he seldom perpetrated a jest the force of which lay solely in its cruelty. Perhaps the most harsh and reprehensible outburst of satiric humor recorded of him is the crushing speech by which he ruined a young man for life. "The *unfortunate* client for whom it is my privilege to appear," said a young barrister, making his first essay in Westminster Hall—the unfortunate client, my lord, for whom I appear—hem! hem!—I say, my lord, my *unfortunate client*—" Leaning forward, and speaking in a soft, cooing voice, that was all the more derisive because it was so gentle, Lord Ellenborough said, "You may go on, sir—so far the court is with you." One would have liked his lordship better had he sacrificed his jest to humanity, and acted as long afterward that true gentleman, Mr. Justice Talfourd, acted, who, seeing a young barrister overpowered with nervousness, gave him time to recover himself by saying, in the kindest possible manner, "Excuse me for interrupting you—but for a minute I am not at liberty to pay you attention." Whereupon the judge took up his pen and wrote a short note to a friend. Before the note was finished, the young barrister had completely recovered his self-possession, and, by an admirable speech, secured a verdict for his client.

Of Lord Ellenborough's sarcastic speeches to counsel who consumed his time to no good purpose, and were so well known among solicitors that a sharp reproof from a judge's lips could do them no serious harm, nothing can be said in the way of regret. The natural ebullitions of irritation from a giant toward men almost as strong and quite as prosperous as himself, they rouse laughter, without, at the same time, offending the reader's generosity and love of fair play. Preston, the great conveyancer, having inflicted on the court an unspeakably dreary oration, toward the close of the day asked when it would be their lordships' pleasure to hear the remainder of his argument; whereupon Lord Ellenborough uttered a sigh of resignation, and answered, "We are bound to hear you, and we will endeavor to give you our undivided attention on Friday next; but as for *pleasure*, that, sir, has been long out of the question."

Notwithstanding his high reputation for wit, Lord Ellenborough would deign to use the oldest jests. To silence a wearisome talker, he would pelt him with puns from Joe Miller; but though his missiles were of the cheapest kind, and picked from public ground, he hurled them with a force and precision that drew the applause of by-standers. Thus of Mr. Caldecott, who over and over again, with dull verbosity, had said that certain limestone quarries, like lead and copper mines, "were not ratable, because the limestone could only be reached by boring, which was matter of science," he gravely inquired, "Would you, Mr. Caldecott, have us believe that every kind of *boring* is matter of science?"

With finer humor he nipped in the bud one of Randle Jackson's flowery harangues. "My lords," said the orator, with nervous intonation, "in the book of nature it is written—" "Be kind enough, Mr. Jackson," interposed Lord Ellenborough, "to mention the page from which you are about to quote."

This calls to mind the ridicule which, at an earlier period of his career, he cast on Sheridan for saying at the trial of Warren Hastings, "The treasures in the Zenana of the Begum are offerings laid by the hand of piety on the altar of a saint." To this not too rhetorical statement, Edward Law, as leading counsel for Warren Hastings, replied by asking, "how the lady was to be considered a saint, and how the camels were to be laid upon the altar?" With greater pungency Sheridan defended himself by saying, "This is the first time in my life that I ever heard of special pleading on a metaphor, or a bill of indictment against a trope; but such is the turn of the learned gentleman's mind, that when he attempts to be humorous no jest can be found, and when serious no fact is visible."

To the last Ellenborough delighted to point the absurdities of orators who, in aiming at the sublime, only achieved the ridiculous. "My lords," said Mr. Gaselee, arguing that mourning-coaches at a funeral were not liable to post-horse duty, "it never could have been the intention of a Christian Legislature to aggravate the grief which mourners endure while following to the grave the remains of their dearest relatives, by compelling them at the same time to pay the horse-duty." Had Mr. Gaselee been a humorist, Lord Ellenborough would have laughed; but as the advocate was well known to have no turn for raillery, the chief justice gravely observed, "Mr. Gaselee, you incur danger by sailing in high sentimental latitudes."

To the surgeon in the witness-box who said, "I employ myself as a surgeon," Lord Ellenborough retorted, "But does any body else employ you as a surgeon?"

Very pungent was his ejaculation at a cabinet dinner when he heard that Lord Kenyon was about to close his penurious old age by dying. "Die! why should he die? what would he get by that?" interposed Lord Ellenborough, adding to the pile of jests by which men have endeavored to keep a grim, unpleasant subject out of sight — a pile to which the latest *mot* was added by Lord Palmerston, who, during his last attack of gout, exclaimed, playfully, "*Die*, my dear doctor! That's the *last* thing I think of doing."

Having jested about Kenyon's parsimony as the old man

lay in *extremis*, Ellenborough placed another joke of the same kind upon his coffin. Hearing that through the blunder of an illiterate undertaker the motto on Kenyon's hatchment in Lincoln's Inn Fields had been painted "*Mors janua vita*," instead of "Mors janua vitæ," he exclaimed, "Bless you, there's no mistake; Kenyon's will directed that it should be 'vita,' so that his estate might be saved the expense of a diphthong."

Capital also was his reply when Erskine urged him to accept the great seal. "How can you," he asked, in a tone of solemn entreaty, "wish me to accept the office of chancellor, when you know, Erskine, that I am as ignorant of its duties as you are yourself?"

THE WITTY AND ACCOMPLISHED MANSFIELD.

Lord Chancellor Mansfield, unanimously allowed to be the most accomplished and learned lawyer of his time, was also one of the wittiest; and many are the stories told of his sparkling pleasantry. His story of his advice to an old army officer who knew nothing of law, and who had been appointed governor of a West India island, is related in exquisite style by Jeaffreson. The most appalling duty which the governor had to perform was the administration of justice, and in his ignorance he addressed Lord Mansfield in a voice of great concern, saying that he knew nothing of law, and asking what he should do as the presiding officer of the local Court of Chancery on the island to which he was going. "Tut, man," said Mansfield, "decide promptly, but never give any reasons for your decisions. Your decisions may be right, but your reasons are sure to be wrong." Acting on this rule, the military chancellor pushed on well enough; but in an evil hour, forgetting the precept, he gave his first good decision, and it was immediately appealed against. Recounting the story to his grandson, Lord Mansfield said, "I was two or three years afterward sitting at the Cockpit on Plantation Appeals, when there was one called from my friend and pupil the general, which the losing party had been induced to bring on account of the ludicrously absurd reasons given for the judgment, which, indeed, were so absurd that he incurred some suspicion of corruption, and there was a clamor for his recall. Upon examining it, I found that the judgment itself was perfectly sound and correct. Regretting that my advice had been forgotten, I was told that the general acquiring reputation by following it, began to suppose himself a great lawyer, and that this case brought before us was the first in which he had given his reasons, and was the first appealed against."

Lord Mansfield had a great abhorrence of the penal system of England, and used every effort to have it modified. His humanity was so shocked by the bare thought of killing a man for committing a trifling theft, that he on one occasion ordered a jury to find that a stolen trinket was of less value than forty shillings, in order that the thief might escape the capital sentence. The prosecutor, a dealer in jewelry, was so mortified by the judge's leniency that he exclaimed, "What, my lord, my gold trinket not worth forty shillings? Why, the fashion alone cost me twice the money!" Removing his glance from the vindictive tradesman, Lord Mansfield turned toward the jury and said, with solemn gravity, "As we stand in need of God's mercy, gentlemen, let us not hang a man for fashion's sake."

Lord Mansfield, when simply Counselor Murray, was one of the managers for the impeachment of Lord Lovat by the House of Commons, in 1747, and, when commenting on the evidence, displayed so much candor and moderation, that the celebrated Lord Talbot, on the conclusion of his speech, felt called upon to pay him the following enthusiastic compliment: "The abilities of the learned manager who has just now spoke never appeared with greater splendor than at this very hour, when his candor and humanity have been joined to those great abilities which have already made him so conspicuous, that I hope to see him one day add lustre to the dignity of the first civil employment in this nation." Lord Lovat himself bore remarkable testimony to the abilities and fairness of his adversary. Alluding to one of the witnesses on the trial, he said, "I thought myself very much LOADED by one Murray, who your lordships knew was the bitterest evidence there was against me. I have since suffered by another Mr. Murray, who I must say is an honor to his country, and whose eloquence and learning is much beyond what is to be expressed by an ignorant man like me. I heard him with pleasure, though it was against me. I have the honor to be his relation, though perhaps he neither knows it nor values it. I wish that his being born in the North may not hinder him from the preferment that his merit and learning deserve."

Lord Mansfield was once presiding at a trial consequent upon a collision of two ships at sea, when a common sailor, while giving testimony, said, "At the time I was standing abaft the binnacle;" whereupon his lordship, with a proper desire to master the facts of the case, observed, "Stay, stay a minute, witness; you say that at the time in question you were *standing abaft the binnacle;* now tell me, where is 'abaft the binnacle?'" This was too much for the gravity of "the salt," who immediately before climbing into the witness-box had taken a copious draught of rum. Removing his eyes from the bench, and turning round upon the crowded court with an expression of intense amusement, he exclaimed at the top of his voice, "He's a pretty fellow for a judge! Bless my jolly old eyes!—[the reader may substitute a familiar form of 'imprecation on eyesight']—you have got a pretty sort of a land-lubber for a judge! He wants me tell him where *abaft the binnacle* is!" Not less amused than the witness, Lord Mansfield rejoined, "Well, my friend, you must fit me for my office by telling me where *abaft the binnacle* is; you've already shown me the meaning of *half-seas over!*"

On one occasion Lord Mansfield covered his retreat from an untenable position with a sparkling pleasantry. An old witness named *Elm* having given his evidence with remarkable clearness, although he was more than eighty years of age, Lord Mansfield examined him as to his habitual mode of living, and found that he had throughout life been an early riser, and a singularly temperate man. "Ay," observed the chief justice, in a tone of approval, "I have always found that, without temperance and early habits, longevity is never attained." The next witness, the elder brother of this model of temperance, was then called, and he almost surpassed his brother as an intelligent and clear-headed utterer of evidence. "I suppose," observed Lord Mansfield, "that you also are an early riser?" "No, my lord," answered the veteran stoutly; "I like my bed at all hours, and specially I like it of a morning." "Ah! but like your brother, you are a very temperate man?" quickly asked the judge, looking out anxiously for the safety of the more important part of his theory. "My lord," responded this ancient Elm, disdaining to plead guilty to a charge of habitual sobriety, "I am a very old man, and my memory is as clear as a bell, but I can't remember the night when I've gone to bed without being more or less drunk." Lord Mansfield was silent. "Ah! my lord," Mr. Dunning exclaimed, "this old man's case supports a theory upheld by many persons, that habitual intemperance is favorable to longevity." "No, no," replied the chief justice with a smile, "this old man and his brother merely teach us what every carpenter knows—that elm, whether it be wet or dry, is a very tough wood."

Sir Fletcher Norton was noted for his want of courtesy. When pleading before Lord Mansfield on some question of manorial right, he chanced to say, "My lord, I can illustrate the point in an instant in my own person—I myself have too little manors." The judge immediately interposed, with one of his blandest smiles, "We all know that, Sir Fletcher."

Mansfield was very intimate with the wits of his time, one of whom wrote of him,

> "Graced as thou art with all the power of words,
> So known, so honored in the House of Lords."

Another, of a more churlish nature but not less wit, Sam Johnson, at once humorously recognized Mansfield's merit, and betrayed his own hatred of the Scotch, by alluding to him as "an instance of what might be made of a Scotchman who had been caught young."

PECULIARITIES OF LORD CHANCELLOR LOUGHBOROUGH.

There are few stories told of Lord Loughborough, though he was one of the most singular characters who ever held the Great Seal of England. Jeaffreson says of him, "A poor conversationalist, he was so incapable of responding to the smart repartees of the wits, that Samuel Johnson petulantly asked Foote, 'What can that barrister mean by coming among us? He is not only dull himself, but the cause of dullness in others.'" But he was a fluent, impetuous, incisive speaker whenever he was permitted to speak without interruption. Devoid of fancy, but overflowing with spite, he poured forth his malignant sentences with a sharp, precise, hissing accentuation that gave a fine edge to each well-chosen word, and drove it home to the adversary's most sensitive point. On the bench he declined to adopt the colloquial tone usual with judges transacting ordinary business, but retained the preciseness and venomous acrimony of the eloquence which had made him dreaded as a counselor.

THE PRESENT LORD-CHANCELLOR.

The present Lord Chancellor of England is the Right Honorable Sir Frederick Thesiger, first Baron Chelmsford. Unlike all others of his predecessors, he came to the wool-

LORD CHELMSFORD.

sack from neither the bar nor the Church, but the navy. He was born in 1794, and entered the English navy as a midshipman in 1803. The only naval battle which he witnessed, however, was the bombardment of Copenhagen in 1807. In 1818, his elder brother dying childless, Sir Frederick succeeded to the titles and estates, and also abandoned his own for his late brother's profession, and commenced the study of law. He rapidly acquired great reputation, particularly in the conduct of election cases, and in 1834 was appointed one of the king's counsel. He entered Parliament in 1841 as member for the borough of Woodstock, and held a seat for different constituencies, but always in the conservative interests, until 1858, when, on the return of Lord Derby to power, he was made Baron Chelmsford, and placed in charge of the seals. On the fall of Derby in the year following, he retired with him, and in 1866 was again elevated with Derby to power, receiving the seals for the second time. Lord Chelmsford made law and politics his stepping-stones to power; he had none of that love of the profession which distinguished many of his predecessors, and consequently few amusing incidents or witty sayings of his are recorded.

2.

Celebrated British Barristers.

CHAPTER II.

ANECDOTES OF CELEBRATED BRITISH BARRISTERS.

REMINISCENCE OF HENRY GRATTAN.

SIR JONAH BARRINGTON, in his pleasant "Sketches," thus relates an interview which took place upon the introduction of Aaron Burr and John Randolph, of South Carolina, to Henry Grattan: "We went to my friend's house on the evening before he was to leave London. I announced that Colonel Burr, Mr. Randolph (from America), and myself wished to pay our respects, and the servant informed us that his master would receive us in a short time, but was, at the moment, much occupied on business of consequence. Burr's expectations were all on the alert. Randolph was also anxious to be presented to the great Grattan, and both impatient for the entrance of this Demosthenes. At length the door opened, and in hopped a small, bent figure—meagre, yellow, and ordinary; one slipper and one shoe; his breeches loose at the knee; his cravat hanging down, his shirt and coat-sleeves tucked up high, and an old hat upon his head. This apparition saluted the strangers very courteously; asked (without any introduction) how long they had been in England, and immediately proceeded to make inquiries about General Washington and the Revolutionary War. My companions looked at each other; their replies were curt, and they seemed quite impatient to see Mr. Grattan. I could scarcely contain myself, but determined to let my eccentric countryman take his own course. He appeared quite delighted to see his visitors, and was the most inquisitive person in the world. Randolph was far the tallest and most dignified-looking man of the two, gray-haired and well dressed. Grattan therefore took him for the Vice-president, and addressed him accordingly. Randolph at length begged to know if they could shortly have the honor of seeing Mr. Grattan. Upon which our host (not doubting but they knew him) conceived it must be his son James for whom they inquired, and said he believed he had at that moment wandered out somewhere to amuse himself. This completely disconcerted the Americans, and they were about to make their bow and their exit, when I thought it high time to explain, and, taking Colonel Burr and Mr. Randolph respectively by the hand, introduced them to the Right Honorable Henry Grattan.

"I never saw people stare so, or so much embarrassed! Grattan himself now perceiving the cause, heartily joined in the merriment; he pulled down his shirt-sleeves, pulled up his stockings, and in his own irresistible way apologized for the *outre* figure he cut, assuring them that he had totally overlooked it in his anxiety not to keep them waiting; that he was returning to Ireland next morning, and had been busily packing up his books and papers in a closet full of dust and cobwebs! This incident rendered the interview more interesting; the Americans were charmed with their reception, and, after a protracted visit, retired highly gratified, while Grattan returned again to his books and cobwebs."

The last words of Grattan to the surgeon general, who saw him in London just before his death, are very patriotic and beautiful:

"I am perfectly resigned; I am surrounded by my family; I have served my country; I have reliance upon God, and I am not afraid of the devil!"

PERSONAL APPEARANCE OF CURRAN.

Barrington, whom I have quoted before, has also given the following pen-and-ink picture of John Philpot Curran, the eloquent champion of Irish liberty: "Curran's person was mean and decrepit, very slight, very shapeless—with nothing of the gentleman about it; on the contrary, displaying spindle limbs, a shambling gait, one hand imperfect, and a face yellow, furrowed, rather flat, and thoroughly ordinary. Yet his features were the very reverse of disagreeable. There was something so indescribably dramatic in his eye and the play of his eyebrow, that his visage seemed the index of his mind, and his humor the slave of his will. His very foibles were amusing. He had no vein for poetry, yet, fancying himself a bard, he contrived to throw off pretty verses. He certainly was no musician, but, conceiving himself to be one, played very pleasingly. Nature had denied him a voice, but he could sing; and, in the rich mould of his capabilities, the desire had also bred in some degree the capacity."

CURRAN'S FIRST BRIEF AND FIRST WITTICISMS.

Not long after his first brief, a circumstance occurred which elicited the first scintillation of Curran's genius, and rendered him a terror alike to the bench and the bar.

Lord Robertson, one of the presiding judges, was very unpopular both as a man and a jurist. He had undertaken to edit an edition of Blackstone, but, being afraid of the critics, he simply gave it the title of "Blackstone's Commentaries, by a Member of the Irish Bar." Soon after the work appeared Curran was pleading a case before his lordship, when the judge interrupted him and said,

"Gentlemen of the jury, the learned counsel has mistaken the law of this case. The law is so and so."

To which Curran tartly replied,

"If his lordship says so, the etiquette of the court demands that I submit, though neither the statute nor common law of the country should sanction his lordship's opinion; but it is my duty and privilege, too, to inform you, gentlemen of the jury, that I have never seen the law so interpreted in any book of my library."

Lord Robertson sneeringly replied, "Perhaps your library is rather small, Mr. Curran."

"I admit," said Curran, "my library is small; but I have always found it more profitable to read good books than to publish bad ones—books which their very authors and editors are ashamed to own."

"Sir," said the judge, "you are forgetting the dignity of the judicial character."

To this Curran promptly replied,

"Speaking of *dignity*, your lordship reminds me of a book I have read—I refer to 'Tristram Shandy'—in which, if your lordship has read it, you will remember that the Irish buffer Roche, on engaging in a squabble, lent his coat to a by-stander, and after the fight was ended he discovered that he had got a good beating and lost his coat into the bargain; your lordship can apply the illustration."

"Sir," said the judge very petulantly, "if you say another word I'll commit you."

"If you do, my lord," replied Curran, coolly, "both you and I shall have the pleasure of reflecting that I am not the worst *thing* your lordship has *committed*."

CURRAN AND HIS YOUNGER BROTHER.

Curran had a younger brother, an attorney like himself, possessing a good deal of his wit and humor, but of exceedingly dissolute habits. He was a great spendthrift, importuned the elder Curran for loans, and was a heavy tax upon his purse. His brother having once refused to advance him any more money, the profligate lawyer devised the following plan to recruit his finances from the usual source.

AN ENGLISH JUDGE.

There was a small space of dead wall directly facing Curran's house in Ely Place, against which the attorney procured a written permission to build a little wooden box. He accordingly got a carpenter to erect a cobbler's stall there for him; and, having assumed the dress of a shoemaker, he wrote over his stall, "CURRAN, COBBLER:—Shoes toe-pieced, soled, or heeled on the shortest notice: when the stall is shut, inquire over the way." Curran, on returning from court, perceived his worthy brother hard at work, with a parcel of loafers lounging round him. His brother just nodded to the attorney, cried "How do you do, Jack?" and went on with his employment. Curran immediately dispatched a servant for the spendthrift, to whom having given some money, the show-board was taken down, the stall removed, and the attorney promised that he would never set up again as a cobbler.

Curran's wit was double-edged, and cut like a sword. His ruling passion was his joke, and it was strong, if not in death, at least in his last illness. One morning his physician observed that he seemed to "cough with more difficulty."

"That is rather surprising," answered Curran, smiling sadly, "for I have been practicing all night."

While thus lying ill, Curran was visited by a friend, Father O'Leary, who also loved his joke.

"I wish, O'Leary," said Curran to him abruptly, "that you had the keys of heaven."

"Why, Curran?"

"Because you could let me in," said the facetious counselor.

"It would be much better for you, Curran," said the good-humored priest, "that I had the keys of the other place, because I could then let you out."

Lundy Foot, a celebrated tobacconist, applied to Curran for a motto when he first established his carriage. "Give me one, my dear Curran, of a serious cast, because I am afraid the people will laugh at a tobacconist setting up a carriage, and for the 'scholarship's sake,' let it be in Latin."

"I have just hit on it," said Curran; "it is only two words, and will at once explain your profession, your elevation, and your contempt for their ridicule, and it has the advantage of being in two languages, Latin or English, just as the reader chooses. Put up '*Quid rides*' upon your carriage."

Curran was once pleading a case before a very facetious judge, who was occasionally rather irritable, and any noise while he was charging a jury annoyed him very much. On such an occasion he was sadly interrupted by the braying of an ass, and turned to the sheriff, ordering him to stop that noise. Curran being present, observed, "May it please your honor, it is merely an echo!"

An Irish judge of the King's Bench, in giving his *dictum* on a certain will case, absolutely said, "He thought it very clear that the *testator* intended to keep a *life interest* in the estate to *himself*." The bar did not laugh outright, but Curran soon rendered that consequence inevitable. "Very true, my lord," said he; "very true. Testators usually do secure life interests to themselves; but in this case I had rather your lordship would take the *will* for the *deed*."

Chief Justice Carleton was a very lugubrious personage. He never ceased complaining of his bad state of health (or, rather, of his hypochondriasm), and frequently introduced Lady Carleton into his "Book of Lamentations." Thence it was remarked by Curran to be very extraordinary, that the chief justice should appear as plaintiff (*plaintive*) in every cause that happened to come before him.

One day Lord Carleton came into court looking unusually gloomy. He apologized to the bar for being necessitated to adjourn the court and dismiss the jury for the day, "though," proceeded his lordship, "I am aware that an important issue stands for trial; but the fact is, I have met with a domestic misfortune which has altogether deranged my nerves!—poor Lady Carleton (in a low tone to the bar) has most unfortunately *miscarried*, and—"

"Oh, then, my lord!" exclaimed Curran, "there was no

F

necessity for your lordship to make any apology, since it now appears that your lordship has *no issue* to try."

Curran's avoidance of a duel by the exercise of his wit is a story not less amusing than familiar. He was waited on one morning before he had left his bed by a gentleman whom he had cross-examined with needless cruelty and unjustifiable insolence on the previous day.

"Sir!" said this irate man, presenting himself in Curran's bedroom, and rousing the barrister from slumber to a consciousness that he was in a very awkward position, "I am the gintleman whom you insulted yesterday in his majesty's court of justice in the presence of the whole bar, and I come to demand justice!"

Curran measured at a glance the huge person of the intruder, and concluded that he had a poor chance in a combat with him. So, lying still, he asked,

"Surely, you wouldn't strike a man when he's down?"

"No, sir, no; certainly not."

"Then I wish you a very good-morning," said Curran, turning over on his side and pulling the cover closer about his ears; "I'm going to take a nap."

The scene was so ridiculous that the stranger dropped his uplifted arm, burst into a hearty roar of laughter, and asked the counselor to shake hands with him. Of the genuineness of this piquant story the writer is compelled to entertain some unpleasant doubts, since he has found it in books, with numerous minor variations, told of half a dozen different Irish barristers.

Very sarcastic was Curran's reply to a prosy member of Parliament who had asked him,

"Have you read my last speech?" Curran replied, turning away,

"I hope I have."

More bitter still was his answer to the poet who, fishing for compliments, asked him,

"Have you seen my 'Descent into Hell?'

"No," said Curran warmly, "I should be delighted to see it."

Terribly sarcastic was the denunciation of his political enemy, whom he described as "buoyant by putrefaction, rising as he rotted."

ENGLISH COUNSELORS.

Curran was once engaged in a legal argument. Behind him stood his colleague, a gentleman whose person was remarkably tall and slender, and who had originally intended to take orders. The judge observed that the case under discussion involved a question of ecclesiastical law. "Then," said Curran, "I can refer your lordship to a *high* authority behind me who was once intended for the Church, though, in my opinion, he was fitter for the steeple."

ANECDOTES OF DR. JOHNSON.

Dr. Sam Johnson, poet and counselor, noted for his gruffness and his wit, compared plaintiff and defendant in action at law to two men ducking their heads in a bucket, and daring each other to remain longest under water.

Nothing could have been more natural than that Johnson should have married a cross, gruff woman. When he asked the widow Porter to be his wife he told her candidly that he was of mean extraction, that he had no money, and that he had an uncle hanged. The widow replied that she cared nothing for his parentage, that she had no money herself; and though she had not had a relation hanged, she had fifty who deserved hanging. So they made a match of it.

A LAWYER'S "FIRST BEST CAUSE."

One of Charles Lamb's best witticisms was on an embryo lawyer, his young friend Robinson. On receiving his first brief, Robinson called in delight upon Lamb to tell him of it.

"I suppose," said Lamb, "you addressed that line of Milton to it, 'Thou first best cause, least understood.'"

ANECDOTES OF RICHARD BRINSLEY SHERIDAN.

Sheridan studied the art of punning, and many of the most brilliant *mots* of various ages are attributed to him. In this volume they have been given as far as possible to the rightful authors, and what follows are only those of which Sheridan was the undoubted and undisputed author.

As Sheridan was visiting London in one of the public coaches for the purpose of canvassing Westminster at the time when Paul was his opponent, he found himself in company with two Westminster electors. In the course of the conversation one of them asked the other to whom he should give his vote, when his friend replied,

"To Paul, certainly; for though I think him but a shabby sort of fellow, I would vote for any one rather than that rascal Sheridan."

"Do you know Sheridan?" asked the stranger.

"Not I, sir," answered the gentleman; "nor do I wish to know him."

The conversation dropped here; but, when the party alighted to breakfast, Sheridan called aside the other gentleman and said,

"Pray, who is that very agreeable friend of yours? He is one of the pleasantest fellows I ever met with, and I should be glad to know his name."

"His name is Mr. T——; he is an eminent lawyer, and resides in Lincoln's-inn Fields."

Breakfast over, the party resumed their seats in the coach, soon after which Sheridan turned the conversation to the law.

"It is," said he, "a fine profession. Men may rise from it to the highest eminence in the state, and it gives vast scope to the display of talent. Many of the most virtuous and noble characters recorded in our history have been lawyers. I am sorry, however, to add that some of the greatest rascals have also been lawyers; but of all the rascals of lawyers I ever heard of, the greatest is one T——, who lives in Lincoln's-inn Fields."

"I am Mr. T——," thundered the gentleman.

"And I am Mr. Sheridan," was the laughing reply.

The jest was instantly seen; they shook hands, and, instead of voting against the facetious orator, the lawyer exerted himself warmly in promoting his election.

Sheridan was once staying at the house of an elderly maiden lady in the country, who wanted more of his company than he was willing to give. Proposing one day to take a stroll with him, he excused himself to her on account of the badness of the weather. Shortly afterward she met him sneaking out alone. "So, Mr. Sheridan," said she, "it has cleared up." "Just a little, ma'am; enough for one, but not enough for two."

As Sheridan was entering court one day, carrying his books and briefs in a green bag according to the custom of the time, some of his brother barristers, thinking to play a joke on him, urged some boys to ask him if he had old clothes for sale in his green bag.

"Oh no," instantly responded Sheridan; "they are all new suits."

Those who are in the habit of telling prodigious stories ought to have good memories; but, fortunately, their memories are generally short. Richard Brinsley Sheridan dealt with these mendacious pests in a manner peculiar to himself. He would never allow himself to be outdone by a verbal prodigy. Whenever a monstrous story was told in his presence, he would endeavor to outdo it by one of his own coinage, and consign the narrator to confusion by a falsehood more glaring than his own. Once in his hearing a sporting adventurer ran thus: "I was fishing one day, say in a certain cold spring full of delicious trout, and soon caught a large mess. But what was really surprising, not a foot from the cold spring there was one of boiling water; so that, when you wanted to cook your fish, all you had to do, after hooking them from the cold spring, was to pop them directly into the boiling."

The company all expressed astonishment and incredulity at this monstrous assertion, with the exception of Sheridan. "I know," said he, "of a phenomenon yet more surprising:

I was fishing one day, when I came to a place where there were three springs. The first was a cold one stocked with fish, the second a boiling spring, and the third a natural fountain of *melted butter and parsley.*"

"Melted butter and parsley!" exclaimed the first story-teller, "impossible!"

Sheridan was one day much annoyed by a fellow-member of the House of Commons who kept crying out every few minutes "Hear! hear!" During the debate he took occasion to describe a political contemporary that wished to play rogue, but who only had sense enough to act fool. "Where," exclaimed he, with great emphasis, "where shall we find a more foolish knave or more knavish fool than he?" "Hear! hear!" was shouted from the troublesome member. Sheridan turned round, and, thanking him for the prompt information, sat down amid a general roar of laughter.

Sheridan is said to have remarked, on entering a crowded committee-room, in parliamentary language, "Will some member move that I may take the chair?"

GRIM JOKES OF HANGING JUDGES.

Horrible are the flippant tales told about the "hanging judges" of the days, not far distant, when women were judicially murdered by English law for offenses that would not nowadays get them six months' imprisonment, and when sentence of death was recorded against children for misdeeds that would have been amply punished by a single application of a birch rod. And of all these bloodthirsty wearers of the ermine no one, since the opening of the eighteenth century, has fared worse than Sir Francis Page—the virulence of whose tongue and the cruelty of whose nature were marks for successive satirists. In one of his Imitations of Horace, Pope says,

> "Slander or poison dread from Delia's rage,
> Hard words or hanging, if your judge be Page."

In the same spirit the poet penned the lines of the "Dunciad"—

> "Morality, by her false guardians drawn,
> Chicane in furs, and Casuistry in lawn,
> Gasps, as they straighten at each end the cord,
> And dies when Dullness gives her—the sword."

Powerless to feign insensibility to the blow, Sir Francis openly fitted this black cap to his dishonored head by sending his clerk to expostulate with the poet. The ill-chosen embassador performed his mission by showing that, in Sir Francis's opinion, the whole passage would be sheer nonsense, unless "Page" were inserted in the vacant place!

Johnson and Savage took vengeance on the judge for the judicial misconduct which branded the latter poet a murderer; and Fielding, in "Tom Jones," illustrating by a current story the offensive levity of the judge's demeanor at capital trials, makes him thus retort on a horse-stealer: "Ay! thou art a lucky fellow; I have traveled the circuit these forty years, and never found a horse in my life; but I'll tell thee what, friend, thou wast more lucky than thou didst know of; for thou didst not only find a horse, but a halter too, I promise thee."

It is said of Page that in his last year he pointed the ignominious story of his existence by a speech that soon ran the round of the courts. In answer to an inquiry for his health, the octogenarian judge observed, "My dear sir, you see how it fares with me; I just manage to keep *hanging on, hanging on.*" This story is ordinarily told as though the old man did not see the unfavorable significance of his words; but it is probable that he uttered them wittingly and with a sneer—in the cynicism and shamelessness of old age.

One of the humorous aspects of this repulsive subject is seen in the curiosity and fastidiousness of prisoners on trial for capital offenses with regard to the professional *status* of the judges who try them. A sheep-stealer of the old bloody days of English law liked that sentence should be passed upon him by a chief justice; and, in the present time, murderers awaiting execution sometimes grumble at

ENGLISH ATTORNEYS.

the unfairness of their trials because they have been tried by judges of inferior degree. Lord Campbell mentions the case of a sergeant, who, while acting as Chief Justice Charles Abbott's deputy, was reminded by the prisoner in the dock that he was "merely a temporary." Being asked in the usual way if he had aught to say why sentence of death should not be passed upon him, the same prisoner answered surlily, "Yes; I have been tried before a journeyman judge!"

Among the grimly humorous addresses attributed to judges speaking from the bench to prisoners at the bar, Baron Alderson's rejoinder to a man convicted of swindling is memorable. In reply to the final inquiry why sentence should not be passed upon him, the prisoner, with blasphemous obstinacy, persisted in asserting his innocence. The miserable fellow concluded his address by saying deliberately, and in a singularly solemn tone, "May God strike me dead, now at this moment, and here where I stand, if I am not innocent!" As the speaker's guilt had been clearly ascertained, every hearer was painfully moved by this abominable self-imprecation. A thrill of horror ran through the court. A minute of painful silence ensued; and then the judge substituted another emotion in the minds of all present by saying, in a cold matter-of-fact voice, "Prisoner at the bar, as Providence has not interposed in the behalf of society, the sentence of the court is that you be transported for twenty years."

Lord Norbury, celebrated equally for his wit and his severity, while sitting as a special commissioner to try the culprits in one of the Irish rebellions, convicted a great many in a single day.

"You are going on here swimmingly, my lord," said one of the counsel for the prisoners.

"Yes," answered his lordship significantly, "seven knots an hour."

Chief Justice Hale was strongly opposed to the severity of the English law, and took occasion, whenever he found opportunity, to show his repugnance to its needless severity. Once he tried a half-starved lad on a charge of burglary. The prisoner had been shipwrecked upon the Cornish coast, and on his way through an inhospitable district had endured the pangs of extreme hunger. In his distress, the famished wanderer broke the window of a baker's shop and stole a loaf of bread. Under the circumstances, Hale directed the jury to acquit the prisoner; but, less merciful than the judge, the gentlemen of the box returned a verdict of "guilty"—a verdict which the chief justice stoutly refused to act upon. After much resistance the jurymen were starved into submission, and the youth was set at liberty. Several years elapsed; and Chief Justice Hale was riding the Northern Circuit, when he was received with such costly and excessive pomp by the sheriff of a northern county, that he expostulated with his entertainer on the lavish profuseness of his conduct. "My lord," answered the sheriff, with emotion, "don't blame me for showing my gratitude to the judge who saved my life when I was an outcast. Had it not been for you, I should have been hanged in Cornwall for stealing a loaf, instead of living to be the richest landowner of my native county."

Chief Justice Hale had been in his youth a rather wild young man, and more than one of his companions were brought in after years before him for judgment. On one occasion, before sentencing to death a culprit whom he had known in better days, he asked him some questions touching their old associates.

"They are all hanged, my lord," said the knave, "except you and me."

In a note to a passage in one of the Waverley novels Scott tells a story of an old Scotch judge, who, as an enthusiastic chess-player, was much mortified by the success of an ancient friend, who invariably beat him when they tried their powers at the beloved game. After a time the humiliated chess-player had his day of triumph. His conqueror happened to commit murder, and it became the judge's not altogether painful duty to pass upon him the sentence of the law. Having in due form, and with suitable solemnity, commended his soul to the Divine mercy, he, after a brief pause, assumed his ordinary colloquial tone of voice, and nodding humorously to his old friend, observed, "And noo, Jamie, I think ye'll alloo that I hae checkmated you for ance."

An Irish judge, familiarly known as the "hanging judge," was never seen to shed a tear but once, and that was during the representation of *The Beggar's Opera*, when Macheath got a *reprieve*!

It was between the same judge and Curran that the following passage of wit once took place at table:

"Pray, Mr. Curran," said the judge, "is that hung beef beside you? If it is, I will try it."

"If *you* try it, my lord," replied Mr. Curran, "it is sure to be hung."

COKE DONE INTO VERSE.

About 1742 a volume appeared in England purporting to be the "Reports of Sir Edward Coke, Knight, in Verse." Though the book does not now survive, the humorous story which inspired the droll volume is yet remembered. The story is alike commendable for its subtlety and inoffensive humor. An amiable and upright, but far from brilliant judge, Sir Lyttleton Powys, had a few pet phrases,—among them "I humbly conceive," and "Look, do you see"—which he sprinkled over his judgments and colloquial talk with ridiculous profuseness. Surprised at Philip Yorke's sudden rise into lucrative practice, this most gentlemanlike worthy was pleased to account for the unusual success by maintaining that young Yorke must have written a law-book which had brought him early into favor with the inferior branch of the profession. "Mr. Yorke," said the venerable justice, while the barristers were sitting over their wine at a "judges' dinner," "I can not well account for your having so much business, considering how short a time you have been at the bar; I humbly conceive you must have published something; for look you, do you see, there is scarcely a cause in court but you are employed in it on one side or the other. I should therefore be glad to know, Mr. Yorke, do you see, whether this be the case." Playfully denying that he possessed any celebrity as a writer on legal matters, Yorke, with an assumption of candor, admitted that he had some thoughts of lightening the labors of law-students by turning Coke upon Littleton into verse. Indeed, he confessed that he had already begun the work of versification. Not seeing the nature of the reply, Sir Littleton Powys treated the droll fancy as a serious project, and insisted that the author should give a specimen of the style of his contemplated work. Whereupon the young barrister—not pausing to remind a company of lawyers of the words of the original, "Tenant in fee simple is he which hath lands or tenements to hold to him and his heirs forever"—recited the lines,

"He that holdeth his lands in fee
Need neither to quake nor to quiver,
I humbly conceive; for look, doy ou see,
They are his and his heirs' forever."

The mimicry of his voice being not less perfect than the verbal imitation, Yorke's hearers were convulsed with laughter; but so unconscious was Sir Lyttleton of the ridicule which he had incurred, that, on subsequently encountering Yorke in London, he asked how "that translation of Coke upon Littleton was getting on."

A REMARKABLE COUNTENANCE.

Charles Yorke, the less honorable, more ambitious, and successful brother of the foregoing, was not less inclined to the humorous. It is recorded of him that, after his election to serve as a member for the University of Cambridge, he, in accordance with etiquette, made a round of calls on members of senate, giving them personal thanks for their votes; and that, on coming to the presence of a supporter—an old "fellow" known as the ugliest man in Cambridge—he addressed him thus, after smiling "an aside" to a knot of by-standers—"Sir, I have reason to be thankful to my friends in general, but I confess myself under particular obligation to you for the very *remarkable countenance* you have shown me on this occasion."

A CALUMNY ON THE PROFESSION DISPROVED BY ITS AUTHOR.

Lord Keeper Williams, one of the most honest of the Chancellors of England, is the author of a reflection on the purity of the legal profession which is improperly quoted to this day as justification of the common and vulgar idea that there are no honest lawyers. The remark of Williams, not unjust at that time, though inapplicable with truth to lawyers in every age, was, that "A proneness to take bribes may be generated from the habit of taking fees." A story of this same lord keeper is preserved, which at once refutes his own calumny, and illustrates the prevalence of judicial corruption in the seventeenth century, and the jealousy with which the right reverend slanderer watched for attempts to tamper with his own honesty. While he was taking exercise in the great park of Nonsuch House, his attention was caught by a church recently erected at the cost of a rich chancery suitor. Having expressed satisfaction with the church, Williams inquired, "Has he not a suit depending in chancery?" and on receiving an answer in the affirmative, observed, "He shall not fare the worse for building of churches." These words being reported to the pious suitor, he not illogically argued that the keeper was a judge likely to be influenced in making his decisions by matters distinct from the legal merits of the case put before him. Acting on this impression, the good man forthwith sent messengers to Nonsuch House, bearing gifts of fruit and poultry to the holder of the seals. "Nay, carry them back," cried the judge, looking with a grim smile at the presents, "nay, carry them back, and tell your master that he shall not fare the better for sending of presents."

More familiar and more ridiculous are the stories told of the manner in which Chief Justice Hale displayed his aversion to any thing having the appearance of bribery. A less familiar one is told by Sir John Graham of his own experience:

"There was a baronet of ancient family with whom the judges going the Western Circuit had always been accustomed to dine. When I went that circuit I heard that a cause, in which he was plaintiff, was coming on for trial; but the usual invitation was received, and, lest the people might suppose that judges could be influenced by a dinner, I accepted it. The defendant, a neighboring squire, being dreadfully alarmed by this intelligence, said to himself, 'Well, if Sir John entertains the judge hospitably, I do not see why I should not do the same by the jury.' So he invited to dinner the whole of the special jury summoned to try the cause. Thereupon the baronet's courage failed him, and he withdrew the record, so that the cause was not tried; and, although I had my dinner, I escaped all suspicion of partiality."

This story puts Jeaffreson, who tells it, in mind of another which he had heard told in various ways, and which he relates in the following neat manner:

Less than twenty years since, in one of England's southern counties, two neighboring landed proprietors differed concerning their respective rights over some uninclosed land, and also about certain rights of fishing in an adjacent stream. The one proprietor was the richest baronet, the other the poorest squire, of the county, and they agreed to settle their dispute by arbitration. Our master in chancery, slightly known to both gentlemen, was invited to act as arbitrator after inspecting the localities in dispute. The invitation was accepted, and the master visited the scene of disagreement on the understanding that he should give up two days to the matter. It was arranged that on the first day he should walk over the squire's estate, and hear the squire's uncontradicted version of the case, dining at the close of the day with both contestants at the squire's table; and that on the second day, having walked over the baronet's estate, and heard without interruption the other side of the story, he should give his award, sitting over wine after dinner at the rich man's table. At the close of the first day the squire entertained his wealthy neighbor and the arbitrator at dinner. In accordance with the host's means, the dinner was modest, but sufficient. It consisted of three fried soles, a roast leg of mutton, and vegetables; three pancakes, three pieces of cheese, three small loaves of bread, ale, and a bottle of sherry. On the removal of the viands, three magnificent apples, together with a magnum of port, were placed on the table by way of dessert. At the close of the second day the trio dined at the baronet's table, when it appeared that, struck by the simplicity of the previous day's dinner, and rightly attributing the absence of luxuries to the narrowness of the host's purse, the wealthy disputant had resolved not to attempt to influence the umpire by giving him a superior repast. Sitting at another table, the trio dined on exactly the same fare—three fried soles, a roast leg of mutton, and vegetables; three pancakes, three pieces of cheese, three small loaves of bread, ale, and a bottle of sherry; and for dessert three magnificent apples, together with a magnum of port. The dinner being over, the apples devoured, and the last glass of port drunk, the arbitrator (his eyes twinkling brightly as he spoke) introduced his award with the following exordium: "Gentlemen, I have with all proper attention considered your *sole* reasons; I have taken due notice of your *joint* reasons; and I have come to the conclusion that your *des(s)erts* are about equal."

FALSE WITNESS ADROITLY EXPOSED.

A few years since, a man of high respectability was tried in England on a charge of forging a will, in which it was discovered that he had an indirect interest in a large amount. Samuel Warren, author of the "Diary of a London Physician," "Ten Thousand a year," etc., was the associate prosecuting attorney, and the case was tried before Lord Denman. The prisoner was arraigned, and the formalities gone through with; the prosecutor, placing his thumb over the seal, held up the will, and demanded of the prisoner if he had seen the testator sign the instrument, to which he promptly answered he had.

"And did you sign it at his request as subscribing witness?"

"I did."

"Was it sealed with red or black wax?"

"With red wax."

"Did you see him seal it with red wax?"

"I did."

"Where was the testator when he signed and sealed this will?"

"In his bed."

"Pray, how long a piece of red wax did he use?"

"About three inches long."

"Who gave the testator this piece of wax?

"I did."

"Where did you get it?"

"From the drawer of his desk."

"How did he light that piece of wax?"

"With a candle."

"Where did that candle come from?"

"I got it out of a cupboard in the room."

"How long was that candle?"

"Perhaps four or five inches long."

"Who lit that candle?"

"I lit it."

"With what?"

"With a match."

"Where did you get that match?"

"On the mantle-shelf in the room."

Here Warren paused, and, fixing his large deep blue eyes upon the prisoner, he held the will up before his eyes, his thumb still resting upon the seal, and said, in a solemn, measured tone,

"Now, sir, upon your solemn oath, you saw the testator sign that will—he signed it in his bed—at his request you signed it as a subscribing witness—you saw him seal it—it was with red wax he sealed it—a piece of wax about three inches long—he lit the wax with a piece of candle which you procured from a cupboard—you lit the candle with a match which you found on a mantle-shelf?"

"I did."

"Once more, sir—upon your solemn oath, you did?"

"I did."

"My lord, *it is sealed with a wafer!*"

SARCASM OF LORD CHATHAM.

Lord Chatham rebuked a dishonest Chancellor of the Exchequer by finishing a quotation the latter had commenced. The debate turned upon some grant of money for the encouragement of art, which was opposed by the Chancellor of the Exchequer, who finished his speech against Lord Chatham's motion by saying, "'Why was not this ointment sold and the money given to the poor?'" Chatham rose and said, "Why did not the noble lord complete the quotation, the application being so striking? As he has shrunk from it, I will finish the verse for him—'This Judas said, not that he cared for the poor, but because *he was a thief and carried the bag.*'"

WISE MEN FROM THE EAST.

Sergeant Davy made a reputation at the London bar for wit by a single smart saying. Davy had great contempt for Devonshire and other Western country lawyers, and particularly for Maynard, one of the rudest and most offensive counselors at the bar of London. Intending once to affront Maynard, Davy observed in a very loud tone,

"The farther I journeyed toward the West, the more convinced I was that the wise men come from the East."

CHICANERY OF AN EXTORTIONATE LAWYER.

Of the many piquant stories about the chicanery and extortionate practice of attorneys with which the jest-books of the last century are crammed, few are more humorous than the variously-told anecdote, for which the *London Chronicle*, January 11, 1781, gives the following statement of facts: "An attorney in Dublin, having dined by an invitation with his client several days pending a suit, charged 6*s.* 8*d.* for each attendance, which was allowed by the master on taxing costs. In return for this, the client returned the master-attorney with a bill for his eating and drinking, which the attorney refusing to pay, the client brought his action, and recovered the amount of his charge. But he did not exult in his victory; for in a few days after the attorney lodged an information against him before the Commissioners of Excise for retailing wine without a license; and not being able to controvert the fact, to avoid an increase of costs he submitted, by the advice of counsel, to pay the penalty, a great part of which went to the attorney as informer." This account of an improbable but laughable story gave rise to the following song, which was communicated to *Notes and Queries* by a correspondent:

"A lawyer quite famous for making a bill,
And who in good living delighted,
To dinner one day with a hearty good will
Was by a rich client invited.
But he charged six-and-eightpence for going to dine,
Which the client he paid, though no ninny,
And in turn charged the lawyer for dinner and wine,
One a crown, and the other a guinea.
But gossips, you know, have a saying in store,
He who matches a lawyer has only one more.

"The lawyer he paid it, and took a receipt,
While the client stared at him with wonder;
With the produce he gave a magnificent treat,
But the lawyer soon made him knock under.
That his client sold wine, information he laid,
Without license, and, spite of his storming,
The client a good thumping penalty paid,
And the lawyer got half for informing.

But gossips, you know, have a saying in store,
He who matches a lawyer has only one more.

A LAME CASE MENDED BY WIT.

Sergeant Gardiner, an English barrister of some repute, who was lame of one leg, was once pleading before Sir John Fortescue-Aland, who was disfigured by a nose which was purple, and hideously misshapen by morbid growth. Having checked the ready counsel with the needlessly harsh observation, "Brother, brother, you are handling the case in a very lame manner," the angry advocate gave vent to his annoyance by saying, with a perfect appearance of *sang froid*,

"Pardon me, my lord; have patience with me, and I will do my best to make the case as plain as—as—the nose on your lordship's face."

A CHIEF JUSTICE IN THE STOCKS.

Readers of Sir Edward Lytton Bulwer's novel of "Varieties in English Life" will remember the amusing episode of Dr. Riccabocca's rescue of Leonard Fairfield from the stocks, and his own incarceration therein. Sir Edward had his authority for this ludicrous scene, though the original of the story did not prove such a philosopher as did the worthy Italian under the same circumstances.

While Lord Camden held the chiefship of the Court of Common Pleas of England, he was walking with his friend Lord Dacre on the outskirts of an English village, when they passed the parish stocks.

"I wonder," said the chief justice, "whether a man in the stocks endures a punishment that is physically painful? I am inclined to think that, apart from the sense of humiliation and other mental anguish, the prisoner suffers nothing, unless the populace express their satisfaction at his fate by pelting him with brickbats."

"Suppose you settle your doubts by putting your feet into the holes," rejoined Lord Dacre carelessly.

"By Jove, I will!" exclaimed the chief justice; and in a trice he was sitting on the ground, with his feet some fifteen inches above the level of his seat, and his ankles encircled by hard wood.

"Now, Dacre!" he exclaimed enthusiastically, "fasten the bolts, and leave me for ten minutes."

Like a courteous host, Lord Dacre complied with the whim of his guest, and having placed it beyond his power to liberate himself, bade him "farewell" for ten minutes. Intending to saunter along the lane and return at the expiration of the stated period, Lord Dacre moved away, and falling into one of his customary fits of reverie, soon forgot all about the stocks, his friend's freak, and his friend. In the mean time the chief justice went through every torture of an agonizing punishment—acute shootings along the confined limbs, aching in the feet, angry pulsations under the toes, violent cramps in the muscles and thighs, gnawing pain at the point where his person came in immediate contact with the cold ground, pins and needles every where. Among the various forms of his physical discomfort, faintness, fever, giddiness, and raging thirst may be mentioned. He implored a peasant to liberate him, and the fellow answered him with a shout of derision. He hailed a passing clergyman, and explained that he was not a culprit, but Lord Camden, Chief Justice of the Common Pleas, and one of Lord Dacre's guests.

"Ah!" observed the man of cloth, not so much answering the wretched culprit as passing judgment on his case, "mad with liquor. Yes, drunkenness is sadly on the increase; 'tis droll, though, for a drunkard in the stocks to imagine himself a chief justice!" and on he passed. A farmer's wife jogged by on her pillion, and hearing the wretched man exclaim that he should die of thirst, the good creature gave him a juicy apple, and hoped that his punishment would prove for the good of his soul. Not ten minutes, but ten hours did the chief justice sit in the stocks, and when at length he was carried into Lord Dacre's house, he was in no humor to laugh at his own miserable plight. Not long afterward he presided at a trial in which a workman brought an action against a magistrate who had wrongfully placed him in the stocks. The counsel for the defense happening to laugh at the statement of the plaintiff, who maintained that he had suffered intense pain during his confinement, Lord Camden leaned forward, and inquired in a whisper,

"Brother, were you ever in the stocks?"

"Never, my lord," answered the advocate, with a look of lively astonishment.

"I have been," was the whispered reply; "and let me assure you that the agony inflicted by the stocks is—*awful!*"

A DIRTY JUDGE.

One of Joseph Jekyll's best displays of brilliant impudence, and the origin of one attributed to Sheridan, was perpetrated on a Welsh judge, who was alike notorious for his greed of office, and his want of personal cleanliness. "My dear sir," Jekyll observed in his most amiable manner to this most unamiable personage, "you have asked the minister for almost every thing else, why *don't* you ask him for a piece of soap and a nail-brush?"

A JOHN BULL JURY.

QUARRELS AT THE BAR.

Disreputable squabbles between rival barristers, and between the bench and the bar, occasionally occur in our own times, and the ruffianism of the prisoners is now and then surpassed by the ruffianism of the advocates; but we should be astounded if lawyers of to-day were to imitate the violence of Coke in his outburst against Bacon, as is thus related by the latter:

Coke. "Mr. Bacon, if you have any tooth against me,

pluck it out, for it will do you more hurt than all the teeth in your head will do good."

Bacon (coldly). "Mr. Attorney, I respect you; I fear you not; and the less you speak of your own greatness, the more I will think of it."

Coke. "I think scorn to stand upon terms of greatness toward you, who are less than little—less than the least (adding other such strange light terms, with that insolence which can not be expressed)."

So runs the report. Bacon adds, "With this he spake, neither I nor himself could tell what, as if he had been born attorney general, and in the end bade me not meddle with the queen's business but with mine own, and that I was unsworn." This was in the Elizabethan age, and in the Old Bailey Court. Of late years there has been a visible improvement in the conduct of proceedings in that court; but in the days when that good scholar and man, Sergeant Adams, acted as assistant judge, the collisions between the bench and bar were of scandalous frequency and violence. The last words spoken by the sergeant in his official character comically illustrate the state of affairs during his time. Having concluded a summing up with reference to an altercation which had occurred during the trial between himself and certain barristers, he ended his remarks by saying, "*And so, gentlemen of the jury, there was a shindy.*" With these memorable and suggestive words ended the last judicial address of an excellent judge. Indulging in his coarse personalities on another occasion, Coke described Garnet, the Jesuit, as "a Doctor of Jesuits; that is, a Doctor of six D's—as Dissimulation, Deposing of princes, Daunting and Deterring of subjects, and Destruction."

A BEAUTIFUL THOUGHT.

Sir William Jones, whose reputation as a barrister has been almost forgotten in his fame as a linguist and scholar, is the author of the famous and exquisite epigram which follows, and which has been attributed at various times to almost every standard author in the English tongue:

"A NEW-BORN CHILD.

"On parent knees, a naked, new-born child,
Weeping thou sat'st, while all around thee smiled;
So live, that sinking in thy last, long sleep,
Calm thou mayst smile, while all around thee weep."

A LEGAL IMPOSSIBILITY.

Counselor Garrow, during his cross-examination of a prevaricating old female witness, by whom it was essential to prove that a tender of money had been made, had a scrap of paper thrown him by the opposing counsel, in which was written,

"Garrow, submit: that tough old jade
Will never prove—a *tender made.*"

POPULAR PREJUDICES AGAINST LAWYERS.

Strange prejudices have existed against lawyers from time immemorial. Oliver Cromwell's officers were inclined to think that the country should be governed by pious soldiers; and notwithstanding the number and influence of the lawyers who had served the republic in camp as well as at Westminster, the more zealous Puritans entertained strong prejudices against the legal profession, and were almost unanimous in holding that non-military wearers of the long robe should be excluded from the House of Commons. Lawyers were then commonly known by the title of "sons of Zeruiah." In the autumn of 1649 a republican soldier warmly urged upon the Commons that they should exclude all lawyers from Parliament, and that, if they could not find heart to take so decided a course, they ought at least to resolve that while lawyers sat in Parliament they should relinquish practice. Bulstrode Whitelock, who was then keeper of the seals, replied in a speech strong with reason and sarcasm. From the days of the Parliamentum Indoctum, which lawyers were forbidden to enter, till the days of his own connection with Sir Edward Coke, Whitelock set forth the services which his profession had rendered to the country, and pointed out the blunders into which Parliaments had fallen when they presumed to act without the guidance, or in opposition to the advice of legal authorities. "As to the sarcasms," he continued, "on lawyers for not fighting, I deem that the gown does neither abate a man's courage or his wisdom, nor render him less capable of using a sword when the laws are silent. Witness the great services performed by Lieutenent General Jones and Commissary Ireton, and many other lawyers, who, putting off their gowns when the Parliament required it, have served stoutly and successfully as soldiers, and have undergone almost as much and as great hardships and dangers as the honorable gentleman who so much undervalued them. With respect to the proposal for compelling lawyers to suspend their practice while they sit in Parliament, I only insist that, in the act for the purpose, it be provided that merchants forbear from their trading, physicians from visiting their patients, and country gentlemen from selling their corn or wool while they are members of that House." The motion was of course withdrawn, and the maker well laughed at. The same prejudice was continually reappearing. Some four years later the Barebones Parliament showed their low opinion of the "sons of Zeruiah" by proposing to abolish

Chancery on the expiration of a month after their decision. By resolution the Parliament actually suspended Chancery for a month; and when the bill for the total abolition of the court came to a decision, it was thrown out by the speaker's casting vote.

ENGLISH LEGAL IGNORANCE.

Americans have not a greater appreciation of the intelligence of their Anglo-Saxon brethren over the water than the latter have of their American cousins, and we love to recall such illustrations of English legal ignorance as the following:

A jury was once empaneled in Surrey County, England, to try a man charged with having house-breaking implements in his possession, with intent to commit a felony. The foreman delivered the intelligent verdict, "We find the prisoner guilty, with the benefit of a doubt." Of course the presiding magistrate refused to receive such a verdict; whereupon the foreman explained that there was a doubt among them, but they thought the prisoner was guilty. The explanation did not make matters clearer, and the doubting jury were sent back to consider the evidence again. They failed to agree, and were discharged, the prisoner being remanded to the next sessions, to be then tried.

In London, in 1863, at the trial of a divorce case, the parties to which were a nobleman of advanced years and his young wife, Sir Creswell Creswell, the presiding judge, remarked that the case on trial was another instance of the evil effects of "marriages contracted between May and December." Shortly afterward the learned judge received a letter from the secretary of a Scotch statistical society, intimating that the body he represented would be much obliged if Sir Creswell would favor them with an account of the facts from which he had derived the singular rule enunciated by him as to the infelicity of marriages solemnized during certain months of the year, and adding that some of the members of the society wished to draw up the information which might thus be afforded them in the shape of a paper to be read before the society, with a view to public discussion.

3.

Chief Justices of the United States.

CHAPTER III.

THE CHIEF JUSTICES OF THE UNITED STATES.

THE FIRST CHIEF JUSTICE.

JOHN JAY was the first to hold the office of Chief Justice of the United States. He was born in New York, December 12, 1745, graduated at King's (now Columbia) College in 1764, and four years later he was admitted to the bar. He bore a distinguished part in our Revolutionary struggle, and was the youngest member of the First Congress, which convened in 1774. He prepared the draft of the first Constitution of the State of New York in 1777, and was appointed its first chief justice. Two years after he was sent on an important mission to Spain. He also, in conjunction with Adams, Franklin, and Laurens, negotiated the treaty by which Great Britain recognized the independence of the United States. On his return to this country he was appointed Secretary of Foreign Affairs. When the Union superseded the old Confederation, Washington, as a mark of his personal esteem and a recognition of Mr. Jay's important services, offered him any office which he might prefer. He chose that of chief justice, and received his appointment in 1789. In 1794 he was sent to Great Britain as envoy extraordinary, to negotiate an important treaty. He was absent a year, during which time he was elected Governor of New York. He then resigned the chief justiceship, was twice re-elected governor, and then, in 1801, at the age of fifty-six, resolved to retire from public life. President

Adams, wishing to retain his services for the public, nominated him for his former place as chief justice, then vacant by the resignation of Oliver Ellsworth.

Jay declined, on the ground that he had deliberately made up his mind to retire from public life, and duty to his country did not then require him to accept office. He retired to his farm in Bedford, New York, where he died May 17, 1829, in the eighty-fourth year of his age. While the question of the adoption of the Federal Constitution was before the people, Hamilton, Madison, and Jay projected the famous series of essays called the *Federalist.* Jay wrote the second, third, fourth, and fifth numbers, furnishing no more until the sixty-fourth number. During the greater part of the interval he was lying between life and death. A party of medical students had violated the grave to acquire subjects for dissection. They were put in prison, but a mob threatened their lives. Jay and others, under the lead of Hamilton, joined to prevent the outrage; they were set upon by the rioters, and Jay was struck on the temple by a stone, and almost killed. He recovered only in time to write the single additional paper, on a subject which he was especially requested to undertake. To this accident it is owing that the *Federalist*, valuable as it is, was not rendered still more valuable by contributions from one who was recognized as the ablest political writer in the United States. Mr. Jay was one of the noblest and purest characters in our history.

Mr. Jay was a zealous but not bigoted member of the Episcopal Church; took great interest in the religious movements of his day; was president of several religious societies, and frequently presided at their anniversary meetings. He always observed family worship, morning and evening, and never postponed or suspended it on account of the presence of company.

The quality of the man is well illustrated in the following incident: After he had lived twenty-eight years in retirement, devoting his time to agriculture, visiting, recreation, study, benevolent works, and the duties of a Christian, upon being asked how it was possible to occupy his mind in seclusion and retirement, he replied, with a smile, "I have a long life to look back upon, and an eternity to look forward to."

THE SECOND CHIEF JUSTICE.

Upon the resignation of Mr. Jay, John Rutledge was nominated by the President as Chief Justice of the United States. He was born in 1739, in South Carolina, whither his father had emigrated from Ireland four years before. He studied law in the Temple in London, and returned to Charleston in 1761, where he at once gained the highest rank at the bar. He espoused the cause of the colonies at the outset of the troubles with Great Britain. In 1776 he was appointed president and commander-in-chief of the colony of South Carolina. It was owing to him that Fort

Moultrie was not abandoned to the enemy without a struggle. General Lee, who commanded the Continental troops, pronounced the fort a "slaughter-pen," and wished to evacuate it. Rutledge wrote to Moultrie, "General Lee wishes you to evacute the fort. You will not without an order from me. I would sooner cut off my hand than write one." When the Constitution of South Carolina was framed, Rutledge refused his assent on the ground that it was too democratic. He finally yielded his scruples, and was appointed governor, with the real power of dictator. In 1789 he was appointed Associate Judge of the Supreme Court of the United States. The treaty negotiated by Jay with Great Britain excited a storm of indignation in South Carolina. Rutledge made a violent speech against it at Charleston just two days before his appointment as chief justice reached him, in which he spoke in bitter language of the leaders of the then dominant Federal party, of which he had hitherto been considered a member. In August, 1795, he presided at a session of the Supreme Court, and in November started to hold a circuit in North Carolina, when he was attacked by sickness, and his mind was apparently affected. This, and the remembrance of his recent Charleston speech, induced the Senate to refuse to confirm his nomination—a refusal by no means disagreeable to the President, who was strongly in favor of Jay's treaty. Mortification at this rejection extinguished the last remnant of Rutledge's sanity, and he died in 1800 at the age of sixty-one.

THE THIRD CHIEF JUSTICE.

After the death of Rutledge the President nominated Judge William Cushing, of Massachusetts, as chief justice. The nomination was confirmed; but Mr. Cushing, after holding the commission a few days, resigned on account of ill health. As he never acted in that capacity, his name only belongs technically to the list of chief justices.

THE FOURTH CHIEF JUSTICE.

Oliver Ellsworth was then nominated and confirmed as chief justice. He was born at Windsor, Connecticut, April 29, 1745. His studies, commenced at Yale, were completed at Princeton, where he graduated at the age of twenty-three. For a time he was a teacher; then commenced the study of theology, but subsequently decided on the profession of law. He had then married, and his father gave him a farm

of wild land and an axe. While slowly working his way at the bar, he cleared his wild farm with his own hands. His early career gave no promise of future eminence, but, the first upward steps once taken, his progress was sure. He was appointed state's attorney, and yearly elected to the General Assembly. In 1777 he was chosen delegate to Congress; in 1784, judge of the Superior Court of Connecticut; and in 1789, senator in Congress. In 1796 he was appointed Chief Justice of the United States. His unquestioned probity and the soundness of his judicial decisions gained him the highest respect. In 1799 he was sent, against his wishes, as minister to France, though still retaining for two years his seat on the bench. His health failing, he resigned his office in 1801. He died November 26, 1807, at the age of sixty-two.

When young Ellsworth was at Yale College, an anecdote is related of him which indicated his aptness for special pleading, and betokened the future lawyer.

The students were prohibited from wearing their hats in the college yard. Ellsworth, on one occasion, was arraigned for violating the law of the institution. He defended himself upon the ground that a hat was composed of two parts, the crown and the brim, and as his hat had no brim —which, by-the-by, he had torn off—he could be guilty of no offense. This ingenious plea seemed to have satisfied the scruples of his judges, and he escaped all punishment.

After Ellsworth had obtained reputation both in professional and political life, a friend asked him what was the secret of his intellectual power. He said, in reply, that early in his career he discovered that he had no imagination; that the qualities of his mind promised so little that he became almost discouraged; that he then determined to study but one subject at a time, and not abandon it until he had mastered it. He said also that, in the practice of his profession, he had, as a rule, given his attention to the main points of the case, leaving the minor ones to shift for themselves.

Ellsworth was a man of great pertinacity of character, as well as wisdom in the conduct of affairs, and acquired immense influence while a member of the United States Senate. While he was one of this body Aaron Burr said of him that, "if Ellsworth should chance to spell God with two *d*'s, it would take the Senate three weeks to make up its mind to expunge the superfluous letter."

In all his tastes and habits Ellsworth exhibited an unaffected simplicity. He often visited a mineral spring in Suffield, Connecticut, for the benefit of his health. On one occasion the wife of the proprietor of the springs declined his application for board, saying that "she could not entertain a great man like him in a suitable manner." "But, madam," said he, "do you not have bread?" "Oh, yes, sir, and milk too." "Very well," was the reply, "that is all the food I need." The fears of the good woman were soon dissipated, and she received him willingly.

THE FIFTH CHIEF JUSTICE.

John Marshall, the most eminent of our chief justices, was born in Fauquier County, Virginia, September 24, 1755. His father was a farmer in narrow circumstances, but of decided ability. There were no schools in what was then the frontier region, and the early education of the future chief justice was conducted by his father, aided for about a year by the clergyman of the parish, with whom he began to read Horace and Livy. By his own unaided exertions he subsequently became a fair classical scholar, and was intimately acquainted with English literature. He had just begun the study of law when the war of the Revolution broke out. In 1775 he was appointed lieutenant in a company of minute-men. He afterward became captain in a Virginia regiment of the Continental army, and was present at the battles of Brandywine, Germantown, and Monmouth. He pursued his legal studies at intervals during the war, and at its close commenced practice. He soon rose to eminence at the bar and in politics. He was one of the small but distinguished body of men through whose influence Virginia was induced to accept the Federal Constitution. In 1794 Washington offered him the post of Attorney General, and subsequently the mission to France. Both offers were declined. The French government having refused to accept Mr. Pinckney as minister, Mr. Adams, who was then President, appointed Mr. Marshall as one of three envoys to that country. Shortly after his return he yielded to the personal solicitations of Washington, and consented to become a candidate for Congress. President Adams at the same time offered him a seat on the bench

of the Supreme Court, which was declined. He was elected to Congress after a sharp contest, taking his seat in December, 1799. During the excited session which followed he was one of the ablest supporters of the administration of Mr. Adams. In May, 1800, he was nominated and confirmed as Secretary of War, but he declined to accept the appointment. Shortly after he accepted the post of Secretary of State. On the 31st of January, 1801, he was appointed Chief Justice of the United States, a position which he held for thirty-five years, until his death in July, 1835, at the age of eighty years. His unquestioned character, sound judgment, and felicitous diction, added to the long period during which he held his seat, and the magnitude of the questions which came before him for decision, entitle Mr. Marshall, beyond all question, to the first place in the noble list of our chief justices. Besides his judicial labors, he was the author of a "History of the American Colonies," and of a "Life of Washington," which we must still regard as the best yet written.

Marshall, in the first years of his practice, was one morning strolling through the streets of Richmond, attired in a plain linen roundabout and shorts, with his hat under his arm, from which he was eating cherries, when he stopped in the porch of the Eagle Hotel, indulged in some little pleasantry with the landlord, and then passed on. Mr. P., an elderly gentleman from the country, then present, had a case coming on in the Court of Appeals, and was referred by the landlord to Marshall as the best advocate for him to employ; but the careless, languid air of the young lawyer had so prejudiced Mr. P. that he refused to engage him. On entering the court Mr. P. was referred a second time, by the clerk of the court, to the same lawyer, and a second time declined. At this moment entered Mr. V., a venerable-looking legal gentleman, in a powdered wig and a black coat, whose dignified appearance produced such an impression on Mr. P. that he at once retained him. In the first case which came on, Marshall and Mr. V. each addressed the court. The vast inferiority of his advocate was so apparent, that, at the close of the argument, Mr. P. introduced himself to young Marshall, frankly stated the prejudice which had caused him, in opposition to advice, to employ Mr. P.; that he regretted his error extremely, but did not know how to remedy it. He had come into the city with one hundred dollars as his lawyer's fee, which he had paid, and had but five left, which, if Marshall chose, he would cheerfully give him for assisting in the case. Marshall, pleased with the incident, accepted the offer, not, however, without passing a sly joke at the *omnipotence* of a powdered wig and a black coat.

Marshall, returning from North Carolina, wrapped in profound thought on some knotty point, found himself suddenly brought to a halt by a small tree, which intervened between the front wheel and the body of his buggy. Seeing a servant at a short distance, he asked him to bring an axe and cut down the tree. The servant told the judge that there was no occasion for cutting down the tree, but just to back the buggy. Pleased at the good sense of the fellow, he told him that he would leave him something at the inn hard by, where he intended to stop, having then no small change. In due time the negro applied, and a dollar was handed him. Being asked if he knew who it was that gave him the dollar, he replied, "No, sir; I concluded he was a gentleman by his leaving the money, but I think he is the biggest fool I ever saw."

Chief Justice Marshall once indorsed a bond amounting to several thousand dollars, and, the drawer having failed, he was called upon to pay it. He knew the bond could be avoided, because the holder had advanced the money at a usurious rate of interest; but he was utterly incapable of throwing off the moral obligation in that way, and paid it voluntarily.

In passing through Culpepper on his way to Fauquier, the chief justice fell in company with Mr. S., an old fellow-officer in the army of the Revolution. In the course of the conversation, Marshall learned there was a lien upon the estate of his friend to the amount of three thousand dollars about due, and he was greatly distressed at the prospect of impending ruin. On bidding farewell Marshall privately left a check for the amount, which being presented to Mr. S.

after his departure, he, impelled by a chivalrous independence, mounted and spurred his horse till he overtook his friend. He thanked him for his generosity, but refused to accept it. Marshall strenuously insisted on its acceptance, and the other as strongly refused. Finally it resulted in a compromise, by which Marshall took security on the lien, but never called for pay. This incident only illustrates the active benevolence of his whole life.

The following pen-sketch of the eminent and popular chief justice is from the journal of an English traveler, who spent a week in Richmond in the spring of 1835: "The judge is a tall, venerable man, about eighty years of age, his hair tied in a cue, according to the olden custom, and with a countenance indicating that simplicity of mind and benignity which so eminently distinguish his character. As a judge he has no rival, his knowledge being profound, his judgment clear and just; and his quickness in apprehending either the fallacy or truth of an argument is surprising. I had the pleasure of several long conversations with him, and was struck with admiration at the extraordinary union of modesty and power, gentleness and force which his mind displays. What he knows he communicates without reserve; he speaks with clearness of expression, and in a tone of simple truth which compels conviction; and on all subjects on which his knowledge is not *certain*, or which admit of doubt or argument, he delivers his opinion with a candid diffidence, and with a deference for that of others amounting almost to timidity; still, it is a timidity which would disarm the most violent opponent, and win respect and credence from any auditor. I remember having often observed a similar characteristic attributed to the immortal Newton. The simplicity of his character is not more singular than that of his life; pride, ostentation, and hypocrisy are "Greek to him," and he really lives up to the letter and spirit of republicanism, while he maintains all the dignity due to his age and office. His house is small, and more humble in appearance than those of the average of successful lawyers or merchants. * * * In short, blending, as he does, the simplicity of a child and the plainness of a republican with the learning and ability of a lawyer, the venerable dignity of his appearance would not suffer in comparison with the most respected and distinguished-looking peer in the British House of Lords."

Miss Martineau, who visited Washington the winter preceding the decease of the venerable Chief Justice Marshall, speaks as follows of one trait of his beautiful character: "He maintained through life, and carried to his grave, a reverence for woman as rare in its kind as in its degree. It had all the theoretical fervor and magnificence of Uncle Toby's, with the advantage of being grounded upon an extensive knowledge of the sex. He was the father and grandfather of women; and out of this experience he brought not only the love and pity which their offices and position command, and the awe of purity which they excite in the minds of the pure, but a steady conviction of their intellectual equality with men, and with this a deep sense of their social injuries. Throughout life he so invariably sustained their cause that no indulgent libertine dared to flatter and humor, no skeptic, secure in the possession of power, dared to scoff at the claims of woman in the presence of Marshall, who, made clear-sighted by his purity, knew the sex far better than either."

The chief justice, fearing the effects of age upon his mind, and anxious that in "life's last scenes" he might not exhibit another instance of the "follies of the wise," had charged his confidential friends to let him know whenever they perceived the slightest abatement in his intellectual vigor, and he would at once retire from the bench. But they never had occasion to perform this delicate task. At the age of eighty years, his intellect remained unclouded and undimmed to the last moments of his life.

THE SIXTH CHIEF JUSTICE.

Roger Brooke Taney was born in Calvert County, Maryland, March 17, 1777. In 1831 President Jackson appointed him Attorney General of the United States. Two years later, Mr. Duane, then Secretary of the Treasury, refused to remove the government deposits from the United States

Bank; he was removed, and Mr. Taney was appointed in his place. The Senate refused to confirm the nomination; but in the mean while Mr. Taney had obeyed the orders of the President, and removed the deposits. Jackson then nominated him as Associate Judge of the Supreme Court, to fill a vacancy occasioned by the resignation of Judge Duval. The Senate refused to confirm the nomination. Chief Justice Marshall died in 1835, and Jackson at once nominated Mr. Taney for the place. The Democrats, having now a majority in the Senate, confirmed the nomination, and Mr. Taney became chief justice—a position which he retained until his death, October 12, 1864, a period of twenty-seven years. Chief Justice Taney is best known by his famous "decision," or rather "opinion," in the Dred Scott case, in which, going beyond the question before the court, he endeavored to settle the general question of the *status* of persons of African descent in the United States. Undeserved obloquy has been attached to him on account of a sentence in this opinion which apparently affirmed that blacks had no rights which whites were bound to respect. The context shows that this was the very reverse of the meaning intended to be conveyed by Judge Taney. He says thas it is now difficult to realize the state of opinion on this subject held at the formation of our government. Blacks were then regarded as beings of an inferior order, "*and so far inferior that they had no rights which the white man was bound to respect.*" This outrageous sentiment is mentioned only to be impliedly condemned—the "opinion" of the chief justice, harsh enough as he gave it, being to the effect that no person whose ancestors were imported and sold as slaves had any right to sue in a court of the United States, or could become citizens of the United States. It is due to the honor of our highest judicial tribunal to state that the opinion of the chief justice did not affirm, but did, by plain implication, condemn the doctrine that such persons "had *no* rights which whites were bound to respect." Mr. Taney's last notable public act was in May, 1861, when the case of John Merryman came before him. This man was arrested near Baltimore on a charge of being an officer in a company raised to aid the rebellion. He was imprisoned by the military authorities in Fort M'Henry. He prayed for a writ of *habeas corpus*, which was granted by Judge Taney. General Cadwalader, the commander, refused to obey, on the ground that the execution of the writ of *habeas corpus* had been suspended by the President in the State of Maryland. The judge issued an order for the arrest of General Cadwalader. The marshal was not allowed to serve the writ. Judge Taney thereupon prepared an opinion denying the right of the President to suspend the writ, and affirming that it was the duty of all military officers to obey it. He added that if the officer had been brought before him he should have punished him by fine and imprisonment; but, as he had no force capable of carrying his order into effect, he should report the whole case to the President, and call upon him to enforce the process of the court. No farther action was had on the case. Mr. Taney was aged eighty-seven at the time of his death, nearly forty of which had been spent in the public service. He owed his appointment as chief justice to the purely partisan services which he rendered to President Jackson. As a jurist, he can not be ranked with the great men who had occupied his seat before him. His judicial integrity has never been impeached, even in the case of his unfortunate opinion in the Dred Scott case, or the later and equally unfortunate course in the Merryman case, by which he will be chiefly remembered in after years.

THE SEVENTH CHIEF JUSTICE.

Salmon Portland Chase, now Chief Justice of the United States, was born in Cornish, New Hampshire, January 13, 1808. His father having died, he was sent, at the age of twelve, to Ohio, and placed under the care of his uncle, Bishop Chase. After studying for a year at Cincinnati College he entered Dartmouth College, in New Hampshire, from which he graduated in 1829. He went to Washington, where he opened a school, at the same time studying law under the direction of William Wirt. Having been admitted to the bar, he went to Cincinnati, and entered upon the practice of his profession. To this for some years he applied himself exclusively, taking no prominent part in politics, though he belonged to the Democratic party. In 1841 he first took a decided part in politics.

He was then a member of the Convention of those opposed to the farther extension of slavery, and was the author of the address unanimously adopted by that body. He took a prominent part in all the subsequent movements having this end in view, and was president of the Free Soil Democratic Convention at Buffalo in 1848. The Democratic party in Ohio had at this time assumed the position of hostility to slavery in the Territories. Mr. Chase was chosen United States senator in February, 1849, rceeiving the votes of all the Democratic members of the Legislature, together with those of others who were in favor of free soil. Though elected as a Democrat, he declared that if the party withdrew from its position in regard to slavery, he should withdraw from it. This he did formally, in consequence of the action of the Democratic Convention held at Baltimore in 1852. When the Republican party was organized, Mr. Chase took the position of one of its acknowledged leaders. Soon after the close of his senatorial term in 1855 he was elected Governor of Ohio. He was re-elected, his second term closing in 1860. In the Republican Convention at Chicago in that year he was next, after Mr. Lincoln and Mr. Seward, the leading candidate for the presidency. He had in the mean time been again elected to the Senate of the United States, and, had he taken his place, would undoubtedly have been the leader in that body. But he resigned his seat in order to accept the position of Secretary of the Treasury—a position for which he was especially pointed out by the success of his financial policy while Governor of Ohio. It is honorable to all the persons that the three leading competitors of Mr. Lincoln for the presidential nomination should have received and accepted his nomination as members of his cabinet. As the presidential canvass of 1864 approached, a strong effort was made to bring forth Mr. Chase as the Union candidate; but the current of popular feeling was so unmistakably in favor of the re-election of Mr. Lincoln that Mr. Chase refused to become a candidate, and gave his cordial support to Mr. Lincoln. Meanwhile, finding that Congress hesitated to carry out the financial system which he proposed, Mr. Chase had, on the

30th of June, 1864, resigned the post of Secretary of the Treasury. Almost the first important public act of Mr. Lincoln after his re-election was to appoint Mr. Chase to the most important position within the executive nomination. Mr. Chase entered upon the duties of his high office at the age of fifty-six, with a sound legal reputation, and with a physical vigor which gives reason to hope that he may be able to perform its duties for a period as long as that of his predecessor.

Chief Justice Taney was the author of the saying found in his opinion in the case of Dred Scott, and which will always be associated with his name, "A black man has no rights that a white man is bound to respect." The present Chief Justice Chase uttered the eloquent aphorism, "Congress has no more power to make a slave than to make a king."

The following has been told of Judge Chase's father:

"In New Hampshire they used to choose all their state, county, and town officers, from governor down to hog-reeves, at one town-meeting—the annual March meeting. As the town officers were very numerous, it was customary, as fast as they were chosen, to walk them up before a justice of the peace, and have them sworn into office 'by companies, half companies, pair, and single.' 'Squire Chase,' of Cornish (father of Secretary Chase), being the most prominent justice, had this task to perform, and a severe task it was, occupying much of his time from morning till night.

"It was on one of these occasions, after the labors and toils of the day were over, he returned to his home weary and overcome with the fatigues of his employment, and, throwing himself into his easy-chair, fell into a sound sleep. In the mean time, a couple, who had been waiting impatiently for some time for the justice to join them in wedlock, presented themselves in another part of the house, and made known their interesting desire to Mrs. Chase, who, somewhat confused and agitated, attended them to the sleeping justice, whom she found it difficult to arouse. Shaking him by the shoulder, she called out, 'Mr. Chase, Mr. Chase, do pray wake up; here is a couple come to be married.' The justice, having administered oaths all day, was dreaming of nothing else. Half waked, rubbing his eyes, and looking at the wistful pair, he asked,

"'Are you the couple?'

"They nodded assent.

"'Well, hold up your hands.' They did so, with some hesitation. 'You severally solemnly swear that you will faithfully perform the duties of your offices respectively according to your best skill and judgment, so help you, etc.'

"The astonished couple looked wild; the justice added, soothingly, 'That's all, excepting the fee—one dollar,' which was quickly dropped into his hand, and they were off, doubting as they went the legality of the process; but they concluded to go according to the oath."

THE SUPREME COURT IN 1835.

Miss Martineau, who was in Washington in the winter of 1835, speaks as follows of a session of the Supreme Court of the United States, when the venerable and accomplished Marshall was the chief justice: "This court presents a singular spectacle. I have watched the assemblage while the chief justice was delivering a judgment, the three judges on either hand gazing on him more like learners than associates; Webster standing firm as a rock, his large, deep-set eyes wide awake, his lips compressed, and his whole countenance in that intent stillness which instantly fixes the eye of the stranger; Clay leaning against the desk in an attitude whose grace contrasts strangely with the slovenly make of his dress, his snuff-box for the moment unopened in his hand, his small gray eye and placid half smile conveying an expression of pleasure, which redeems his face from its usual unaccountable commonness; attorney general, his fingers playing among his papers, his quick black eye, and thin, tremulous lips for once fixed, his small face pale with thought, contrasting remarkably with the other two: these men, absorbed in what they are listening to, thinking neither of themselves nor of each other, while they are watched by the groups of idlers and listeners around them—the newspaper corps, the dark Cherokee chiefs, the straggler from the far West, the gay ladies in their waving plumes, and the members of either House that have stepped in to listen—all these have I seen at one moment constitute one silent assemblage, while the mild voice of the venerable chief justice sounded through the court."

4.

Advocates of the United States.

CHAPTER IV.

ANECDOTES OF DISTINGUISHED ADVOCATES OF THE UNITED STATES.

ANECDOTES OF RUFUS CHOATE.

Rufus Choate and Chief Justice Shaw, of Massachusetts, often indulged in wordy combats, and wit was generally freely expended by both sides. Choate was once arguing a cause before the chief justice (who was one of the homeliest men ever elevated to the bench), and, to express his reverence for the conceded ability of the judge, said, in yielding to an adverse decision,

"In coming into the presence of your honor, I experience the same feelings the Hindoo does when he bows before his idol. I know that you are ugly, but I feel that you are great!"

It is said that Choate had a command of language, and his brain teemed with a wealth of diction truly marvelous. When Judge Shaw first heard that there was a fresh edition of Worcester's Dictionary out, containing 2500 new words, he exclaimed, "For heaven's sake, don't let Choate get hold of it."

Choate, in an important assault and battery case at sea, had Dick Barton, chief mate of the clipper ship Challenge, on the stand, and badgered him so for about an hour that Dick got his salt water up, and hauled by the wind to bring the keen Boston lawyer under his batteries.

At the beginning of his testimony Dick said that the

night was as "dark as the devil, and raining like seven bells."

Suddenly Mr. Choate asked him,

"Was there a moon that night?"

"Yes, sir."

"Ah, yes! a moon—"

"Yes, a full moon."

"Did you see it?"

"Not a mite."

"Then how do you know that there was no moon?"

"The Nautical Almanac said so, and I'll believe that sooner than any lawyer in this world."

"What was the principal luminary that night, sir?"

"Binnacle lamp aboard the Challenge."

"Ah! you are growing sharp, Mr. Barton."

"What in blazes have you been grinding me this hour for—to make me dull?"

"Be civil, sir. And now tell me what latitude and longitude you crossed the equator in?"

"Sho'—you're joking."

"No, sir, I am in earnest, and I desire you to answer me."

"I sha'n't."

"Ah! you refuse, do you?"

"Yes—I can't."

"Indeed! You are the chief mate of a clipper ship, and are unable to answer so simple a question?"

"Yes, 'tis the *simplest* question I ever had asked me. Why, I thought every fool of a lawyer knew that there ain't no *latitude* at the equator."

That shot floored Rufus.

As Mr. Choate was cross-questioning a witness, he asked him what profession he followed for a livelihood. The witness replied,

"I am a candle of the Lord—a minister of the Gospel."

"Of what denomination?" asked the counselor.

"A Baptist," replied the witness.

"Then," said Mr. Choate, "you are a dipt, but I trust not a wick-ed candle."

In 1841 Mr. Choate was engaged in a divorce suit on the part of the husband to procure a bill of separation from his wife. The principal witness for his client was a woman named Abigail Bell. On the cross-examination, Mr. Sumner, the opposing counsel, asked her,

"Are you married?"

"No."

"Have you children?"

"No."

"Have you a child?"

Then there was a long and distressing pause. At last the monosyllable "Yes" was fully uttered by the witness. Instantly the counsel ceased the cross-examination. Of course, her evidence, where there was a conflict of testimony, was immensely damaged in the eyes of the jury by this fact confessed by the maiden mother. Choate did not ask any question in reply or explanation, and she stepped down from the witness-stand a blackened woman.

When he came, in the course of his argument, to reply to that part of his case which rested on her evidence, he took her character in hand. The court-room hushed the moment he said, "Abigail Bell's evidence, gentlemen, is before you." Raising himself up with great firmness, he went on, "I solemnly assert there is not the dream of a shadow of a shade of doubt or of suspicion on that evidence, or on her character."

Every body looked stupefied with astonishment at these words. Solemnly he proceeded:

"What though, in an unguarded moment, she may have trusted too far to the young man to whom she had pledged her untried affections, to whom she was to have been wedded on the next Lord's day, and *who was suddenly struck dead at her feet* by a stroke of lightning out of the heavens!"

Then he made another of his tremendous pauses, snuffing the air, and his strange, dark eyes lowered over the jury, while they took in this romantic and extraordinary explanation. The whole court-room felt its force, and lighted up as if a feeling of relief had been experienced by every one present. There was a buzz, a stir, a universal sensation, and then again Choate rolled along under full headway. He won his case, and this tragic story, to save the character of the fair witness, was the offspring of his fertile fancy.

The use of the expression from Sophocles, "the dream of the shadow of a shade," in the last anecdote of Choate, shows that he could be extravagant when necessary. In a speech at the beginning of the Mexican War Mr. Choate opposed an invasion of the Mexican territory, advocating the policy of keeping the United States army within the line of boundary claimed by our government. In answer to this, it was urged that such a policy would prolong the war; that the Mexicans did not agree to this boundary, and that they would be sending armies continually into the field to harass our troops. This Mr. Choate energetically denied. "No, sir," said he; "draw a line with the sword where the United States are resolved it should be drawn, and no *Mexican army will dare come within a thousand miles of that line for a thousand years!*"

In maintaining the worthlessness of certain testimony offered upon the other side, in a case in which he was engaged, Mr. Choate said, "It would be as difficult to find a grain of truth in that testimony as to find *a drop of water spilled in the Desert of Sahara in the times of the Crusaders!*"

Speaking in excuse of a man who had borrowed largely

in the prosecution of an enterprise that failed of success, and thus cruelly disappointed his creditors, Mr. Choate said, "Suddenly, as the lightning blazes in the summer sky, *all his vernal hopes of promise perished in autumnal rigor.*"

In a speech in defense of the judiciary in a Constitutional Convention, Choate was inquired of directly by a suspicious member as to whether he had not heard particular acts of the judges commented on very unfavorably. He proceeded to answer very slowly and solemnly, saying,

"Sir, I have known and loved many men, many women"—(here there was a subdued titter in the house: he raised himself up erect, his eyes flashed with a sublime ardor as he repeated in a most solemn tone)—"ay, many beautiful women, of the living and of the dead, of the purest and the noblest of earth and skies, but I never knew one, I never heard of one, if conspicuous enough to attract any considerable observation, whom the breath of calumny or sarcasm always wholly spared. Did the learned gentleman who interrogates me ever know one?

"'Be thou as chaste as ice, as pure as snow,
Thou shalt not escape calumny.'"

It is related that Mr. Choate wrote three hands: one which he could read, and his clerk could not; one which his clerk could read, and himself could not; and a third which nobody could read. Some of his friends used to tell him jestingly that he had better get the appointment of minister to China, where he could employ his leisure in lettering tea-chests with his pen.

GRACEFUL COMPLIMENTS.

Judge Story and Edward Everett were once the prominent personages at a public dinner in Boston. The former, as a voluntary toast, gave the following:

"Fame follows merit where Everett goes!"

The gentleman thus delicately complimented at once arose, and replied with this equally felicitous impromptu:

"To whatever height judicial learning may attain in this country, there will always be one Story higher."

AN INCORRUPTIBLE JUDGE.

The integrity of Judge Sewall, of Massachusetts, like that of Chief Justice Marshall, is a favorite recollection with the members of the legal profession. It is related of him that he went one day into a hatter's shop to purchase a pair of second-hand brushes for cleaning his shoes. The master of the shop presented him with a couple.

"What is your price?" said the judge.

"If they will answer your purpose," replied the other, "you may have them and welcome."

The judge, upon hearing this, laid them down, and bowing, was leaving the shop, upon which the latter said to him,

"Pray, sir, your honor has forgotten the principal object of your visit."

"By no means," answered the judge. "If you please to set a price, I am ready to purchase; but ever since it has fallen to my lot to occupy a seat on the bench, I have studiously avoided receiving any present to the value of a single copper, lest at some future period of my life it might have some kind of influence in determining my judgment."

ANECDOTES OF HENRY CLAY.

In the long dispute between the States of Virginia and Kentucky, growing out of what was termed the "occupying claimant laws," Henry Clay was retained by Kentucky to maintain her rights before "that tribunal in the last resort," the Supreme Court of the United States. The then Speaker of the House of Representatives was to appear for the first time before that elevated, dignified, and venerable body, and a large concourse of spectators was attracted by a natural curiosity to determine whether the orator of the West would be able to sustain his reputation upon this new and untried theatre.

When he rose, it was with some slight agitation of manner; but he soon recovered his wonted composure, and held his auditors in admiring attention while he pronounced a most beautiful eulogium upon the character of the sons of Kentucky. The judges sat, in their black robes of office, sedate and attentive. Judge Washington, who was in the habit of indulging himself with an occasional pinch of snuff,

had taken out his snuff-box for a little of that titillating restorative, and Mr. Clay, on observing it, instantly stopped, and advancing gracefully to the bench, participated with the judge in the refreshment of his nasal organs.

As he applied the pinch, he observed,

"I perceive that your honor sticks to the Scotch," and immediately resuming his stand, he proceeded in his argument without the least embarrassment. So extraordinary a step over the usual barrier which separates the court and the barristers excited not a little astonishment and admiration among the spectators, and it was afterward aptly remarked by Judge S., in relating the circumstance to a friend, that "he did not believe there was a man in the United States who could have done that but Henry Clay."

It is known that Mr. Clay was remarkable for his recollection of faces. A curious incident of this wonderful power is told of his visit to Jackson, Mississippi, in the year 18—. On his way the cars stopped at Clinton for a few moments, when an eccentric, but strong-minded old man made his way up to him, exclaiming, as he did so, "Don't introduce me, for I want to see if Mr. Clay will know me."

"Where did I know you?" said Mr. Clay.

"In Kentucky," answered the keen-sighted, but one-eyed old man.

Mr. Clay struck his long, bony finger upon his forehead, as if in deep thought. "Have you lost that eye since I saw you, or had you lost it before?" inquired Mr. Clay.

"Since," said the man.

"Then turn the sound side of your face to me, that I may get your profile."

Mr. C. paused for a moment, his thoughts running back many years. "I have it!" said he. "Did you not give me a verdict as juror, at Frankfort, Kentucky, in the great case of the United States *vs.* Innis, twenty-one years ago?"

"I did! I did!" said the overjoyed old man.

"And is not your name," said Mr. Clay, "Hardwicke?"

"It is, it is," replied Dr. Hardwicke, bursting into tears. "Did I not tell you," he said to his friends, "that he knew me, though I have not seen him from that time to this? Great men never forget faces."

ANECDOTES OF AARON BURR.

When Aaron Burr returned to New York city to practice law after his voluntary exile in Europe, he found the late Rev. Jedediah Burchard, then a celebrated revivalist, holding a series of protracted meetings in his family church. He attended from habit, always went late, and disturbed the services by attracting to himself the attention of the audience on account of his infamous notoriety as the man who shot Alexander Hamilton, and who had been tried for

treason. Mr. Burchard resolved to rebuke him openly. The next Sabbath, when he came in and got about half way up the aisle, the clergyman paused in his discourse, and pointing at Colonel Burr, said, in the most scathing manner, "You hoary-headed old sinner, I'll appear against you at the day of judgment!" The proud, defiant old man, standing erect as ever, with that perfect composure which never deserted him, and fixing his fine gray eyes on the occupant of the pulpit, replied, "Mr. Burchard, I have observed through a long course of professional experience that the very meanest class of criminals are those who turn *States' evidence!*"

It was a favorite saying of this astute legal practitioner, "That *is* law which is clearly stated and plausibly maintained."

When Burr was being tried for treason at Richmond, among the young gentlemen of the town who had succeeded in forcing their way into the room was Winfield Scott, then just admitted to the bar. He stood at the massive lock of the great door, above the crowd, in full view of the prisoner, who observed him, harassed even as he was by the incidents of the great trial. Years afterward they met. Scott was then the lauded hero of the War of 1812, Burr was a ruined adventurer. On the evening of the day on which he was first named *General*, Scott found himself at the house of a distinguished politician in Albany, where a little supper was to celebrate his promotion.

"Have you any objection, general, to be introduced to Colonel Aaron Burr?" inquired the giver of the feast.

"Any gentleman whom you may choose to invite to your house," replied the general, "I shall be glad to know."

Colonel Burr entered; the introduction took place; the party sat down to whist until the supper was announced. At the table the old colonel and the young general sat opposite to each other, but no particular conversation occurred between them for some time. Meanwhile General Scott, ever as courteous as brave, forbore to pronounce the word *Richmond* or even *Virginia*, lest it should excite painful feelings in the mind of a fellow-man. Suddenly Colonel Burr looked up and said,

"General Scott, I've seen you before."

"Have you, indeed?" rejoined the general, supposing that he referred to some military scene, or other public occasion in which he had figured.

"Yes," continued Burr, "I saw you at my trial."

On one occasion, when Burr was a prisoner in Louisville, Ky., on his way to Richmond to be tried for treason, the populace outside the building was excited to the highest degree, and made a demonstration as if they would seize and maltreat him. Henry Clay, just then rising into fame, became somewhat alarmed for Burr's safety, and in that courtly manner for which he was always so remarkable, said,

"Mr. Burr, whatever may be the excitement in the street, depend upon it I will be answerable for your personal safety."

At the remark the fine eye of Burr flashed with lurid fire, and, drawing himself up with a dignity that seemed overpowering, he replied,

"Mr. Clay, I have never been placed in any circumstances where I could not protect myself."

OUT OF THE JURISDICTION.

The late Judge Pearce, of the Supreme Court of the State of Ohio, was a noted wag. A young lawyer was once making his first effort before him, and had thrown himself, on the wings of his imagination, far into the upper regions, and was seemingly preparing for a higher ascent, when the judge struck his rule on the desk two or three times, exclaiming to the astonished orator,

"Hold on, hold on, my dear sir. Don't go any higher, for you are already out of the jurisdiction of this court."

RELATED TO THE JUDGE.

Judge B——, late one of the judges of the Eighth District of the State of New York, was a most amiable man, whose honor was unsullied, and who hated a mean action as every such character must. At the Genesee Circuit he was hearing an action in which one of the parties happened to be a namesake of his. During the trial, the party, having an opportunity, and thinking probably to gain some advantage by it, approached the judge and said,

"We are of the same name, judge. I've been making inquiries, and find we are some relation to each other."

"Ah!" said the judge, "is that so? Are you sure of it?"

"Oh yes," said he, "no doubt of it."

"Well," said the judge, "I'm very glad to hear that—*very glad indeed.* I shall get rid of your case; I shall dismiss it, because I can not sit in a suit where I am related to one of the parties."

This was a little more than the party had bargained for, and he began at once to paddle off. After a few inquiries as to the judge's ancestry, and their residence, etc.,

"I think, judge," said he, "I was mistaken. We are of quite different families, and not at all related."

"Ah!" says the judge, "is that so?"

"Oh yes," said he, "there is no mistake about it."

"Well," replied the judge, in a very emphatic tone, "I'm glad to learn that—very glad. I should hate awfully to be related to a man mean enough to attempt to influence a court as you have!"

HANDLING A WITNESS WITHOUT GLOVES.

Colonel L——, who was at one time one of the most distinguished practitioners in the criminal courts of the city of Philadelphia, on a certain occasion was for the prosecution, and his witnesses had been subjected to a terrible cross-examination from Mr. Ingraham, who appeared for the defense. After the testimony for the state had closed, Colonel L—— said to his opponent,

"Now, Mr. Ingraham, I intend to handle your witnesses without gloves."

"That is more than I would like to do with yours," responded Mr. Ingraham.

ANECDOTES OF JOHN RANDOLPH.

When John Randolph visited Richmond it was his habit to stop at the Eagle Hotel, and to drive his own horse around to the stables on another street. On one of these occasions, while performing this latter operation, he was arrested by a country wagon standing before a grocery store kept by one Simpson and his wife—the wife being the man of the two—and Randolph, being impeded in his passage of the narrow street, ordered the countryman to get out of his way. The frightened fellow tried to do so, but Randolph was too impatient, and, springing out of his own wagon, put after the countryman, who took refuge in the grocery. As Randolph rushed in, Mrs. S. was coming out with a bucket of dirty water in her hand, and, seeing the excitement of the intruder, demanded of him where he was going.

"Madam," said Randolph, in his shrillest key, "do you know who you are speaking to?" And then, drawing himself up to his fullest *lankitude*, he exclaimed, "I am John Randolph, of Roanoke."

"I don't care," said she, "who you are; but if you ain't out of this house in a minute, you'll get this bucket of slops in your face."

Suiting the action to the threat, she raised the bucket, and would have dashed it over the statesman had not his discretion, for the first and only time, got the better of his valor. Turning on his heel, he beat a hasty retreat, and left the woman mistress of the field.

John Randolph was once in a tavern, lying on a sofa in the parlor, waiting for the stage to come to the door. A dandified chap stepped into the room with a whip in his hand, just come from a drive, and, standing before the mirror, arranged his hair and collar, quite unconscious of the presence of the gentleman on the sofa. After attitudinizing a while, he turned to go out, when Mr. Randolph asked him,

"Has the stage come?"

"Stage, sir! stage!" said the fop; "I've nothing to do with it, sir."

"Oh! I beg your pardon," said Randolph, quietly; "*I thought you were the driver!*"

Mr. Randolph was traveling through a part of Virginia in which he was unacquainted with either people or routes, and stopped during one night at an inn near the forks of two roads. The inn-keeper was a fine gentleman, and, no doubt, of one of the *first families of the Old Dominion.* Knowing who his distinguished guest was, he endeavored during the evening to draw him into a conversation, but failed in all his efforts. But in the morning, when Mr. Randolph was ready to start, he called for his bill, which, on being presented, was paid. The landlord, still anxious to have some conversation with him, began as follows:

"Which way are you traveling, Mr. Randolph?"

"Sir?" said Mr. Randolph, with a look of displeasure.

"I asked," said the landlord, "which way are you traveling?"

"Have I paid you my bill?"

"Yes."

"Do I owe you any thing more?"

"No."

"Well, I'm going just where I please; do you understand?"

"Yes."

The landlord by this time got somewhat excited, and Mr. Randolph drove off. But, to the landlord's surprise, in a few minutes he sent one of the servants to inquire which of the forks of the road to take. Mr. Randolph not being out of hearing distance, the landlord spoke at the top of his breath, "Mr. Randolph, you don't owe me one cent; just take which road you please."

It is said that the air turned blue with the curses of Randolph.

AN AUGUST TRIBUNAL.

The late Justice Butterfield was well known as one of the most eminent lawyers of Illinois. With a cold and impassive manner, he was capable of enlivening the dryest legal argument with the keenest wit.

On one occasion he was retained by the celebrated Joe Smith, the Mormon prophet, to defend him upon an indictment for treason before the United States Court at Springfield. Judge Pope had permitted, with his usual gallantry, a large number of fair ladies to occupy the ample room in close proximity to the judge. A large number of spectators from all parts of the state crowded the court-room. Mr. Butterfield arose in his usual solemn and dignified manner, and began the defense in this wise:

"May it please the court and gentlemen of the jury—I arise before the 'Pope,' in the presence of Angels, to defend the Prophet of the Lord." The inspiration of the *defender* continued to the termination of a successful *defense* of the defended.

AN OLD-TIME ANECDOTE.

The following legal anecdote, belonging to the history of another age, is thus graphically related by an eye-witness to the scene:

"It was, I think, in the winter of 1816–'17, or '17–'18, that business called me to Trenton, New Jersey. While there I was informed that an interesting trial was in progress before the chancellor, Mahlon Dickerson (who was also governor), to test the validity of a will. By the will property to the amount of $100,000 had been bequeathed to a man whom we will call H——, who, if I remember aright, was not related to the testator, but who had been much with him during his last illness. The heirs-at-law determined to contest the will on the ground of fraud, and had employed as counsel Joseph Hopkinson, author of 'Hail Columbia,' and Alexander J. Dallas, both of Philadelphia, and both, as you know, of great celebrity. When I entered the court-room Mr. Dallas was delivering the closing argument for the plaintiffs. He was standing immediately opposite the chancellor, at a table some three feet wide, on the other side of which sat H——, his head resting on his hand, and looking directly in the face of the speaker, his countenance wearing an expression of mingled rage and anxiety, which he endeavored to conceal by a sort of sickly smile. All at once Mr. Dallas ceased speaking; a breathless silence of about half a minute succeeded, when the following episode took place:

"'Mr. Chancellor,' he resumed, 'ever since the commencement of my argument, in which I have endeavored, to the best of my ability, to trace and expose this most atrocious attempt to defraud my clients of their rightful inheritance, this man, the defendant, who, during the whole of this trial, has exhibited an effrontery that I have rarely seen equaled, has chosen to place himself in most offensive proximity to my person; and in hope, I presume, that he may embarrass me, has been smiling and smirking in my face. May it please your honor, smiles are as multiform as the characters and dispositions of men. There is the smile of conscious innocence, which sparkles in the eye and mantles on the cheek, and, wherever encountered, it exerts a power that is always irresistible. Whether in the marble palace or the lowly cottage, that heaven-born smile unconsciously challenges, and as surely receives, the instinctive homage of every true-hearted man. But, sir, there is another smile, and of a far different character. It is that which the blackest villainy can assume when it would hide the loathsomeness of its own deformity. It was that which sat upon the features of the regicide of Claudius, whom Hamlet, if my memory serves me, thus apostrophizes:

> "'Oh! villain, villain, smiling, damned villain!
> My tables—meet it is I set it down
> That one may smile and smile, and be a villain!'"

The effect of this withering rebuke, deriving its force not more from the words than the manner of the speaker, was electrical upon bench, bar, and auditory; and the pitiable creature against whom it was directed, his face reddening to the very roots of his hair, seized his hat, and, elbowing his way through the dense crowd, made his escape, and was seen no more in that court-room. The will was set aside.

That was the last speech of Alexander J. Dallas. He was taken sick that night; the next morning he and Mr. Hopkinson started for home, but he died before he reached it, and then was lost to his country a man who, as orator, jurist, statesman, and patriot, had but few superiors.

WIRT AND WEBSTER IN A TRIAL OF WIT.

Daniel Webster was once engaged in the trial of a case in one of the Virginia courts, and the opposing counsel was William Wirt, author of the "Life of Patrick Henry," which has been criticised as a brilliant romance. In the progress of the case, Mr. Webster produced a highly respectable witness, whose testimony (unless disproved or impeached) settled the case, and annihilated Mr. Wirt's client. After getting through the testimony, he informed Mr. Wirt, with a significant expression, that he was through with the witness, and that he was at his service. Mr. Wirt rose to commence the cross-examination, but seemed for a moment quite perplexed how to proceed, but quickly assumed a manner expressive of his incredulity as to the facts elicited, and, coolly eying the witness a moment, he said,

"Mr. K——, allow me to ask you if you have ever read a work called the 'Baron Munchausen?'"

Before the witness had time to reply, Mr. Webster quickly rose to his feet, and said,

"I beg your pardon, Mr. Wirt, for the interruption; but there was one question I forgot to ask the witness, and if you will allow me that favor, I promise not to interrupt you again."

Mr. Wirt, in the blandest manner, replied, "Yes, most certainly;" when Mr. Webster, in the most deliberate and solemn manner, said,

"Sir, have you ever read 'Wirt's Patrick Henry?'"

The effect was irresistible, and even the judge could not control his rigid features. Mr. Wirt himself joined in the momentary laugh, and, turning to Mr. Webster, said, "Suppose we submit this case to the jury without summing up," which was assented to, and Mr. Webster's client won the suit.

BEAUTIFUL IMPROMPTU OF WILLIAM WIRT.

This eloquent and distinguished advocate, in the trial of a case, stated a legal proposition, the soundness of which was doubted by his opponent, who asked him for his authority—to cite a precedent, and name the book and page.

Mr. Wirt turned upon the questioner, and instantly replied in his most gorgeous manner,

"Sir, I am not bound to grope my way among the ruins of antiquity, to stumble over obsolete statutes and delve in black-letter lore in search of a principle written in living letters upon the heart of every man."

PATRICK HENRY'S REPLY TO A CHALLENGE.

Governor Giles, of Virginia, once addressed a note to Patrick Henry, demanding satisfaction:

"Sir, I understand that you have called me a 'bob-tail' politician. I wish to know if it be true; and if true, your meaning. WM. B. GILES."

To which Mr. Henry replied in this wise:

"Sir, I do not recollect having called you a bob-tail politician at any time, but think it probable I have. Not recollecting the time or occasion, I can't say what I did mean, but if you will tell me what you think I meant, I will say whether you are correct or not. Very respectfully,

"PATRICK HENRY."

ANECDOTES OF THOMAS. F. MARSHALL.

The Hon. Thomas F. Marshall, of Kentucky, once a prince of good fellows, was defending a man charged with murder in Jessamine County, Judge Lusk presiding. The testimony against the prisoner was strong, and Tom struggled hard on the cross-examination, but to little purpose, for the old judge was inflexible in his determination to rule out all the improper testimony offered on the part of the defense. At last Tom worked himself into a high state of excitement, and remarked that "Jesus Christ was convicted upon just such rulings of the court that tried him."

"Clerk," said the judge, "enter a fine of ten dollars against Mr. Marshall."

"Well, this is the first time I ever heard of any body being fined for abusing Pontius Pilate," was the quick response of Tom.

Here the judge became very indignant, and ordered the clerk to enter another fine of twenty dollars.

Tom arose with that peculiar, mirth-provoking expression that no one can imitate, and addressed the court with as much gravity as circumstances would permit, as follows:

"If your honor pleases, as a good citizen, I feel bound to obey the order of this court, and intend to do so in this instance; but as I don't happen to have thirty dollars about me, I shall be compelled to borrow it of some friend, and, as I see no one present whose confidence and friendship I have so long enjoyed as your honor's, I make no hesitation in asking the small favor of a loan for a few days, to square up the amount of the fines that you have caused the clerk to enter against me."

This was a stumper. The judge looked at Tom, and then at the clerk, and finally said,

"Clerk, remit Mr. Marshall's fines; the state is better able to lose thirty dollars than I am."

Marshall was once a candidate against General James S. Pilcher, at one time mayor of Louisville, Kentucky. The general made a long and telling speech, for it was replete with good stories, if not good language and deep learning, and had closed by telling his audience that he was raised a plain country lad, and had never been to school more than about three months in his life. Marshall arose, and, in that humorous way peculiar to himself, remarked,

"My friend has told you that his school education was confined to the short period of three months' time; for myself, I was much surprised to hear that the gentleman had been to school at all!"

In an important suit before the Kentucky Court of Appeals, Marshall was pitted against Henry Clay, for whom he had as great hatred as dread. Marshall spoke first, and attacked with all his energy the positions he *supposed* Clay would assume.

"You can barely imagine," said he, subsequently, alluding to the case, "my immense mortification when Clay concluded a splendid speech without even alluding to any thing I had said."

On another occasion Marshall was engaged in a trial before a justice of the peace, whom he tried to convince that he had made an erroneous decision on a certain point of law, and for this purpose he cited authorities from King Solomon all the way down, piling tome on tome, till the justice was ready to swear that he didn't care a button for all his books or Tom Marshall either. After Tom had exhausted all his fund of argument and eloquence to no effect, he said,

"Will your honor please fine me ten dollars for contempt of court?"

"For *what?*" asked the astonished magistrate. "You have committed no contempt of court."

"But," replied the illustrious Tom, in his own provokingly ludicrous way, "I assure you that I have an infernal contempt for it."

A young limb of the law, named M'Kay, who had heard of this anecdote of Marshall, once attempted to imitate it, and was punished as all imitators deserve to be. He was employed to prosecute a man indicted for larceny before a committing court composed of three magistrates. On hearing the testimony, they refused to commit the prisoner to jail. M'Kay concluded to take revenge on the magistrates. He accordingly began the attack.

"I wish your worships would fine me five dollars for contempt of court."

"Why, Mr. M'Kay?"

"Because I feel a very decided contempt for the court."

"Your contempt for the court is not more decided than the court's contempt for you," was the response of one of the magistrates.

This was a stinging retort, and Mac felt it; but another worshipful member of the court—a dry, hard-looking old blacksmith—put in a blow that finished the work, and completely demolished the young lawyer:

"We mout fine you," he said, "but we don't know which one of us you'd want to borry the money from to pay it with."

A few years since Marshall was delivering an address before a large audience in Buffalo, when some one in the hall every few moments shouted "Louder! louder!" Tom stood this for a while, but at last, turning gravely to the presiding officer, he said, "Mr. Chairman, at the last day, when the angel shall with his golden trumpet proclaim that time shall be no longer, when the quick and dead shall appear before the mercy seat to be judged, I doubt not, sir, that the solemnity of that solemn and awful scene will be interrupted by some drunken fool from Buffalo shouting 'Louder, Lord! louder!'" Tom went on with his speech, but there were no more cries of "louder."

At a great political meeting Tom began his speech, and had made but little progress before he was assailed with a torrent of abuse by an Irishman in the crowd. Not at all disconcerted, Tom sung out at the top of his voice,

"Be jabers, that's me fren', Patrick Murphy—the man that spells God with a little *g*, and Murphy with a big *M!*"

If Pat had any elevated ideas of his smartness, the roars of laughter that greeted this shot must have caused him to doubt the propriety of giving words to more.

In his life Marshall represented at once the genius, passion, wit, and worst follies and weaknesses of humanity. In his latter days he did not belong to more than two or three temperance societies at a time; and once, in a wild fever of dissipation, was taken to a room in the Mansion House at Lexington by a friend. When there, he found the old school-boy warning that "what goes up must come down" entirely reversed, and his friend, hearing the up-heavings from the vasty deep, said,

"Are you unwell, Mr. Marshall?"

"Oh no," was the reply; "only throwing up for fun!"

RIDICULE VERSUS ELOQUENCE.

The celebrated legal orator, Elisha Williams, of Columbia County, was a most graceful speaker, and his voice, particularly in its pathetic tones, was melody itself. All who remember Ogden Hoffman's voice (he was called "the Flute" by his fellow-members of the bar of New York) can appreciate the mellifluous organ of Mr. Williams. His power over a jury was astonishing. He swayed as with the wand of an enchanter, and it was very seldom that he failed to secure a verdict for his client; but on one occasion he did, in such a perfectly ridiculous manner, that a crowded court and grave judges on the bench were convulsed with laughter at the burlesque of the result. He was completely discomfited by an ignorant, impudent, unlettered pettifogger who knew no law, but somehow or other had obtained the credit of shrewdness, and the reputation among his farmer neighbors of being hard to beat.

The case was an act of murder. Mr. Williams, of course on the ground of his power over the jury, was for the defense. His peroration was exceedingly touching and beautiful.

"Gentlemen of the jury," said he, "if you can find this unhappy prisoner at the bar guilty of the crime with which he is charged after the adverse and irrefragable arguments which I have laid before you, pronounce your fatal verdict; send him to lie in chains upon the dungeon floor, waiting the death which he is to receive at your hands; then go to the bosom of your families, go lay your heads on your pillows—*and sleep if you can!*"

The effect of the closing words of the great legal orator was at first thrilling, but by-and-by the pettifogger, who had volunteered to follow the prosecuting attorney, arose and said,

"Gentlemen of the jury, I should despair, after the weeping speech which has been made to you by Mr. Williams, of saying any thing to do away with its eloquence. I never heerd Mr. Williams speak that piece of his'n better than what he spoke it now. Onct I heerd him speak it in a case of stealin', down to Schaghticoke; then he spoke it ag'in in a case of rape, up to Æsopus; and the last time I heerd it, before jest now, was when them niggurs was tried—and convicted, too, they was—for robbin' Van Pelt's hen-house, over beyond Kingston. But I never know'd him to speak it so elegant and effectin' as what he spoke it jes now."

This was a poser. The jury looked at one another, whispered together, and our pettifogger saw at once that he had got them. He stopped at once, closing with a single remark: "If you can't see, gentlemen of the jury, that this speech don't answer all cases, then there's no use of my saying any thing more."

And there wasn't; he had made his case, and they awarded him their verdict.

A VALUABLE WATCH.

The following anecdote, illustrative of the character of Judge Parsons, is sublime in thought and language. A gentleman had been concerned in a duel; the ball of his antagonist struck his watch, and remained there. It thus saved his life. The watch was afterward exhibited, with the ball remaining in it, in a company where Judge Parsons was present. It was observed by several that it was a valuable watch. "Yes," said Parsons, "very excellent; *it has kept Time from Eternity.*"

REMINISCENCES OF JOHN VAN BUREN.

The late John Van Buren, or "Prince John," as he was familiarly called, was noted for his "infinite jest." He

was, besides, a very remarkable character, though not a successful man. He did not, in fact, possess the peculiar endowments which give a man success in this practical country of ours. His talents and his information were too general, and he developed a readiness in all things, but greatness in none. He was not a business man, but a man of society; not a sharp financier, but a witty diner-out; not a dry, and fusty, and learned lawyer, but a genial, lively, and generous gentleman of elegant leisure. It was the business of his life to entertain, and none could be more entertaining or more elegant, or be so more unflaggingly than himself. His wit and humor intruded itself in every thing, and all his law cases are distinguished by his witticisms, and every political campaign for many years past has its hundreds of reminiscences of John Van Buren's jokes and dry humor. Although lacking in practicability, in fact, though terribly deficient in purpose (and the fixedness of purpose often makes a man out of small material), John Van Buren became a leading spirit among the politicians of New York, and a powerful one, too, among the Democracy. Smooth (but not oily) as a courtier, elegant and princely in manner, and naturally a beautiful and effective orator, John Van Buren swayed the wayward masses, and controlled them by his wise and witty, shrewd and plain phrases.

His oratorical efforts were always not merely elegant and witty, but eminently effective. Perhaps the most potent evidence of his eloquence might be found in his Tammany Hall speeches, where he had to deal with the roughest elements of the community. With his suave manner and soft voice he held the surging and often noisy mass in a control which was as absolute as it was remarkable. Oftentimes, when the turbulence of the crowd would break out into hand-to-hand fights—when fists would ply to the right and left with apparent indiscrimination, and the proceedings would be completely disorganized, and the voice of the speaker drowned in the tumult, John Van Buren would wait his time patiently, until the sudden outbreak had exhausted itself, and then, with a wave of his hand, a pleasant smile, a merry twinkle of his eye, he would arrest the attention of the peaceably disposed elements, hanging on the outskirts and around the platform, and, by some happy allusion or witty phrase, he never failed to gather in the floating turbulence of the quarrelsome part of the meeting, and keep it in easy subjection until all thoughts of fighting were forgotten in laughter at the fun, or absorbed by the close logic of the speaker.

As an instance of his wit, it is told of him that he was once angrily accosted by a suitor whose case he had overthrown with,

"I believe, sir, you would take a fee from the greatest scoundrel on earth!"

"Softly, my dear sir," half whispered Van Buren, with well-affected concern; "walk aside with me, if you please. Now, sir," presenting his ear to the man, "tell me what you have been doing!"

One of the phrases which Van Buren once used in regard to some popular candidate, who, he said, "would run like the cholera," is in common use to this day. To Mr. Van Buren belongs the paternity of another phrase as frequently used as the above. "Vote early and vote often" was the witty advice which he gave a Democratic meeting twenty odd years ago.

In 1865 Mr. Van Buren ran on the ticket with General Slocum for attorney general of New York, and, though satisfied at all times of his defeat, appeared at all times most sanguine of success. One day he went to one of the newspaper offices, and announced that he would bet $10,000 in gold that Slocum would be elected. The next day he received a note accepting the bet from, as he described him, "one Lawrence Jerome, a Wall Street broker, who was popularly supposed to have a little surplus cash." He wrote to Mr. Peter Cagger, one of the rich members of the Albany Regency, relating what Mr. Jerome proposed to do, and suggesting to him to furnish the funds, but Mr. Cagger answered that he was busy. He telegraphed to Dean Richmond, who answered that he was deep in New York Central matters; to Governor Seymour, who replied that he was busy stumping the state. Finding none of these were open to a good thing, Van Buren called on Mr. Jerome, discussed the bet as the most serious of matters, announced that it was open for acceptance only until one o'clock (it was then twelve), and then deliberately disputed as to what bank should be the holder of the stakes until the hour expired, when he announced the bet as withdrawn.

He was one of the counsel for Edwin Forrest in the famous divorce case, and, being opposed by Charles O'Conor, of course lost his suit. When the decision in Mrs. Forrest's favor was rendered, Mr. Van Buren quietly arose and addressed the jury, informing them that nothing remained to be done but to fix the amount of the allowance to be granted to the divorced wife, and raised a laugh throughout the court by saying, with a merry twinkle of the eye, that he had examined the English authorities on the subject, and found that precedent justified the jury in fixing the matter of allowance to any sum between a farthing and sixpence.

In 1848 Mr. Van Buren followed his father into the Free-soil camp. This step was the occasion of some pretty sharp attacks on the Prince, who, in characteristic style, parried the thrusts of his adversaries with an anecdote. And this was the anecdote: A traveler, passing along a corduroy road in the Empire State, came to a load of hay overturned on the side of the road. Observing a lusty youth pitching the hay right and left in a very unaccountable way, the traveler said, "My young friend, why do you do that?"

Wiping the sweat from his brow, and pointing to the pile of hay, the boy replied, "*Stranger, dad's under there!*" Of course this anecdote required no application from the son of his father, and, amid general merriment, the prince would pass on to the graver topics of the canvass.

A COUPLE OF RIVAL EPIGRAMS.

At a trial of a cause before a referee, in Delaware County, New York, Hon. Daniel S. Dickinson was counsel for the plaintiff, and Mr. H——, of Binghamton, for the defendant. Mr. H——, albeit a lawyer of some eminence, was so interminably *slow* on this occasion as to utterly weary out both referee and witnesses. One of the latter, while waiting with eager impatience to give his evidence and be dismissed, perpetrated the following, and handed it to the ex-senator for perusal:

"When Job was tempted by the devil,
His patience saved his soul from evil;
But were he living in our day,
And thrown by chance in H——'s way—
If forced to hear him try a case,
I fear poor Job would fall from grace;
He never could endure, I trow,
What we poor devils suffer now!"

Mr. Dickinson read the lines, and rapidly dashed off the following rejoinder:

"There were no lawsuits in these days,
As any one can plainly see,
For, had there been, the devil would
Have made poor Job a referee,
And sent for H—— to try the case,
And spin it out till Job would cry
'I give it up—my patience's gone;
Now must I curse my God and die!'"

"VERY INDIFFERENTLY INDEED."

Richard O'Gorman was recently trying a case before a rather ignorant judge of the New York Superior Court, who appeared strongly prejudiced, if not partisan, in favor of the side against which Mr. O'Gorman was pleading. Of this fact Mr. O'Gorman gave a pretty broad hint, intimating that his honor should not have remained on the bench to hear a case in which he was so clearly interested in behalf of one side.

"You are wrong, sir," thundered the judge, growing red in the face; "I am no partisan in the matter. I have no interest in either of the parties to this suit. I administer justice in the case indifferently."

"Very indifferently indeed, your honor!" replied O'Gorman, with a courteous bow, and there the matter dropped, the judge believing he had received a compliment.

"WOULD MAKE A POOR LAWYER."

The plaintiff in a suit brought against the city of New York had been injured by a fall, caused by what is termed "a corporation hole," and during the trial, Dr. Willard Parker being upon the stand in behalf of the plaintiff, the associate counsel of the city cross-examined him, and elicited the remark that "the plaintiff was so injured that he could *lie* only on one side." The answer was no sooner given than the counsel says,

"I suppose, doctor, you mean he would make a very poor lawyer!" The court did not maintain its gravity.

A FORGETFUL JUDGE.

Chief Justice Jones, of New York, who had been chancellor of the state, chief justice of the Superior Court, judge of the Court of Appeals, and presiding justice of the Supreme Court, had some peculiarities. One was, never to decline an invitation to a dinner or evening party. Another was, that his desk at home, where he studied his cases, was the strangest pile of heterogeneous papers one ever saw. They would accumulate for months, until the table could hold no more, and then he would get a basket or a barrel, and empty into them the contents of his table, and begin and go over the process of accumulation again. Sometimes a paper would be required, and then would come a grand rummage, during which there would not unfrequently turn up some forgotten thing of interest. He had probably been recently engaged in some such work, when, one evening, about nine o'clock, he walked into the house of an acquaintance — a gentleman of fortune, who often gave parties—dressed for a party with white kids, etc. Upon being ushered into the parlor, he found the host sitting there alone, reading the paper, but no signs of a party. He was received very cordially, for the host had great respect for him — as who had not? But the chief said, "I'm afraid I have made a mistake."

"If you have," said mine host, "I am obliged to the mistake, for it has given me the honor of your company."

"But haven't you a party to-night?"

"No, sir."

The chief drew forth a small note from his pocket, and inquired, "Is not that from you, sir?"

"Certainly, judge," said the host, "but that was for this day of the month last year, when I can not forget that we had the pleasure of your company."

ANECDOTES OF DANIEL WEBSTER.

The following characteristic and amusing anecdotes of the late lamented statesman, Daniel Webster, are undeniably authentic. They proceed from personal friends of Mr. Webster.

Some years ago Mr. Webster paid a professional visit to Northampton, Massachusetts, one of the pleasantest inland towns in the state. His presence there was expected, and, being the political idol of a large portion of the community, preparations had been made to give him a cordial reception by eminent private citizens. The landlord, too, of the principal inn had prepared a very handsome suite of apartments for his express accommodation, and had made arrangements to have the great man occupy them.

At length Mr. Webster arrived, and stopped at the hotel in question. He was shown to his quarters, with which he expressed himself well pleased, until it was incidentally remarked by some friend present that "Northampton was a temperance town, and that that was a temperance house."

"Won't you ring the bell for the landlord?" asked Mr. Webster of a gentleman who stood near the bell-pull.

He rang the bell, and the landlord soon came up.

"Mr. Brewster," said Mr. Webster, "can you direct me to General L——'s house. I think I will take up my quarters with him."

The landlord, with great disappointment expressed in his face and manner, said,

"Why, Mr. Webster, I was in hopes my rooms would meet with your entire approbation. We had taken great pains to have their arrangements such as should please you."

"Your rooms, Mr. Brewster, are excellent every way. Nothing need be more so; and I understand your table is abundantly supplied with well-cooked viands. But, Mr. Brewster, I understand that your house is conducted upon rigid temperance principles. Now, sir, I am an old man; my blood is thin, and now and then I require a little stimulus. Have you any pure old brandy, Mr. Brewster?"

"I have some of the oldest and purest in Massachusetts, I think," answered the landlord.

"Well, Mr. Brewster, have the kindness to bring me up a bottle, and place it on the little stand behind that door."

Mr. Brewster departed, and soon came back with the desiderated fluid, which he deposited as directed.

"Mr. Brewster," continued Mr. Webster, "have you any fine old Madeira?"

"Yes, Mr. Webster, of the oldest and best vintage."

"Do you know how to ice it properly, so that it shall be only just gratefully cool?"

The landlord answered in the affirmative, and went down to the cellar for a bottle. When he came back, he placed it in a graduated cooler, and was about to retire, when Mr. Webster said,

"You need be under no apprehension, Mr. Brewster, that this infraction of the temperance law of your town will be discovered. I must needs honor law, being one of its humble ministers, and would not exhibit even a justifiable evasion of its commands. No, Mr. Brewster, you leave those bottles there, where they will be unobserved, and in a short time *I will put them where no human eye can see them.*"

But among the Websteriana there is nothing of his better than the answer to the French minister, who asked him, while Secretary of State, whether the United States would recognize the new government of France.

The secretary assumed a very solemn tone and attitude, saying,

"Why not? The United States has recognized the Bourbons, the Republic, the Directory, the Council of Five Hundred, the First Consul, the Emperor, Louis XVIII., Charles X., Louis Philippe, the—"

"Enough! enough!" cried the French minister, perfectly satisfied by such a formidable citation of consistent precedents.

When Daniel Webster was a young man, about commencing the study of law, he was advised not to enter the legal profession, for it was already crowded. His reply was, "*There is room enough at the top!*"

Lewis Gaylord Clark has thus described a scene illustrating Webster's impressiveness in manner and delivery:

"I had often seen Mr. Webster walking up Pennsylvania Avenue to the Capitol, but had never happened to be in Washington when any public question was before Congress in which he was to speak. At length one day, however, a friend said to me, 'If you want to hear Webster speak, go up to the United States Supreme Court-room at eleven o'clock; he is going to address the court at that hour in a very important case.' Well, about half past eleven I was there. The judges ('terrible show') were there in a row, in their black silk canonicals, dignified and impressive, and, what is rare in any of our less important tribunals, utterly unconscious of their impressiveness. There were not, I venture to say, fifty persons among the audience in the room. Mr. Webster was on his feet, and addressing the court. His were commercial figures, and not 'figures of speech' at first, and I must say I thought them very dry. But at length he warmed up a little.

"The case before the court had been a long time before the public, and every body had become tired of it. It was the Wheeling Bridge case, which had been the 'Jarndyce *vs.* Jarndyce' of the times. After stating facts and figures, and previous conclusions and decisions upon them, Mr. Webster said:

"'Now, your honors, we desire this legitimately unauthorized company to send in complete returns from the first; to present a bill of entire receipts; to render up strict and unimpeachable accounts; to settle up, and pay up; in other words, your honors, we demand that they DISGORGE!'

"That single word, as Webster brought down his hand upon the desk before him, seemed to me to weigh a hundred pounds; and the court thought so too, it appears, from their decision."

When Hayne, of South Carolina, urged on by his Southern friends, had made his speech which called forth that immortal reply of the great "Northern Lion," many of Webster's friends, struck with Hayne's real ability, began to say to each other, "*Can Webster answer that?*" Mrs. Webster was present at the Capitol, and was greatly agitated at the fire and force of the hero of South Carolina. She rode home with a friend in advance of her husband. At last the "Lion" came tramping up to the door, and marched in in an easy, unconcerned way. His wife hastened into the hall just as she was, and, with tears in her eyes, said to him, "*Can* you—*can* you answer Mr. Hayne?"

With a sort of grunt or quiet roar, her lord turned upon her: "Answer him! "*I'll gr-i-n-d him finer than that snuff in your box!*"

In due time the Websterian thunder rolled through the arches of the Capitol, and Hayne was *ground fine.*

"What do you think now," says the general's friend to his Southern acquaintances, "of our Northern Lion?"

The reply came quick, but rather angrily: "He's a long-clawed, strong-jawed, tough-hided devil!"

What but a suppressed sense of humor, in both speaker and auditors, could possibly have carried off such a speech as this, which is attributed to Webster?

"Men of Rochester, I am glad to see you, and I am glad to see your noble city. Gentlemen, I saw your falls, which I am told are one hundred and fifty feet high. That is a very interesting fact. Gentlemen, Rome had her Cæsar, her Scipio, her Brutus, but Rome, in her proudest days, had *never* a waterfall a hundred and fifty feet high! Gentlemen, Greece had her Pericles, her Demosthenes, and her Socrates, but Greece, in her palmiest days, NEVER had a waterfall a hundred and fifty feet high! Men of Rochester, go on. No people ever lost their liberties who had a waterfall one hundred and fifty feet high!"

The kind of humor (such as it is) to which this belongs has been named by the Americans as *highfalutin*.

MISAPPLICATION OF SHAKSPEARE.

Hon. Benjamin F. Wade and the late Hon. Joshua Giddings used to be constant competitors at the bar in "old, benighted Ashtabula," their place of residence. In the early part of his practice, Wade was defending a man against an action of slander, and, after having concluded a very effective speech to the jury, sat awkwardly leaning backward, his feet on the counsel table, and facing Giddings, who was attempting to be eloquent in behalf of his slandered client. "Old Gid," as he was familiarly called, knew a little smattering of Shakspeare, and now determined to bring that great author to his aid.

"Gentlemen of the jury," said he, with much ardor,

> "'He that steals my purse, steals trash;
> But he that robs me of my good name—'"

(Ahem!)

At this point, to his great discomfiture, Shakspeare deserted him. He repeated,

> "'But he that robs me of my good name—'"

(Another pause.)

"Takes that I never had," whispered Wade, as if prompting him, and so distinctly as to be heard by all in the room.

Amid the laughter and his own confusion, Giddings brought his speech to such a "lame and impotent conclusion," that his client recovered but six and a quarter cents for his lost character.

A SCATHING REBUKE.

Judge B—— was not only one of the best judges, but also one of the best and most successful criminal lawyers in Philadelphia some years ago. He was once defending a notorious rascal who was indicted for larceny. The evidence for the prosecution was overwhelming, and Judge B—— not only made no attempt to refute it, but offered no testimony in favor of his client. The judge on the bench, for whom Judge B—— did not entertain the most profound respect, suggested that, as the case was a clear one, it had better be submitted without argument. But the prisoner's counsel thought differently, and stated that he should address the jury. The attorney general opened the case, and Judge B—— followed in a speech that partook of the character of a Fourth of July oration, a lecture on Shakspeare, and a history of the French Revolution. In his flight of eloquence he forgot both his client and the flight of time. He was brought to a sudden check in one of his most beautiful bursts by the voice of the judge, who had been on nettles for the last half hour.

"Judge B——," said he, pulling out his watch, "are you aware of the time of day? It is half past one o'clock, sir."

"Well, what of that?" quietly returned the orator.

"You know very well, sir," answered the judge, who was a sallow, meagre-looking, and exceedingly irritable man, "that the court is in the habit of adjourning every day at one o'clock for dinner. The court has waited half an hour, expecting you to finish your speech."

This was too much for Judge B——, and, turning full upon the dignitary of the bench, with his long finger extended, exclaimed,

"I know your honor is a great lover of Shakspeare—I

know your honor is a great admirer of the poetry of the immortal bard—but there is one great truth in Shakspeare that must have escaped the attention of your honor. I allude to that scene in King Lear where the poet with great truth says, "'The lean, lank, and hungry judge would hang the guiltless rather than eat his mutton cold.' With your honor's permission, I will here close my speech."

ANECDOTES OF THOMAS CORWIN.

Hon. Tom Corwin, the most amusing and popular of our modern orators, who kept his audiences in a roar, and often disturbed the gravity of the United States Senate, regarded his life as a failure because he had not been successful in more serious veins. A friend relates that he was riding with Corwin in the summer of 1860, when Corwin remarked of a speech made the evening before,

"It was very good, indeed, but in bad style. Never make the people laugh. I see that you cultivate that. It is easy and captivating, but death in the long run to the speaker."

"Why, Mr. Corwin, you are the last man living I expected such an opinion from."

"Certainly; because you have not lived as long as I have. Do you know, my young friend, that the world has a contempt for the man who entertains it? One must be solemn—solemn as an ass—never say any thing that is not uttered with the greatest gravity, to win respect. The world looks up to the teacher and down upon the clown. Yet, in nine cases out of ten, the clown is the better fellow of the two."

"We who laugh may be well content if we are as successful as you have been."

"You think so, and yet, were you to consult an old fellow called Thomas Corwin, he would tell you that he considered himself the worst used man in existence; that he

has been slighted, abused, and neglected, and all for a set of fellows who look wise and say nothing."

Mr. Corwin uttered this with much feeling, and we have no doubt but that he expressed what he believed to be the net purport and upshot of his whole life.

His very dark complexion was often made the subject of jokes by Corwin and his friends. Thomas F. Marshall, of Kentucky, once told an adventure which he had with Mr. Corwin at Lebanon, Ohio, Mr. Corwin's place of residence. Marshall had stopped at Lebanon overnight, and registered himself at the hotel as "Mr. Marshall, of Kentucky." While sitting in the public room in the evening he noticed a neatly-dressed colored man enter the hall, and, approaching the register, begin to read it. When he had reached Marshall's name he read it aloud, and asked the clerk "if Mr. Marshall was in the hotel." The clerk replied by pointing him to the gentleman in question. The colored man approached Marshall, saluted him very respectfully, and asked if he belonged to the Lexington family of Marshalls. Marshall was, as he expressed it afterward, "somewhat put out by the familiar manner of the 'cullerd gemman,'" but answered civilly that he did. The colored man was delighted to hear it, and to meet him.

"I had," he said, "the honor and pleasure of serving with Mr. Thomas A. Marshall from 1831 to 1835."

Mr. Marshall, thinking he had met with one of the old family servants who had "run away" from slavery in Kentucky to freedom in Ohio, was about to ply him with questions, but found no opportunity of "getting in a word edgeways." The colored man asked in rapid succession after the various members of the family, spoke feelingly and familiarly of old Humphrey Marshall, the head of the Kentucky Marshall family, and at last asked if the gentleman was acquainted with Mr. Henry Clay. On Marshall replying in the affirmative, the colored gentleman began to tell, in a voice intended for the little crowd of listeners who had gathered around, some reminiscences of Henry Clay, one of which he began by the remark,

"When I was in Congress with Mr. Clay—"

"You in Congress with Mr. Clay?" interrupted Marshall—"you in Congress?"

"Yes, sir; yes, sir. My name is Tom Corwin."

"Tom Corwin!" exclaimed Marshall. "Excuse me, my dear sir, but I thought you were some runaway negro."

It will be remembered that Corwin, in the Senate in 1845 or 1846, arguing seriously against the morality of the projected war against Mexico, permitted his appreciation of broad humor to lead him into the extravagant expression, "If I were a Mexican, as I am an American, I would welcome you with bloody hands to hospitable graves." A few years after, when this expression had been quoted by the newspapers until it had become familiar as "household words," Mr. Corwin was retained as counsel for a man charged with murder, and who, he claimed, acted in self-defense. In his closing speech to the jury Corwin pictured the condition of his client as endeavoring to avoid the difficulty, portrayed the murdered man as forcing it upon him, dogging his steps, denouncing him as a coward, and at last threatening to strike him. "What," he exclaimed, "would you have done in such an emergency? What, sir," turning to the prosecuting attorney, "would you have done?"

"Done!" replied the attorney, with great gravity—"done! I would have welcomed him with bloody hands to a hospitable grave."

The jury was convulsed with laughter, and Corwin lost his case.

TRUE ANECDOTE OF MR. LINCOLN.

The following anecdote of the late President Lincoln has

never been published, and unlike, perhaps, some of the stories attributed to him, is an actual fact. During Mr. Lincoln's practice of his profession of the law, long before he was thought of for President, he was attending the Circuit Court which met at Bloomingdale, Illinois. The prosecuting attorney, a lawyer by the name of Lamon, was a man of great physical strength, and took particular pleasure in athletic sports, and was so fond of wrestling that his power and experience rendered him a formidable and generally successful opponent. One pleasant day in the fall, Lamon was wrestling near the court-house with some one who had challenged him to a trial, and in the scuffle made a large rent in the rear of his unmentionables. Before he had time to make any change he was called into court to take up a case. The evidence was finished, and Lamon got up to address the jury, and having on a somewhat short coat, his misfortune was rather apparent. One of the lawyers, for a joke, started a subscription paper, which was passed from one member of the bar to another as they sat by a long table fronting the bench, to buy a pair of pantaloons for Lamon, "he being," the paper said, "a poor but worthy young man." Several put down their names with some ludicrous subscription, and finally the paper was laid by some one in front of Mr. Lincoln, on a plea that he was engaged in writing at the time. He quietly glanced over the paper, and immediately took up his pen and wrote after his name, "I can contribute nothing *to the end in view.*"

MARK HARDIN'S MOCK ARGUMENTS.

Mark Hardin, of Kentucky, was a soldier, lawyer, politician, and wag when Kentucky was young. He lived in the county (Hardin) named after his father, one of the pioneers of the state. A proposition arose while he was a candidate for the Legislature to cut off a new county from Hardin, to be called Larue. The county seat was not determined upon, but Hodgenville was the favorite in the race. Mark opposed the division bitterly, but, he soon found, uselessly. Both sections wanted it to go. The candidate, seeing farther resistance was useless, made an appointment to speak at Hodgenville, the very hot-bed of county secession, and duly appeared on the stump. He began his speech somehow in this way:

"Fellow-citizens, I hear every where that there is a decided wish to divide our county, and some, I regret to say, oppose it. Why? I ask, why? fellow-citizens. Look at this end of Hardin. It comes out of the way. It is detached naturally from Hardin. It projects like the toe of a boot; and, fellow-citizens, the toe of that boot ought to be applied to the blunt end of any candidate who opposes this just, proper, and natural division. [Cheers.] Having shown you that this end (Larue) is thus by nature, and should be divided by law from the other, my next consideration is the county seat. To gentlemen as intelligent as you, and as familiar with the section to be divided off, I need not point out that Hodgenville will be the centre of the proposed county; and where, but at the centre, should the county seat be? [Cheers.] Gentlemen, you have doubtless heard the removal of our state capital spoken of. As it is, it is tucked up in a north corner of the state, where it is about as convenient a situation for the capital of the whole state as Elizabethtown (the county seat of Hardin) is to be the county seat of Larue. The same reasons that induce us to separate this part of the county from the other should make us move the capital. We must move it, and to the centre of the state. Now take a map. Kentucky is 420 miles long by about 140 (in the centre) wide. Now Larue county is on a perpendicular line just 70 miles from the Ohio River, and 210 from each end of the state, and Hodgenville is the centre of Larue county. I have thus mathematically demonstrated to you that the state capital should be removed to Hodgenville. [Enthusiastic cheering.] Fellow-citizens, I have been inadvertently led into these questions, but I will proceed farther. In the late war (the War of 1812) Washington City was burned by the British; and why? Because it was on our exposed border. The national capital should be removed from the Atlantic coast, and to the centre of the Union. Kentucky is the great seal set in the centre of our mighty republic, as you will see by enumerating the surrounding states, and, as I have already shown you that this is the centre of Kentucky, the national capital should be removed to Hodgenville." As some had begun to smell a large Norway by this time, the cheering was not quite so loud. "Nay," said the orator, in a burst of enthusiasm, "Hodgenville is the centre of God's glorious and beautiful world!"

"How in the devil do you make that out?" said an irritated voice in the crowd.

The speaker, drawing himself up, and sweeping his forefinger in a grand circle about the horizon, said, "*Look how nice the sky fits down all around!*"

Hardin didn't go to the Legislature that time, though he had mathematically demonstrated every point he made.

AN ABSENT-MINDED JUDGE.

The late Judge W——, formerly Chief Justice of the Supreme Court of Wisconsin, was a man of deep thought, and often so engrossed in his "cases" as to be wholly unconscious of conversation in his presence. Colonel S—— is one of your courteous Virginia gentlemen, quick, sensitive, and a good talker withal. The colonel has a farm near Madison, on which he had just discovered a valuable peat-bed, and, being much elated by the prospect of "sudden fortune," was apt to talk about it. Meeting the judge in company with several gentlemen of the bar and legislators, then convened at the capitol, the favorite subject of the colonel's opened. He, anxious to enlighten the judge, directed his conversation particularly to that individual, who was sitting head in hands, thinking-cap on, apparently an attentive listener, while the merits of economy, inexhaustible supply, great manufacturing advantages, etc., etc., were expatiated on in all the earnestness for which the colonel is remarkable. After concluding his statements with statistical and divers explanations, he asked the judge what he thought of it.

"Of what?" says the judge, looking up.

"Of peat," replied S——.

"What Pete?" again asked the judge.

"Why, Irish peat," says S——, somewhat perplexed at the apparent stupidity.

"I don't know him, sir," replied the judge, not having heard a word of the subject.

This story naturally leads to the relation of the following incident of the same character. There lives in Wisconsin a certain Judge J——, who is noted for his learning, ability, and for being remarkably absent-minded when intoxicated to a certain degree. Judge J—— and Senator B—— had been on a visit to Madison on some political errand, and had both become somewhat "blue" when they started for home—a distance of about thirty miles. The two friends lived in the same town, had gone to Madison together in the same buggy, and were to return together, and *did* start home in the company of each other about one o'clock P.M. At the "Half-way House" they stopped to take a drink, of course, and Senator B—— alighted to procure the "red-eye," while the judge remained in the buggy. In due time the senator returned with decanter and tumbler, and the two drank, and B—— returned to deliver the "implements" to mine host. B—— deposited the tumbler and decanter, paid for the "exhilarator," then called for a cigar, and proceeded to light the same. Meantime the judge, having taken his drink, sat quietly for the space of a minute, and, forgetting that he was waiting for B——, started up the team at a 2.40 rate, and was off.

After driving about five miles he met a friend going to Madison, whom he hailed as follows:

"I say, D——, just stop at the Half-way House and ask the landlord if I left any thing there. It seems to me I came away and forgot something, and I have been trying to think for an hour what it is, but I can't; so just stop, won't you, and inquire, and if I left any thing just bring it out when you come back."

D—— agreed, and the judge drove home.

Two or three days after B—— arrived, and immediately called on the judge, when occurred what followeth:

Senator B——. "You are a pretty man, to leave a fellow that way, fifteen miles from home, ain't you?"

Judge J——. "Why, B——, what's the matter?"

B——. "What's the matter! Sure enough, I have a good will to thrash you!"

J——. "Why, B——, what's the—I—I—don't understand."

B——. "Don't understand, eh? As though leaving me at the Half-way House wasn't enough, but you must send back by D—— 'to inquire if you hadn't left something!' and now make strange, as though you didn't know it!"

J——. "Ha! ha! ha! That's it. I knew there was something wrong! I told D—— I had left something, but couldn't think what. Tried to remember all the way home. Asked my wife what was missing when I got home. Have thought of it ever since, and could make nothing of it; *and, sure enough, it was you!* Ha! ha! ha! Sorry, 'pon my soul! Let's drink."

And they did drink.

NO COMPLIMENTS UNDER OATH.

In the lifetime of the noted counselor, B. F. Hallett, Dr. Whittemore was on the stand as a witness in an important case. The doctor's testimony not helping at all the case which Hallett was pleading, he took occasion to say, rather frequently, as he had been wont to do to other witnesses of less probity,

"Now, Mr. Whittemore, I want you to remember that you are testifying *under oath.*" This reminder was rather stinging to the doctor's sense of right; but he submitted with as good grace as possible till the testimony was closed, when Mr. Hallett observed, rather testily,

"Well, Mr. Whittemore, you have contrived to manage your case pretty well."

Mr. Whittemore found his turn now, and, with a peculiar twinkle of his eye, replied,

"Thank you, Mr. Hallett; perhaps I might return the compliment if I were not testifying under oath."

A DIRTY AND ECCENTRIC JUDGE.

Hon. A. B. Woodward, a native of Virginia, was appointed by President Jefferson, in 1805, Chief Justice of Michigan Territory. The judge was a bachelor, and used to buy a dozen shirts, with broad cambric ruffles, at a time, and would put one of the dozen on, and wear it until it became soiled; then put on shirt No. 2 over the first, and so one after another, until he had the whole twelve upon his person at the same time. When the exterior one was too dirty to wear longer, this one was taken off, and No. 11 came into view. Thus he proceeded until the entire lot (save No. 12) had been twice exposed to view. Then the whole dozen were sent to his laundress, and he would lie in bed until they were purified and returned to him, when he would go through the same rotation month after month, until they were all worn out, and then he got another dozen. The judge would buy at a slop-shop *one* flannel undershirt, put it on and wear it, without change and unwashed, until it literally came off him in shreds.

A LEGAL WAG.

Judson T. Mills, of South Carolina, was judge of a district court in Northern Texas, fond of a joke, but very decided in his discharge of duty. Thomas Fannin Smith was a practicing lawyer at the bar, and having shamefully misstated the law in his address to the jury, turned to the court, and asked the judge to charge the jury accordingly. The judge was indignant, and replied,

"Does the counsel take the court to be a fool?"

Smith was not abashed by the reproof, but instantly responded,

"I trust your honor will not insist on an answer to that question, as I might, in answering it, truly be considered guilty of contempt of court."

"Fine the counsel ten dollars, Mr. Clerk," said the judge.

Smith immediately paid the money, and remarked it was ten dollars more than the court could show.

"Fine the counsel fifty dollars," said the judge.

The fine was entered by the clerk, and Smith, not being ready to respond in that sum, sat down. The next morning, on the opening of the court, Smith rose, and with much deference of manner began,

"May it please your honor, the clerk took that little joke of yours yesterday about the fifty dollars as *serious*, as I perceive from the reading of the minutes. Will your honor be pleased to inform him of his error, and have it erased?"

The coolness of the request and the implied apology pleased the judge, and he remitted the fine.

BITTER SARCASM OF TRISTAM BURGESS.

During the debate on the tariff in 1828, an amendment was offered to increase the duty on molasses ten cents per gallon, being an increase of a hundred per cent. *ad valorem.* Its object was to choke off the Northern members, and indirectly to kill the bill. The moment the amendment was announced by the chairman in Committee of the Whole, Mr. Burgess, of Rhode Island, arose, and implored the mover to withdraw it. He showed its effects upon the trade between the Eastern States and the adjacent islands in timber, and the return cargoes of molasses, which was the daily food of the poor. His speech was short, and to the point. As he took his seat, Henry Daniel, of Kentucky, sprang to his feet, and roared out at the top of his voice,

"Mr. Speaker, let the constituents of the gentleman from Rhode Island sop their bread only on one side in molasses, and they will pay the same duties they do now."

Mr. Bartlett, of New Hampshire, here remarked,

"Now look out for Tristam; Harry will catch it."

Mr. Burgess arose, with fire beaming from his countenance, and addressed the chair:

"The relief proposed by the gentleman from Kentucky is but adding insult to injury. Does not that gentleman know that established habit becomes second nature, and that all laws are cruel and oppressive that strike at the innocent habits of the people? To illustrate: What would the gentleman think of me if I should offer an amendment that neither himself or his constituents shall hereafter have more than a pint of whisky for breakfast instead of a quart? Does he not know that the disposition of all animals partakes, in a greater or less degree, of the food on which they are fed? The horse is noble, kind, and grateful; he is fed on grain and grass. The bear (looking at Daniel, who was a heavy, short man, dressed in a blue coat with a velvet collar) will eat hog and raw hominy. You may domesticate him, dress him in a blue coat with a velvet collar, and learn him to stand erect, and to imitate the human voice, as some showmen have done, but examine him closely, sir (looking at Daniel some seconds), you will discover he is the bear still. The gentleman told us, in a speech some days ago, that his district produced large numbers of jackasses, hogs, and mules. No stronger proof of the truth of his statements can be given than a look at its representative. I ask the gentleman to keep this extra duty off molasses, and commence its use among his constituents, and, as feeble as our hold upon life is, Mr. Chairman, a man may yet, before we die, be permitted to go to his grave with two eyes in his head in the gentleman's district."

Daniel wilted under the sarcasm, and few members afterward felt disposed to arouse the eminent son of Rhode Island.

FRANKLIN'S OPINION OF LAWYERS.

Dr. Franklin thought that judges ought to be appointed by lawyers, for, added the shrewd man, in Scotland, where this practice prevails, they always select the ablest member of the profession, in order to get rid of him, and share his practice among themselves.

ANECDOTES OF CALHOUN.

Few anecdotes of the late Hon. John C. Calhoun are floating in the public mind. He was not a man *of the people*, but his genius and his habits placed him above the

masses, whom he nevertheless held with a fascination as hard to explain as to resist. The following is remarkably characteristic of Mr. Calhoun, and well deserves to be preserved:

In the early days of his political career Mr. Calhoun had a powerful rival and opponent in the Abbeville District. South Carolina was at this time in a state of high excitement, and party feeling raged fiercely in a struggle to overthrow an aristocratic feature of the Constitution. The issue was upon topics that enlisted the interests and prejudices of parties, and they waged the contest with the energy of a civil war. Mr. Calhoun and Mr. Yancey were on opposite sides, the leaders of hostile bands, and the idols of their respective hosts. There was, and is, for he still lives, a man named Marvin, one of the most violent of Mr. Yancey's party, warmly attached to him as a personal and political friend, and following him blindly as an infallible guide. He was a very eccentric man, and his peculiarities had perhaps led the people to call him "Uncle Jacob," by which name he was better known than that of Marvin. Bitter in his prejudices and strong in his attachments, he could see no right in an enemy, no wrong in a friend. On the other hand, Mr. Yancey was one of the most amiable and candid of men. The strength of his mind, combined with the tolerance of his feelings, raised him above the meanness of clinging to error when reason opposed it. In the discussion that ensued, Mr. Calhoun's arguments overpowered him, and he candidly confessed himself a convert to his great rival's opinions. Great was the rage of "Uncle Jacob" when he heard that Yancey had struck his colors to Calhoun. He swore a big oath that he would *thrash* Calhoun if the story was true. He soon found that it was so, and started at once to put his threat into execution.

He found Mr. Calhoun walking slowly and calmly back and forth, for exercise, on the piazza of the hotel where he was boarding. Mr. Calhoun had been informed of Marvin's intention, and, as soon as he saw him coming, prepared himself for a triumph, not of force, but of manner and address. Marvin took his stand where Mr. Calhoun was to pass, and awaited the trying moment. Mr. Calhoun approached, spoke kindly, and passed on with his blandest smile. Again he passed, and again, each time repeating his soothing salutation, and expecting the man to commence his attack. But a strange fascination had seized upon "Uncle Jacob." The spell which genius throws over those who approach it had unmanned him. At last he could stand it no longer, but, bursting into tears, he grasped the proffered hand of Mr. Calhoun, told him frankly the errand on which he had come, and begged his pardon. Mr. Calhoun then began to press his arguments cautiously, but forcibly, and in a few minutes Marvin was one of his converts, and a decided friend. From that day onward Mr. Calhoun had no more ardent follower than Marvin, and of all "rabid Nullifiers" Uncle Jacob was the rabidest, and to this day he believes there never was such a man in this world as that same John C. Calhoun whom he tried to whip, and who conquered him without raising a finger or saying a word.

NONCHALANCE OF WILLIAM H. POLK.

William H. Polk, the brother of the late President, was once an independent candidate for Congress in the Columbia (Tennessee) Congressional district. Mr. Thomas, his opponent, habitually in discussions charged him with inconsistency. He said on one occasion to Mr. Polk,

"Sir, in 1850–'51 you were a Compromise man; since that time you have been a Fire-eater; and you were again a *quasi* American; and then, again, you were 'soft' on the 'nigger question;' and now, sir, how are you to-day, Mr. Polk?"

In an instant Polk was on his feet, and, with a bow, and his hand extended, replied,

"Pretty well, I thank you, Colonel Thomas. How do you do yourself?"

LESLIE COOMBS AND JOHN C. BRECKINRIDGE.

Soon after John C. Breckinridge had been elected Vice-President of the United States, he and General Leslie Coombs, a bitter party opponent but warm personal friend, happened to meet in the hat store of Hiram Shaw, in Lexington. The conversation naturally turned upon politics, when Breckinridge remarked that "no man living had for his party done *more* and received *less* than the general."

"That is so," replied the old wag; "and, Breckinridge, between ourselves, no man has done *less* and received *more* from his party than you."

A roar of laughter followed, in which the Vice-President joined heartily.

"A CHARGE TO KEEP."

Not many summers ago a case of considerable interest was tried before Justice Loomis, of Binghamton, New York. It seems that the orchard of one of the neighboring farmers had been at different times visited, and many of the best trees robbed of their fruit. Of course, Farmer E—— had a curiosity to find out who was in the habit of appropriating his apples. So, cautiously concealing himself in the shadow of the fence, he discovered a fellow in the act of filling a bag with his best fruit. Farmer E—— started for the youth with his gun, but the fellow took to his heels, and was just getting over the fence, when a discharge from the gun "laid him low." On the trial the boy was introduced to prove the assault, and the injury inflicted. He swore that a large number of shot entered his back, and, although many had been removed, still there were many left "that plagued him considerably." The doctor who was called testified to the fact of finding a number of shot in the flesh, of the impossibility of removing all, and of the strong probability that complainant would always carry about his person a supply of lead. The lawyers rested the case, and the learned justice arose to instruct the jury, when from the farther corner of the room appeared the form of a very benevolent but extremely seedy-looking individual, who, peering over a large and very rusty pair of iron spectacles, and pointing his long finger at the injured boy, exclaimed,

"Young man! young man! you can truly say with the poet,

"'A charge to keep I have.'"

The effect was irresistible. Justice, jury, lawyers, and audience were instantly convulsed with uncontrollable laughter, and for ten minutes or more business was completely suspended. The verdict, when rendered, was, "No cause of action."

THOMAS H. BENTON'S SARCASM.

Thomas H. Benton had a way of telling a story that the wits of the day might be proud of, if they could beg, or borrow, or steal it. In the year 1841, the famous John Tyler Bank Bill was introduced into the United States Senate with the protracted title of "An act to provide for the better collection, safe keeping, and disbursement of the public revenue, by means of a corporation, to be styled the Fiscal Corporation of the United States." Instantly on the title being read, Mr. Benton exclaimed,

"Heavens, what a name! long as the moral law. The people will never stand it. They can not go through all that. Corporosity! that would be a great abridgment; but still it is too long. It is five syllables, and people will not go above two syllables, or three at most, and they often

hang at one. I go for short names. The people will have them, though they spoil a good long one to make a bad short one. There was a most beautiful young lady in New Orleans some years ago, as there always has been, and still are many such. She was a *Creole*. A gentleman, who was building a splendid steam-boat, took it into his head to honor this beautiful young lady by connecting her name with his vessel, and he bestowed upon it, in golden letters, the captivating designation of *La Belle Creole*. The vessel was beautiful, and the name was beautiful, and the lady was beautiful; but all the beauty on earth could not save the name from the catastrophe to which all long titles are subjected. At first they called her the *bell*—not the French *belle*, which signifies *fine* or *beautiful*, but the plain English bell, defined in Scripture to be a tinkling cymbal. This was bad enough, but worse was coming. It so happens that the vernacular pronunciation of *creole* in the Kentucky waters is cre-*owl;* so they began up there to call this beautiful boat the *Creowl*. But things did not stop here. It was too extravagant to employ two syllables when one would answer as well, and be so much more economical, so the first half of the name was dropped and the last retained, and thus *La Belle Creole*—the beautiful Creole—sailed up and down the Mississippi all her life by the name, style, title, and description of THE OWL."

Roars of laughter in the Senate followed this story, and on went Benton with another:

"I do not pretend to impose a name upon this bantling; that is a privilege of paternity, or sponsorship, and I stand in neither relationship to this babe. But a name of brevity—of brevity and significance—it must have, and if the fathers and sponsors do not bestow it, the people will, for a long name is abhorred and eschewed in all countries. Remember the fate of John Barebone, the canting hypocrite, in Cromwell's time. He had a very good name—John Barebone; but the knave composed a long verse, like Scripture, to sanctify himself with it, and entitled himself thus, 'Praise God Barebone; for if Christ had not died for you, you would be damned Barebone.' Now this was very sanctimonious, but it was too long—too much of a good thing—and so the people cut it all off but the last two words, and called the fellow '*damned Barebone*,' and nothing else, all his life after. So let this corporosity beware; it may get itself damned before it is done with us, and Tyler too."

One who knew him well thus writes of Benton's personal character:

"The tone, manner, and bearing of Mr. Benton in the Senate were not suited to the popular taste, nor adapted to win the partiality of the mass of his senatorial brethren. His tone was bold and imperious, his manner precise, and somewhat dictatorial and dogmatical, and his bearing that of a giant among the pigmies. He was by many men considered a savage, egotistical, selfish, vainglorious, and loquacious old aristocrat; and yet, in solid substance, his speeches, on great and small matters, will favorably compare with the best which any other man of our country has produced, and his real character, in fact, was that of a most practical Democrat. As the head of a family, husband, father, companion, and host, he was a model of affection, simplicity, and hospitality. Among his neighbors no man could be more popular. Among his children and grandchildren he was literally worshiped as their best friend, their teacher, their companion, and their guide. At his own table or by his own fireside, his genial spirit, his extensive readings, his great experience, and minute observation concerning men and things, and his wonderful memory, rendered his conversations positively charming, upon whatever subject they might turn. And upon the little trifles of every-day gossip he could talk by the hour, and give an essay upon a lady's bonnet and the changes of the fashions as readily as upon the treaty of Utrecht."

ANECDOTE OF VALLANDIGHAM.

Clement L. Vallandigham, while member of Congress, was on a visit to New Lisbon, Ohio, of which town he is a native. During the visit in question he had occasion to attend court in the adjoining county of Mahoning, town of Canfield. Several members of the New Lisbon bar were going up, and they went in company on horseback. Vallandigham was doing some business for his friend Wright, who owned a bay horse, which he offered to him for the occasion. This horse was remarkable for nothing in particular—a quiet, tractable animal. Arrived at Canfield, the company divided, some stopping at the American House; the others, including Vallandigham, went to the United States Hotel. The session was drawing to a close, and all the New Lisbon members had returned except Anson Brewer and Vallandigham. At last they were ready to go, and the latter arranged to meet Mr. Brewer at the American immediately after dinner. Dinner was dispatched, portmanteau called for, and horse ordered out. The clerk gave the orders, portmanteau was brought, but the horse was not. Impatient with delay, the hostler was again summoned, and again ordered to "bring out Mr. Vallandigham's horse."

"Ay, ay! but please, yer honor, 'pon me soul I don't know which is yer honor's nag."

The clerk desired Mr. V. to describe the horse, remarking that, "where there are so many coming and going, it is hard for the hostler always to remember to whom each belongs."

"Very true," replied Vallandigham; and, after reflecting a moment, continued, "And, upon 'my honor,' it will be hard for me to describe the horse. Indeed, I will not attempt it, but will go into the stable and show the hostler."

Out they went, up and down the stable walked Vallandigham and the hostler. The former looked perplexed, the hostler apologized for forgetting. At last Vallandigham suddenly stopped behind a fine chestnut sorrel, and with much assurance said, "*That's* the horse; bring him out."

Out went the horse, on went the M. C., and away they went together. Mr. Brewer was waiting in front of the American, ready to mount so soon as his friend came up.

They were just about starting, when a countryman (a farmer) came running up almost out of breath. Seizing hold of the bridle-rein of Vallandigham's horse, and looking him fiercely in the eyes, he demanded, "Where are you going to?"

"Why, what's the matter? I'm going home."

"Matter! I shall have you arrested for horse-stealing, you villain! Where did you get this horse?"

Vallandigham looked at the stranger as if he thought he was playing off a joke; but he saw by the fire in his eyes that it was no joke. He looked at the horse, then at Brewer—he saw fun in Brewer's eye—then at the stranger again, and replied,

"My dear sir, this horse belongs to my friend Wright, of New Lisbon. I rode him up several days ago, and now I am going back. Brewer, isn't it so?"

Brewer said, "No, Val, you're caught. Stranger, arrest him; he has stolen your horse."

Stranger smiled, said he was sorry to give any trouble, but if V. would treat he would let him off. He acquiesced, and then, with Brewer, rode back to the United States stables, and the horse was exchanged. Brewer, knowing Wright's horse, pointed him out at first sight.

THE CLERGY ATTACKED AND DEFENDED.

Soon after the War of 1812, and when party politics ran very high between the Federalists and Democrats, the Rev. Mr. H—— published, in a newspaper edited by him, a libelous article on a Democrat who stood high with his party. An action was brought against Mr. H—— by Lawyer Smith, noted for his coarseness and vulgar abuse of parties against whom he was employed. Mr. Daggett was retained to defend the action. In the course of his argument to the jury, Smith went off into a harangue against the defendant and clergymen generally, remarking that the latter were continually fomenting quarrels, and were, on the whole, a very powerful and dangerous class. "Gentlemen," said he, "they are corrupt now, and always have been; we find, as far back as the sacred records extend, that the priest Balaam was so corrupt that even his own ass rebuked him."

Mr. Daggett, in reply, after alluding to the character of his client, and presenting the clergy in a different light from his antagonist, in referring to the remarks of the latter about clergymen, told the jury that the learned counsel had traveled out of the record, and inveighed against the corruptions of the clergy.

"Why, gentlemen," said he, "he has searched among the records of scriptural history, and adduced the case of Balaam and his ass; but, gentlemen, the counsel need not have gone back so far, for even in our own day (turning to Smith) there are plenty of asses to rebuke the clergy, but, unlike Balaam's ass, they don't seem to be very much inspired!"

A REFLECTION ON THE COURT.

When Judge Hewett was on the bench in the Western District of the State of New York, and Colonel Billings was trying a case before his honor, the judge overruled so many of the lawyer's exceptions that Billings got out of patience, and spoke so severely that the judge at last demanded, in a voice of thunder,

"What does the counsel suppose I am here for?"

Colonel Billings looked sadly disconcerted, scratched his head, thought a moment, and at last, with a bland smile on his face, replied,

"I confess your honor has got me now."

THE COURT COULD NOT WHOLESALE.

In an interior county of Ohio, in a criminal court presided over by a judge of considerable humor, a notorious thief was on trial for a larceny. The principal question of fact in the case was whether the property stolen was worth thirty-five dollars, or less than that amount. According to the statutes of that state, if the value amounted to this sum, the offense was grand larceny, and the penalty would be imprisonment in the penitentiary, where the rogue rightfully belonged. After the jury had been out for several hours, they returned into court, and said to the judge that they could not agree unless he charged them whether they should estimate the goods at the wholesale or retail price. Thereupon the judge drew himself up, and enlightened them thus:

"Well, gentlemen, considering the way the rascal came by the goods, I don't think the court can afford to wholesale them to him."

The doors of the penitentiary opened accordingly.

TEN PER CENT. OF MALARIA.

At Hainesville, Alabama, during the trial of the great Lucas will case, Hon. H. W. Hilliard, in an eloquent speech for the contestants, compared the vast estate to a stagnant pool, giving off malaria and affecting the moral atmosphere. It had been proved, however, on the trial, that the agreement between the contestants and their lawyers was that the latter should receive *ten per cent.* of what they recovered for their services. In answering Mr. Hilliard, Hon. Sam. F. Rice replied to the "malaria" argument by saying that he supposed, if Mr. Hilliard's side proved successful, "he would come to his clients, holding his nose with one hand and opening a pocket with the other, and request them, as he was very delicate, and fearful of his health, to drop, *very gently*, a little—about *ten per cent.*—of that 'malaria' into that pocket!" This view of the malaria was too much for the jury, court, and spectators.

A BLACK FLAG.

Among the youngest, handsomest, liveliest, and wittiest individuals on the New York Superior Court bench is Judge R——, a man whose judicial honors have not abated a whit his natural relish for hearing and perpetrating a good thing when occasion offers. The following concerning him will fortify this statement:

"Some years ago, before Judge R—— was appointed to the bench, he happened to be present at a camp-meeting held somewhere in the region of Cape Cod. At the time there was present a middle-aged man, and an outsider at that, who plumed himself on his knowledge of the world, and who spoke rather contemptuously of the object of the meeting, which was exceedingly annoying to those in attendance. Finally the profane individual concluded some derisive remarks by saying, within the hearing of the future judge, that if he 'had a black flag he would give it to them, that it might be hung up to show who they were, and who they worshiped.'

"'That can easily be had,' exclaimed R——; 'make a flag of your character, sir, and none will be blacker.'"

REMINISCENCES OF SARGENT S. PRENTISS.

Sargent S. Prentiss, the great Southern orator and legal luminary, appeared upon the theatre of active life as the meteor appears, dazzling the eye of all who beheld him, and then disappearing, leaving behind scintillations which are impossible to recall by description or fully understand, except as personal witnesses. Mr. Webster, alluding to his great speech in Congress which Mr. Prentiss made when his seat was contested, said he had never heard, in all his public life, any thing equal to it. Mr. Clay, alluding to Mr. Prentiss, said that the theatres of eloquence and public speaking in the United States (without alluding to the pulpit) are the legislative hall, the forum, and the stump. Some of his contemporaries were eminently successful on one of these theatres, without being able to exhibit any remarkable ability in the others; Prentiss was brilliant and successful in them all. It was difficult for such witnesses as Clay and Webster to decide whether Prentiss was most able in an argument before the Supreme Court than he was captivating in a popular address before the people. Chief Justice Marshall listened to his first effort before his court with profound astonishment, and, commenting upon the qualities of Mr. Prentiss's power, remarked, "that if it were not for his surpassing eloquence he would gain the title to the best legal mind in the country." In his management of cases, and in his intercourse with members of the bar and bench, he was a model of fairness and gentlemanly manners. His conversational powers were equal to his eloquence, and his wit, humor, and flowing courtesy

made him perfectly fascinating in usual life. His faculty of mastering a profoundly written book at a superficial reading, or a law case at a glance, was so great that he had little apparent need of labor, yet he was really a most profound student. His memory was so quick and retentive that whatever he read with the least attention he perfectly remembered. He could recite, without missing a word, such poems as "The Lady of the Lake" or "Childe Harold;" the Bible and Shakspeare he knew "from lid to lid." His faculty of memory was so great that he said himself he did not always know whether he was uttering his own thoughts, or dealing out the thoughts, feelings, and language of others. While argument was his forte, he often lessened its effectiveness by the use of tropes. He was a miracle in his gifts and character. Every trait of his nature was in excess; his virtues leaned to faults, and his faults to virtues. He was compounded of all sorts of contradictions, without possessing a single element that could disgust, without one characteristic that did not attract and charm. Except his two appearances before the Supreme Court of the United States and his two years in Congress, his public acts were confined mainly to the southern States of Mississippi and Louisiana, and very little is left, except personal anecdotes, to embalm his memory.

Mr. Prentiss was no duelist on principle, but he accepted the custom as it prevailed in his day in Mississippi as a necessity, and acted accordingly. As he rose in his profession he, of course, made business and political enemies, and, as a last resort to put him down, recourse was had to the "laws of honor." Being a "Yankee," in the Southern acceptation of the word, it was presumed that "he would not fight;" and if he refused, it was held that, as he would be disgraced, his overwhelming influence would be lost. To make the whole thing as unpalatable as possible to Mr. Prentiss, a wretched creature who lived in Vicksburg, who, though once respectable, had lost every thing but a certain physical courage that made him willing to take the chances of a duel with a man of brilliant character who had never fired a pistol, was selected to presume an insult and send a challenge. Upon receiving the "message" Mr. Prentiss at once comprehended the depth of the plot; he was expected to bear the degradation of not only "backing down," but the additional mortification of doing it to an individual who was socially beneath contempt. Having read the challenge attentively, he said he would return an answer at the proper time. The following morning Mr. Prentiss made up a bundle, with a letter neatly tied on the outside, and by the hands of his servant sent it to the challenger. The principal and his friends were confounded at such a proceeding. "Certainly," said they, "Mr. Prentiss must be profoundly ignorant of the 'laws of honor,' else he would not send an answer to a challenge by the hands of a nigger;" but the reading of the note set the matter at rest. It read as follows:

"*Mr.* ——, I have received your challenge to mortal combat; before I can accept it, I insist that you shall have at least one quality of a gentleman, viz., be habited in a clean shirt, which desirable article I send you by the honest bearer of this note. Thus strengthened in your social position by a single quality that makes you worthy of my notice, I will then proceed to arrange farther preliminaries."

It is useless to say that the duel did not take place.

Subsequently Henry S. Foote, whose irritability was proverbial, challenged Mr. Prentiss for some severe language the orator had used in a political discussion. The event attracted, as might be supposed, a good deal of interest; and as the time and place of meeting was days beforehand well advertised, the spectators were innumerable. Mr. Foote, though a very bad shot, was a practiced duelist; Mr. Prentiss at this time was, on the contrary, to make his first appearance in such a field. The first round proving harmless shots, after the combatants were for the second time properly placed, and just as the word was about to be given "to fire," Mr. Prentiss heard a limb of a tree snap just over his head, and, looking up, saw a little boy in the branches, who was thus posted to get a view of the interesting proceedings below. Mr. Prentiss, with a voice distinguished for all its musical softness, said,

"My little fellow, you had better get down from that tree, for Mr. Foote is shooting very wild."

An instant afterward Mr. Foote fell, dangerously but not fatally wounded; Mr. Prentiss was unharmed.

Prentiss, in speaking of his early life, said he commenced in the vicinity of Natchez as a pedagogue, and that while he taught school, to quicken the young idea how to shoot, he cleared ground enough of birchen rods to entitle him to a pre-emption right of public land.

A gentleman, wishing to commend the character of the people of his neighborhood, told Prentiss that there was no jail in the county.

"Ah!" said Prentiss, archly, "possibly the rascals are in the majority, and they won't build one."

Looking at a plantation that was submerged by an overflow, he suggested to the owner that, now it was really *afloat*, he had better pull it out to sea and be done with it.

Prentiss never was off his guard, nor ever lost his presence of mind. While making a stump speech in favor of his political idol, Henry Clay, a rude fellow intruded himself among the audience carrying a banner, on which was inscribed "Hurrah for Polk." The man advanced slowly toward the stand, intending to create a disturbance. No sooner did Prentiss discover the significant motto than he exclaimed,

"In short, fellow-citizens, you have now before you the

sum and substance of all the arguments of the opposite party, '*Hurrah for Polk!*' "

The effect was electrical as the poor fellow with the banner slunk away amid the jeers of the crowd.

On another occasion he was engaged in a political discussion. The gentleman who preceded him on the "opposite side" was very wordy, and very dull, and spoke, by secret agreement with his friends, "against time," so that it was nearly dark before Prentiss rose to speak. It so happened that at that critical moment a jackass in a neighboring pound commenced braying, and kept it up until Prentiss's friends were annoyed, and his political opponents were in ecstacy and roars of laughter. Prentiss waited patiently until the long-eared animal got through, and then, casting a sort of comical look on the previous speaker, he turned to the audience and said, "I did not come here today to reply to *two equally eloquent speeches*," and sat down. The effect of this sally upon a Southern audience can not be described. Prentiss was carried from the stand in the arms of his admirers.

In the year 1844 Mr. Clay was at New Orleans, a guest of the St. Charles Hotel. The largest crowd that ever assembled in that city was collected in front of it, admirers of Mr. Clay, who demanded in wild acclaim that he should make a speech. Mr. Clay came forward, and occupying a place between two of the tall columns that graced the front of the building, said a few words, and, to the disappointment of the crowd, retired. Mr. Prentiss at the same instant was discovered at a side window of the hotel, and was called for so clamorously that he permitted himself to be literally dragged to the front of the portico. His appearance was greeted by the wildest enthusiasm. When silence was restored, he said,

"Fellow-citizens, when the eagle is soaring in the sky,

the owls and the bats retire to their holes." Before the shouts that followed this evident allusion to Mr. Clay had ceased, Mr. Prentiss had disappeared in the surrounding multitude.

The first election of Mr. Prentiss was contested, and he was refused his seat. He returned to Mississippi, and appealed to the people against what he pronounced an unjust decision of the House. It was in this great canvass that he displayed the unrivaled abilities that at the time attracted so much attention. According to Southwestern custom, he made his appointments to speak at designated times all over the state. Crowds followed him wherever he went. The canvass became a sort of political and intellectual carnival. After a while Prentiss discovered that whenever he entered a town that a traveling menagerie was sure to accompany him. It was, on examination, discovered that the proprietor of the wild beasts had advertised his show on the same days that Prentiss had announced himself to make a speech. The "boys," after consultation, decided, that as the showman had made himself a sort of interloping partner in the political campaign, that Prentiss should speak under the menagerie-tent, and on top of the lion's cage. It is unnecessary to say that the show was crowded at the proper time. Prentiss was introduced, and mounted his singular rostrum. For a while the audience and animals were quiet—the former listening, the latter eying the speaker with grave intensity. The first wild burst of applause electrified the permanent inmates of the menagerie. The elephant threw his trunk into the air, and echoed back the noise, while the bears and tigers significantly growled. On went Prentiss, and as each particular animal vented its rage or approbation, he most ingeniously alluded to its habits and appearance as suggestive of some man or passion. In the mean time, the stately king of beasts, who had been quietly treading the mazes of his prison, became alarmed at the footsteps overhead, and, placing his mouth close to the floor of his cage, made every thing tremble by a terrible roar. This, joined with the already excited feelings of the audience, caused the ladies to shriek, and a fearful commotion followed. For an instant it seemed as if some terrible catastrophe was impending, when Prentiss suddenly changed his tone and manner. He commenced a playful strain, and introduced the jackal and hyena, and capped the climax by likening some well-known political opponent to a grim baboon that presided over the cage with the monkeys. The resemblance was instantly recognized, and bursts of laughter followed that literally set many persons present into convulsions. The baboon, all unconscious of the attention he was attracting, suddenly assumed a grimace, and then a most serious face, when Prentiss exclaimed, "I see, my fine fellow, that your feelings are hurt by my unjust comparison, and I humbly beg your pardon." The effect of all this can not be even vaguely imagined.

Mr. Prentiss, when a young man, spent some time in Cincinnati, unknown and unhonored. Years after some business of importance called him to that city. Just then a great public meeting was to be held, and it was desired to have Mr. Prentiss as one of the speakers. A committee, of which Mr. Thomas was a member, was appointed to wait upon him. They found him in the barber's shop of the hotel, in a condition too usual with him.

"No, gentlemen," he replied to their request, "I will not open my lips in Cincinnati. I spent nine long months here, and during that time no man offered me his hand, no woman gave me her smile. I verily believe that in the last great day an indictment will be tried before a jury of the Twelve Apostles charging Porkopolis with being the meanest village on the footstool. I shall be the prosecuting attorney, and I am confident that I shall secure a verdict."

Mr. Prentiss once gave a magnificent dinner to some friends at a hotel in Vicksburg. Early in the evening a stranger entered the room by mistake. Prentiss courteously invited him to join the party. Before long the strange guest began boasting of how much he had drunk during the day—a cocktail here, a smasher there, a julep in this place, a sling in that, and so on apparently without end. At length Prentiss interrupted him:

"Sir," said he, "do you believe in the doctrine of metempsychosis?"

"I don't know," was the reply; "and I don't see that it has any thing to do with what we were talking about."

"It has," rejoined Prentiss, "much—much every way. I have firm faith in that doctrine. I believe that in the next life every man will be transformed into the thing for which he has best qualified himself in this. In that life, sir, you will become a corner groggery."

As the night passed on, Prentiss grew more and more wild and brilliant. "Thomas," he suddenly asked, after a brief pause, "you are lame, like myself. What caused it?"

"A fall from a horse, while I was a boy."

"Ah! there you are more fortunate than I. I was born so. I bear in my body the taint of original sin. Now I know you are a religious man. For what, above all things, do you thank God?"

"I am thankful for health, strength, friends, and the manifold blessings of life."

"So am I. I have all these, and am not, I trust, unthankful for them. But none of these is the thing for which above all others I offer the most devout thanksgiving. I will tell you what that is. Yesterday I was grossly insulted by a six-foot Mississippian. I retired to my chamber, fell on my knees, and poured out my soul in prayer and thanksgiving. I might have thanked my Maker for health and prosperity; but I did not. I might have thanked Him that I was born in an age of light and culture; but I did not. I might have thanked Him that I was *not* born in the State of Mississippi; but I did not even do *that.* But I did thank Him from the very depths of my soul that I was born in an age of gunpowder. I rose from my knees and wrote a message to the man who had insulted me. That brought him down, sir, and he apologized. Ought I not to be thankful that I was born in an age of gunpowder?"

A basket of Champagne stood by the side of Prentiss. High up in the wall of the opposite end of the room was a hole made to receive a stove-pipe. Mr. Prentiss took bottle after bottle of the costly wine, and flung them with unfailing accuracy through this hole into the chimney. All at once a new idea flashed across his mind. "George," said he to the negro waiter in attendance, "would you like to be free?"

"Well, Mass' Prentiss, I think it mout be a nice thing to be free."

"You shall be free this night if you wish. What do you think your master will sell you for?"

"I 'spects I'se one of the best niggers in Massisip. I s'pose marster would want a thousand dollars for me."

"That is not exorbitant. But for ready money your master will sell you for nine hundred dollars. You saw me fling the bottles through that hole?"

"Yes, sir; and mighty nice you did it too. It takes Mass' Prentiss to do that trick."

"Very well. You stand in a chair directly under that hole, with this punch-bowl on your head. I will fling this bottle of wine, and knock the bowl in pieces. I will give you eleven hundred dollars. With nine hundred you shall buy yourself, and to-morrow you may walk off as free a man as treads under the cope of heaven, with two hundred dollars in your pocket. Will you do it?"

"Why, Mass' Prentiss, I do'no. You mout miss your aim, you know, and hit *me!* Then where would this nigger be? I think, Mass' Prentiss, I'd rather not do it."

"There you have it!" exclaimed Prentiss, drawing himself up to his full height. "Here is a slave who says he wishes to be free. Yet for the sake of his freedom, and two hundred dollars in cash to boot, he will not run the little risk of *my* missing my aim. That shows you the character of the race. They are only fit to be slaves. 'A servant of servants shall he be to his brethren. Thus it was in the beginning, is now, and shall be world without end!'"

Many years ago, when Prentiss was engaged in his large practice in Mississippi, he and his friend, Judge Gohlson, were on the circuit in some of the eastern counties of the state, and stopped for the night at Hernando. Late at night Prentiss discovered that Judge Gohlson and himself were not the only claimants for possession of the bed, as he was vigorously beset by a description of vermin which do not make very comfortable bed-fellows. Accordingly he awoke Gohlson, and a consultation was had whether they should beat a retreat, or make an effort to exterminate their assailants. The latter course was, however, adopted, and for this purpose they took from their saddle-bags a brace of pistols, with caps, powder, and other mumitions of warfare. With pistol in hand, they proceeded to raise the bed-clothing, and as one of the creeping reptiles started from his hiding-place, "bang! bang!" would go the pistols. This, of course, aroused and alarmed the worthy landlord, who came in hot haste to the room, and, when he learned the facts, was in great rage. Prentiss demanded he should leave the room, claiming that he was only "exercising the right of self-defense—the right which the law of God and the law of man had given him." Both the entreaty and the threats of the landlord proved unavailing. The firing continued until bed, bedstead, and bedding were completely riddled with balls. At last they succeeded in capturing one of the enemy, when a difference of opinion arose between Prentiss and Judge Gohlson as to what should be his fate. At length it was agreed that the offending vermin should be "fairly and impartially tried by *a jury of his countrymen.*" Three of the landlord's sons were brought in, and forced to sit as members of the jury, and a third lawyer who was present acted as judge. The prisoner was then pinned to the wall. Judge Gohlson (who was a very able lawyer) opened for the prosecution in a speech of two hours in length. Prentiss followed for the defense in a speech of four hours. There were those present who had known Prentiss intimately, and had heard him on great occasions of his life, and who now assert that this was perhaps the most brilliant speech he ever delivered.

JUDGE BRACKENRIDGE'S RESCUE.

Like most men of genius, the late Judge Brackenridge was distinguished by many striking peculiarities. He chose to do every thing in a manner to please himself, without caring for the observations of others. When he resided at Pittsburg he was in the habit of going every morning during the summer months to bathe in the Alleghany, and in order to save time and trouble in undressing, he walked to the river with no other habiliments than his cloak and slippers.

One of those votaries of humor who are to be found in almost every part of the country took it into his head to have a little fun at the learned gentleman's expense, and one morning, just as he had set out to indulge in his customary dip, the wag hired an Irish laborer who was passing by to keep a watch on the "unfortunate gentleman," telling Pat that he was a little out of his head, and that his friends feared he intended to make way with himself. On walked the judge, and, close after his heels, his newly-engaged keeper. Off goes the old cloak, and just as the supposed maniac was about taking the fatal plunge, his faithful guardian seizes him firmly by the arm, exclaiming,

"Och, not so fast, my gay fellow! you sha'n't commit so great sin this time if Paddy Malone can help it."

And sticking fast to the wondering eccentric, he replaced his cloak and slippers, and led him in safety to the hotel, amid the merriment of half the people in the borough, who had been drawn together to enjoy the fun.

THE "TIDE OF PUBLIC FEELING," AND HOW TO CATCH IT.

Much depends in court upon the state of the tide—the tide of public feeling—and in spite of "law and order," so long as jurors are men of like passions with other men, they will be moved as the people are moved. There was Fuller, of the Boston bar, brother of the late Countess Ossoli. He was one of the most solemncholy-looking men in the East, appearing for all the world as if he never had any friends, and had lost them all; but under this gloomy exterior he carried a fund of humor that often shone out in just the right time for himself and his cause. On one occasion the opposing counsel had carried every thing before him, and in a strain of pathetic eloquence that could not be resisted he closed, leaving the whole jury dissolved in tears. Fuller saw that all was lost unless by some sudden turn he could undo the mischief; and rising to reply, putting on his most doleful expression, he said, in slow and measured words, as if he were in a pulpit, and not in court,

"We—will—now—close—these—solemn—services—" But by this time the humor of the thing was seen and felt, and court, jury, audience, and all, laughed till they cried again; but they were now all on the other side.

Another court scene in New York City some years ago, though there was nothing to laugh at, will never be forgotten by those who were present. It was on the trial of Colt for the murder of Adams. Interest as intense as ever marked the trial of any man hung around the proceedings of those days. The theory of the prosecution was, that Adams was *shot* in the head by a pistol having no charge in it, and that a percussion-cap would explode with sufficient force to drive a ball into a man's head, without making noise enough to be heard in the next room. The testimony against the prisoner was clear, conclusive, and so deeply impressive, that when it closed the court-room was as solemn as if sentence of death was then to be pronounced. The first witness called for the defense was Samuel Colt, the great pistol manufacturer, who was asked at once if it were possible for a pistol to be fired with only a cap, and with sufficient force to discharge a ball into a man's head?

"No," he said, promptly.

"Can you prove it?" asked the counsel.

"I can prove it by experiment," he said, and immediately produced a case of pistols, drove in a ball, placed the cap in its place, fired the pistol, and, catching the ball in his hand as he fired, threw it to the counsel. Then he set up a paper mark by the side of the presiding judge, who moved his seat to be a little more out of the range, and as counsel, jury, spectators, and the bar all crowded to see the result, he snapped off ball after ball, every shot exciting more and more ridicule at the idea that any harm could be done by such a discharge. The theory of the prosecution was effectually exploded, and the court-room, which an hour ago was as solemn as the Court of Death, was converted into a shooting-gallery.

Something must be done to recover the ground that was lost. The prosecution was led by Mr. Whiting, the district attorney, and no one was sooner satisfied than he that he was mistaken as to the *mode* in which the murder had been perpetrated. Instantly his ready mind seized upon the most startling expedient to restore the feeling of deep solemnity which had been disturbed, and at the same time to get upon the track to ascertain the nature of the wound by which Adams was killed. The body of the victim, cut into pieces as it was by the murderer, had been buried in the upper part of the city, and Mr. Whiting dispatched an officer, who soon returned with a bundle, and unrolling it, the district attorney presented the head of the murdered man to the court and jury! A thrill of horror passed through the crowded chamber. For the first time during the trial the prisoner buried his face and groaned. The wound was then displayed, and the fact exhibited that it could not have been produced by a pistol ball, but must have been made by the blow of a hammer. This new theory was pressed forward; the awful impression of the ghastly head was never obliterated, and the result is known to the world.

AN AMERICAN RIVAL TO CURRAN.

Curran's witticism in furnishing the motto "*Quid rides*" for the carriage of a rich tobacconist was equaled—to our mind surpassed—by one from S. H. Hammond, formerly District Attorney of Albany County, New York. In the city of Albany, where the court is held, there used to be in the Circuit Court a venerable old crier, who had held the office for many years, and was a universal favorite with the bar. He was always courteous and obliging, and among his voluntary *ex officio* duties was that of supplying the lawyers with tobacco out of a well-filled box which he always carried. When S. H. Hammond closed his last term as district attorney in Albany County, as an acknowledgment of the kindly services of the ancient crier, he presented him with an elegant silver tobacco-box, on which was engraven this motto:

"*Quid pro quo.*"

Mr. Hammond was once trying a case before Judge Bacon, of the Fifth Judicial District (New York), and in questioning a witness named Gunn, said to him when he had finished his examination,

"Mr. Gunn, you can go off."

Judge Bacon saw the pun, and quickly added,

"Yes, Mr. Gunn, you are discharged."

Of course there was an explosion in court.

ANECDOTES OF A. OAKEY HALL.

A. Oakey Hall, having been connected with all the *causes celebres* of New York city for fifteen years (mainly on the side of prosecution as district attorney), has become through the metropolitan press well-known to the nation at large. James T. Brady and himself are well recognized as the witty duo of the New York bar, and a trial is never so "taking" as when both of them appear in it.

Mr. Hall's fun lies almost more in his manner than in his matter. He is capable, when saying his best things, of assuming those imperturbable, or solemn, or apparently innocent expressions of face that generally add so much, by contrast, to the point of jokes and the sparkle of repartee.

At Oakey Hall's election in 1866 he received an enormous majority—nearly forty thousand. An acquaintance, expressing his surprise thereat to the candidate, was answered with a grim shrug, "Few persons have so many *tried* friends as I have, and tried friends are always magnanimous."

At the same election an enthusiastic Radical was found

going from one voting district to another arm in arm with a negro voter possessed of the property qualification.

"What do you think of the spectacle?" asked a disgusted Democrat of Oakey Hall.

"It is political day and night that, in passing from pole to pole, meet on the equating line."

Mr. Hall was a student at Cambridge Law School during the professorship of Judge Story and Simon Greenleaf, the author of the great text-book on Evidence. He has written for William Story's life of the great jurist some witty reminiscences of it—to be found in vol. ii., p. 503. While at the school a new building was finished, and at a *petite souper* given by some of the fledgeling lawyers, he offered the following epigram:

"A magnificent temple of law,
Albeit with only one Story,
Whose 'prudence' with 'jury's' th' *eclat*
Of the Hub-Bar so proud of its glory.
'Tis a Temple that 'Evidence' gives
To the student who loveth history;
How fittingly Fame's laurel climbs
Its Green leaf to the height of one Story.

From Cambridge Oakey Hall went to New Orleans, by advice of Judge Story, to pass a year or two studying civil law. He was a student in the offices of Slidell and Benjamin. Here, as he often said, he learned the law of cession (a civil law phrase), but not that of secession, which after-events showed that his preceptors knew so well. He was listening to a suit brought to enforce a claim against Jacob Barker, who was defending in *propriâ personâ.* The old banker-lawyer made a characteristically egotistic speech, and, among other things, said: "Let me tell this court that I have been a creditor of the government in a time of great emergency; the sails of my ships have whitened every sea; my bills of exchange have gone to every part of the world, and my name has been honorably bandied on the Royal Exchange of London, in the Great Exchange of St. Petersburg, and in the Babel of Calcutta. I have been politician and millionaire, a martyr, and a pauper. I have waded through adversity, and weathered financial gales, but never despaired. I left New York owing hundreds of thousands, and coming here, have paid off every cent. Does the court think I, its servant, am a dog to do such a thing as stand here disputing a just debt?"

"With all respect to my senior," whispered Hall, on hearing these dogmatisms, "he makes me remember that a dog who is so good a barker is nearly always a bad biter."

In a suit of Challeau *versus* Malard, opposing the famous lawyer John R. Grymes (who seldom had forbearance toward an adversary, old or young), Mr. Hall asked him his ideas of the pending proposition.

"Oh, the young man is swimming beyond my depth."

"That is because your logic, for this time only, is in 'Challeau' water."

Mr. Hall returned home to New York in 1848, and was shortly afterward counsel in a church controversy—a class of disputes usually very acrimonious. His opponent, speaking of the argument on the other side, averred that the case was "all ecclesiastical schism against his client, to which his lawyer had added solecism of logic."

"The schism is now on your side," was the repartee, "if that be witticism!"

In the celebrated trial of Mrs. Cunningham for the murder of Dr. Burdell (1857), it was proven for defense, to show her innocent frame of mind, that on the morning succeeding the murder (Sunday) Mrs. Cunningham and her daughters were singing hymns, and one was quoted by her counsel. "Mayhap," said the latter, "there is in the collection some hymn more suitable to our case, but I have been unable to find it."

Alluding to which, in his summing up, District Attorney Hall said he had found an appropriate one for the other side and their witnesses:

> "Hark from the 'Tombs' a doleful sound,
> Mine ears attend the cry!
> Ye living men, come view the ground
> Where ye must shortly *lie*."

In the case of Lewis Baker, charged with the homicide of William Poole, the pugilist, it appeared that George Law had lent a vessel to go after the craft in which Baker had escaped. He was captured just off the Canary Isles.

"An outrageous kidnapping," said Horace F. Clark, Esq., one of Baker's counsel, "and against all law."

"Not so, Brother Clark," retorted the district attorney, "for the capture was made according to George Law."

Later, in the same case, it was said for the prisoner, he was, when captured, within the jurisdiction of the Canaries.

"And we propose a kindred jurisdiction," said the prosecutor—"that of Sing Sing."

During the trial of Dr. Graham for the homicide, at the St. Nicholas Hotel, of a Colonel Loring, Judge Robert H. Morris died. The court took a recess, during which eulogistic speeches were made in memory of the deceased officer of the court. An ex-district attorney, who was remarkable for mixing up his illustrations, closed a feeling speech with this accidental transposition: "He has gone where the weary cease from troubling, and the wicked are at rest."

"Don't blame Brother ——," said District Attorney Hall afterward; "he has so often suffered weariness from others' wickedness that he has insensibly converted the very term wicked."

The colloquies at *nisi prius* between District Attorney Hall and the witnesses are sometimes highly amusing. But he is often overmatched — as happened when (that most dangerous of all witnesses to handle) a shrewd middle-aged Hibernian was on the stand, and a very burly one in this instance. "Were you not once sent up for bigamy?" asked the prosecutor.

"Big Amy? begorra, I was never sent up for any Amy, big or little, or any other woman—"

"The big ami—able witness may pass," was the retort.

Like most humorists, Mr. Hall has great command of pathos, and is quite as effective in infusing that characteristic into his oratory, as in tincturing it with the pun, the sarcastic criticism, or the repartee. He may be said to be perfect master of cross-examination, diplomatic fence, and persuasion before juries. Much of his success therein is due to his extraordinary imperturbability of face and manner, except when he abandons himself to the emotional exigencies of his addresses to bench or jury-box.

In a civil case a few years ago, involving a critique of inventions new and old, foreign and American, Mr. Hall, in the course of his summing up, gave the following universal exposition of how a citizen may exercise daily life under this age of invention:

"He arouses at the awakening of a Yankee alarm-clock, to throw open the outer shutters by pressing an inner spring. The vapors of sleep pleasantly disappear before the perfumes which chemical skill has transplanted from a score of *parterres* to his toilet-table. Dentists have sent him a coral reef of tooth-paste for his sleep-parched mouth; or, if he be a man of middle age, have enabled him to ring the bell, 'bidding the waiter to bring him a fresh auroplastic masticator.' Majestic hair-brushes electrify his ambrosial locks. A beard of hereditary stubbornness yields to the seductive approaches of dainty creams. Pliant bathing utensils invite the ablutions prized of 'gods and men.' He attires himself in linen, glossy from patent mangles, smoothed by patent sad-irons, and buttoned with self-adjusting clasps. Anti-consumptive suspenders are cased beneath a vest with an elastic back. Seamless slippers have coaxed his feet, and a gas stove, lighted by electricity, has warmed his dressing-room, upon a raw morning, to the temperature of May.

"Descending to the breakfast-room, the Hebe of the apartment has taken the silver from the ornamental safe, and spread it upon the magical extension-table. The meal is prepared. Positively the very newest coffee-pot has supplanted the old Parisian toy. The butter has been winner in a 2.40 heat, under pressure of an air-pressure churn. Soapstone warmers embrace the Yankee plates. The eggs for the omelette, after having been proved in the detecter, or *oonoscope*, have been beaten by the elliptic whirligig; or they were poached into the novel drop, and are to be eaten from Columbian glass, that need not blush beside Bohemian or Venetian. Condensed milk has amicably mingled with prepared cocoa, to be drank from cups decorated within a mile of the residence. The beafsteak has arisen from its procrustean bed of late invention. The bread has been kneaded by machinery, and baked in a patent oven. Steam had packed the flour-barrels and made the staves. Marvelous mill-power had presided at the grinding and bolting. The grain was reaped, and threshed, and fanned by three varied combinations of steam, that the season previous, by still another form, had puffed through furrows 'over the hills and far away.' His breakfast over, Betty usurps with the patent carpet-sweeper. *He* retires to a library easy-chair that would have comforted a martyr fresh from the inquisitorial rack. There he consults the Beaumont barometer, and settles down to read a newspaper sheet whose fabric, a week before, was of cellar ropes, and which, while he was that morning playing the part of the Proverb-sluggard, had been born in one hour, with ten thousand brethren, over the Hoe press.

"Soon, preparing for the rainy day, he buttons about him an India-rubber coat. Adjusting his gutta-percha soles, he walks noiselessly through his hall of Vermont tile, with the walls white from new applications of the liquefied quartz, to turn the safety-lock of the front door that is closed by operation of an invisible spring; or he enters his Concord buggy, pulling over his knees the lap robe that successfully imitates the skin of the leopard, to be driven over streets that a combination of mechanical skill has swept over-night; or he hails the omnibus with the patent step, or beckons to the car with the last ventilation and passenger 'registration,' that passengers of all politics agree to be perfectly constitutional.

"Arrived at his place of business, a new stove glows honest welcome in his office (and, thanks to the new ash-sifter, no gaseous vapors). Paper weights, poetical with art-tracery, confine the morning's mail of epistles, covered by adhesive envelopes of the invisible ruling. His penmanship is confused with the stock of patent pens, and patent pencils, and patent inkstands. As the correspondence is answered, a copying-press preserves it for after-years of reference, and the epistle from abroad sleeps between the sheets of the gum-arabic letter-book. His ledgers, ruled by machinery, invite his inspection with their flexible backs. Payments enter the money-drawer in bills, whose colorable devices laugh the counterfeiter's arts to scorn. Seated in rotatory office-chairs, he holds electrical converse with distant correspondents over the exchanges of a dozen cities.

"Walking homeward to the dinner, he hears a cry of fire. He laughs as he thinks of the steam-engine on the next block, and thinks he will get up a new insurance company, by way of relaxation. Relaxation and fire bring thoughts of the juveniles at home, and of the promised presents; so, entering some '*National Bazar*,' he heaves a sigh over the toy-barrenness of his boyhood, and grows distracted amid the philosophical trinkets. He enters the domestic circle, to hear the grateful music of the sewing-machine, over whose purchase were held thirty family councils—corresponding to the numeral choice. Beside it sits grandmamma, with new periscopic spectacles, investigating the mysteries of a knitting-machine. In the corner 'Tom' is reading, as a thing of the past, Thomas Hood's Song of the Shirt! Not far off, a daughter forces him to acknowledge, in her quiet delight, that since the United States government have taken up the proper cudgels of morality, no home *is* complete without the stereoscope. Wifely whispers are heard concerning incredible discoveries in the outskirts of fashion amid crinoline labyrinths, or asking for the new slate globes and the patent orrery for the school-room.

But, hark! the dinner-bell; not that Fejee tomtom of the last century, but one like lovers' tongues at night, silver sweet. It summons the household to a meal whose aroma of food is caught by patent process over the new range—to a meal where vegetables (can-preserved) mock the season—to a board where India-rubber knife-handles and gutta-percha napkin-rings defy their juvenile owner's habits of slovenliness—to the *buffet* where Yankee or Western wine is to be drank from bottles corked by machinery—to a meal where the flies, still buzzing in the temperate zone of the dining-room, enter, one by one, the basket of the clock-work guillotine on the mantle.

"When the meal is finished, he retires to a game of billiards on a Yankee table, with the new billiard register presiding over patent cues and maces.

"Taking a last look before bedtime at the favorite pantry, no more inhabited by the house-beetles that once poured forth, like an army of household Goths and hearth-stone Huns, to vandalize the larder, he places on the doors the burglar guard and examines his patent pistol. Soon, on an elliptic or hydrostatic mattress, beneath a flexible canopy, in a bedstead scrolled by machinery and carved by steam, he falls to sleep, to awaken again to some new daily wonder."

A SMART LAWYER AND A STUPID JUDGE.

James T. Brown, of Greensburg, Indiana, a smart and saucy lawyer, was once employed to defend a case before the Circuit Court of his state. The judge was not very learned in technicalities, knew but little Latin, and much less Greek. The jury were taken from the country, ordinary farmers. The plaintiff's counsel had opened. Brown rose and spoke two hours in the highest possible style, soaring aloft, repeating Latin and translating Greek, using all the technical terms he could bring to the end of his tongue. The jury sat with their mouths open, the judge looked on with amazement, and the lawyers laughed aloud. Brown closed; the case was submitted to the jury without one word of reply. Verdict in the box against Brown; motion for a new trial. In the morning Brown rose and bowed to the court:

"May it please your honors, I humbly rise this morning to move for a new trial; not on my own account; I richly deserve the verdict, but on behalf of my client, who is an innocent party in this matter. On yesterday I gave wings to my imagination, and rose above the stars in a blaze of glory. I saw at the time that it was all Greek and turkey-tracks to you and the jury. This morning I feel humble, and I promise the court, if they will grant me a new trial, I will bring myself down to the comprehension of the court and jury."

The Judge. "Motion overruled, and a fine of five dollars against Mr. Brown for contempt of court."

"For what?"

"For insinuating that this court don't know Latin and Greek from turkey-tracks."

"I shall not appeal from that decision. Your honor has comprehended me this time."

On another occasion, before a circuit judge of the same state, Mr. Brown appeared for the defendant, demurred to the sufficiency of the declaration, and made a short but very pointed argument. The judge, a very stupid specimen of his class, waking up in the midst of the argument, interrupted him, and asked what the *pint* was that he was driving at. Mr. Brown hesitated a moment, and very deliberately replied,

"If the court please, I am about to illustrate it by diagrams, and I hope to make it so plain that it will be comprehended by all the audience, and perhaps I may bring it even within the comprehension of the court."

Mr. Brown then proceeded, and brought his speech to a close; but it is almost needless to say that Judge Dogberry decided against his motion.

A FATHER'S RECOMMENDATION OF HIS SON.

Judge Underwood, of Georgia, had a supreme contempt for fops. A dandy remarked of a gentlemanly planter who was passing that it would be a fine speculation to buy that man for what he *was* worth, and sell him for what he *thought* he was worth.

"Well," says the judge, "I have often seen men selling

jackasses, but this is the first time I ever heard of a jackass offering to sell a gentleman."

The judge was a stanch Clay Whig, but his son, J. W. H. Underwood, was continually changing his politics. A friend asked, "What are John's politics?"

"Really," said the judge, "I can't tell you; I haven't seen the boy since breakfast."

John applied to the old gentleman for a letter of recommendation to his friend, then Governor Crawford, of Georgia. It was immediately given, and, sure of his game, John put off to Milledgeville; but knowing his father's eccentricities, he thought it prudent to open his credentials before presenting them, and, to his astonishment, he read the following:

"MY DEAR FRIEND,—This will be handed to you by my son John. He has the greatest thirst for an office, with the least capacity to fill one, of any boy you ever saw.

"Yours truly, WILLIAM H. UNDERWOOD."

But John has since falsified the old gentleman's opinion by proving himself a shrewd politician and a first-rate lawyer.

The judge was once holding court in the Cherokee District, when log-houses were the only dwellings, and things generally were in a state of nature. It was in the fall, when chestnuts and chincapins were in abundance; the lawyers, witnesses, jurors, spectators, constables, every body were eating them in court and out. The judge wished to maintain something like decency in court, and tired of the ceaseless crack, crack that smote his ears, he at last was provoked to say, "Gentlemen, I am glad to see you all with such wonderful appetites. There is certainly no danger of starvation so long as the chestnuts and chincapins last. I have, however, one request to make of those who compose the juries. I am unable, in the present condition of affairs, to distinguish one body from the other. I must therefore beg the grand jurors to confine themselves to chestnuts, and the petit jurors to chincapins!"

Some years ago Judge Underwood was employed in a lawsuit at Rome, in Georgia. General Jones, a good lawyer and an aspiring politician, was opposed to him in the case. The general had lately changed his politics, to the great astonishment of his friends, of whom the judge had been one. In the progress of the trial Judge Underwood was examining an old-woman witness, who became turbulent and unruly, gesticulating violently, and, in flourishing her long, bony arms about, threatened to hit the judge's head, to the danger of the thatch thereon.

"Take care of your wig—take care of your wig, judge!" said General Jones.

Thinking that his wig was really out of place, and that his opponent was making fun at his expense, the judge turned upon him, and retorted,

"Well, General Jones, this is a free country, and I think a man has as good a right to change his hair as his politics."

The judge had a great dislike to the town of Marietta, Georgia, where he occasionally held court. Some years before his death, while presiding as judge in the court at Marietta, in conversation with General Hamsell, a resident of the town, he remarked,

"General, when my time comes, I am coming to Marietta to die."

"Ah!" replied the general, "I'm glad you think so much of our little town."

"It is not that," replied the judge. "It's because I can leave it with less regret than any other place on the face of the earth."

Singularly enough, he did die there eventually. He arrived on the train about twelve o'clock, was taken suddenly ill about one, and in half an hour was dead.

THE ECCENTRIC JUDGE MARTIN, OF MARYLAND.

Judge Martin, of Maryland, one of the counsel of Aaron Burr in his trial for treason, was very fond of music, but could not distinguish one tune from another. Having made himself very unpopular by his defense of Burr, a crowd surrounded his house with a band of music, playing the Rogue's March. The old gentleman took it as a compliment, walked to the front, and thanked them politely for their music. Not expecting such a reception, the mob stared and moved on, and his family, who were much terrified, gave him a hint to slip away from the door.

He was in the habit of reading the newspapers on his way home of an afternoon, often becoming so absorbed that he would go past his own door; then he would look up and say, "Bless me, I have passed the house!" and, resuming his reading, would perhaps go as far on the other side, to the extreme amusement of the juveniles of the neighborhood, who reported that he once stumbled against a cow, took off his hat, and bowing, said, "I beg your pardon, madam!" without discovering his mistake.

SURGERY VERSUS THE LAW.

Colonel Stone, a practicing lawyer, and Doctor Mason, a practicing physician, were rival candidates for the Senate, and were stumping the district together. Dr. Mason was a warm advocate for law reform, and, in arguing its necessity, he referred to a certain case in which his competitor had been nonsuited upon some technicality.

"Now," said Dr. Mason, "we need to have the law reformed, or Colonel Stone is incompetent to bring a suit correctly—he can take either horn of the dilemma."

Colonel Stone replied,

"Fellow-citizens, the *doctor* has the advantage of me. When I make a mistake in my profession he has only to go to the records of the court, and find it and publish it to the world; but when he makes a mistake *in his profession* he buries it six feet under ground!"

The people appreciated the lawyer's ready wit, and forgave him the blunder charged upon him for the sake of the clever retort he made at the doctor's expense.

REMINISCENCES OF CHARLES O'CONOR.

To perfect the portraiture of Mr. O'Conor the reader must imagine a compact and erect figure of commanding height, clad in an unvarying suit of black; he must endow the eye with an expression of keenness, and light up the face with intellectual fire; he must assume the grayness of hair and whisker as the result rather of excessive mental toil than as a concomitant of age; he must be informed that the countenance can one moment express powerful scorn or indignation, and at the next relax itself to a mould of humor or sympathy. And then the reader, by the aid of the engraving, will be presented to one of the first lawyers in the United States.

Mr. O'Conor is a consummate pleader, and is skilled in all the abstruse branches of law. Those who best know him say he could rise to-morrow in Westminster Hall, or before the master of the rolls, and argue any point which the brief of attorney or solicitor, then and there placed in his hand, might call up. The doctrines of wills, powers, uses, and trusts are to him household words. Nevertheless, in the *trade* of law, as well as in its *profession*, is he a proficient. The tact toward judge, jury, and witness—the play with human nature—the fence with an adversary—the coolness of a repartee—the *sang froid* of cross-exam-

ination—the adroit turn of a position—the dissembling of a fear—the catch of confidence—the wile of diplomacy—the momentary harangue (not at all misplaced, never wordy, keenly put and appropriately dropped)—the *argumentum ad hominem*—the "knacky" quotation—the ingenious diagnosis of motive—the dissection of evidence—the pungent application of proof—all these, which are the *tools* of the *nisi prius* advocate, he wields with dexterity.

His powers as a dialectician are remarkable. Logic pervades even in his repartee, for which he is noted. Woe to the interrupter in the unguarded moment! Even his epithets are rather deductive than in the nature of plain assertion. Mr. O'Conor's speeches, when stenographed, read like review articles—apt words and consecutive arguments being all there. It is so with his conversation. His diction is elegant as well as forcible, and his expressions are particularly crispy and original, without ever being *outré*.

If eloquence consists in meaningless metaphor, turgid sentences, rapid utterance, swollen veins, trick of voice, and dramatic gesture, then Charles O'Conor never had it. But if there practically survives to modern age the idea of Tully—*optimus est orator qui dicendo animos audientium et docet et delectat et permovet*—then the addresses of Mr. O'Conor to jury and judges are worthy of all eloquent attributes. His voice is not so flexible as many could wish, nor his tone so various as some desire, but his matter is so superlatively excellent that there is no room for regret.

He seems to be wanting in what the world calls ambition, and perhaps in professional emulation *per se*. But, phrenologically speaking, his concentrativeness and combativeness are large. As a man, his word is a bond. With his name (as a friend has wittily remarked) there is but one rhyme—*honor*. His generosities are proverbial, and if it were delicate to lift the veil of private confidence, would prove bright exemplars, like "all good deeds in a naughty world." Toward the young he is exceedingly gracious, especially to the junior acquaintances of his profession. At times there is a flush of ancient querulousness (relic of the recluse student-life) in his way of business, but it is only short-lived.

A lawyer from the country once entered the Court of Appeals while Daniel Lord, Jr., of New York, was arguing a case, and inquired of Mr. O'Conor, who was sitting near by, "who that was addressing the court?" Mr. O'Conor, whose feelings must have been nettled by the progress of the argument, replied,

"That is Daniel Lord, *Jr.*, and he puts the *junior* after his name so he may not be mistaken for the Almighty."

A COUNSEL TO WEEP OVER.

General Root and Samuel Sherwood were rival lawyers at Delhi many years ago, and often were opposed in the trial of causes; but in one cause General Root brought a suit for slander in his own behalf, and, like an able politician as he was, he concluded to silence the enemy he most feared by engaging his great adversary as counsel to try his cause at the circuit. Sherwood engaged in the case with his usual zeal, and with all his power and eloquence; and in portraying the sufferings of his client, even exceeded himself. General Root, the client, sat beside him as he closed his argument, and his counsel displayed his wrongs with such pathos that Root was apparently overwhelmed with the picture, and the tears streamed down his rough face.

The jury found a heavy verdict in favor of the general. In the next cause tried the two were opposing counsel, and, as usual, waged their bitter warfare of wit and invective. In the midst of Sherwood's closing argument Root flung at his rival some taunt more savage than ever, when Sherwood, stung by the shaft, suddenly turning on him, called out, "Hadn't you better cry a little, as you did in the last cause?" Root bawled out,

"It would make any body cry to have such a counsel as I had."

The court-house was instantly in roars of tumult and laughter, and Sam took his seat.

SCRATCHING OUT AN ITCHING WITNESS.

The late Judge Oakley, a name held in reverence by the Bench and Bar of New York, was rigid in requiring the attendance of persons summoned as jurors. Excuses, unless very good, were of no avail. On one occasion several whose names had been called stood before the bench, "and they all with one accord began to make excuse." Among them was an insignificant, frowsy-looking little fellow, who said,

"Judge, I wish you'd let me off."

"For what reason?" inquired his honor.

"Well, judge, I don't want to say."

"You must say or serve."

"But, judge, I don't think the other jurors would like to have me serve with them."

"Why not? out with it!"

"Well, judge" (pausing).

"Go on!"

"I've got the *itch!*"

"Mr. Clerk, *scratch* that man out!" was the prompt order of his honor, and the party left the presence.

ANECDOTE OF HON. S. S. COX.

A valiant non-commissioned officer, who left a fair portion of his "corporal" frame at Gettysburg, came to New York in 1866, hoping to obtain some employment by which he could support self and wife. He was well known to

Hon. S. S. Cox, to whom he applied, and who procured for him a situation to look after the interest of the Revenue Department in a distillery that had been seized by the revenue officers, and in which the pay depended on the seizures made for "illicit distilling." The distillers happened to be honest, or very cautious, and no seizures were made —consequently no pay was forthcoming; so the valiant "non-com" had to apply to Mr. Cox again for aid.

"Do you not like your place?" asked Mr. Cox.

"Oh! very well. There is nothing to do, but, unfortunately, I get nothing for doing it. You know, where there are no seizures there is no pay."

"Oh, I see!" exclaimed Cox; "*aut seizure* (*Cæsar*) *aut nihil.*"

REMINISCENCES OF CHANCELLOR BIBB.

The late Chancellor Bibb was one of the most eccentric judges we have ever had. He was known in Washington in 1858–'59, just before his death, as "the last of the small-clothes," from the fact that he refused, at the dictates of fashion, to abandon the dress and customs of his early days, encase his legs in pantaloons, abandon his knee and shoe-buckles, and drop his cue. The chancellor never gave up his broad-brimmed hat, his fine linen, his long waistcoat, his small-clothes, his black silk hose, his silver shoe-buckles, or his snuff-box. Like Henry Clay, he was a lover of the fragrant titillating nose-powder, and right graciously did he dispense it on every hand. Even the boys would often stop him in the streets with "Give us a pinch of snuff, please?" and the chancellor, with an air that would have been admired at the court of Louis Quatorze, would at once tender the snuff-box. The fingers that have entered that same snuff-box have done this country good service with the pen and with the sword. Many a time has it been passed around the Senate and the Supreme Court, nor was it ever refused by President or foreign diplomatist. Yet, as was well said of his prototype, Chief Justice Marshall, what would have been ludicrous in another became in him more than respectable; it absolutely attracted your reverence. Unsightly as were those rusty and snuff-begrimed "tights,"

they yet became, when worn by the chancellor, a kind of ornament, and made the metropolis prize him the more, as we do antique coins and pictures for the rust and smoke that deface them, or a bottle of generous old wine for the dust and cobwebs that cover it.

It was near the close of his senatorial career that Judge Bibb openly avowed himself a disciple of Izaak Walton.

Indeed, his reputation as the most patient and unsuccessful angler in the District was already well established. A bill was before the Senate regulating executive patronage, and it had been insinuated by the opponents of the administration that some of the senators whose terms of office were about to expire would be recipients of Presidential favors. "I deny this," said the judge, at the conclusion of his speech, "so far as I am concerned. I have no personal object in view. I have no ambition. For myself, I prefer to sit with my rod and line on the banks of a pellucid stream, enjoying the pleasures of calmness and contemplation, to any objects that my ambition could achieve." Whatever were his fortunes or his wants, the chancellor always found delight in "casting a line," and by his practice fully indorsed the opinion of Sir Henry Wotton, that angling was "a rest to his mind, a cheerer of his spirits, a diverter of sadness, and a procurer of contentedness." Many are the good stories told of his piscatorial exploits, and he used to enjoy hearing them himself, albeit he would sometimes indorse them rather more emphatically than piously. It was a way he had of expressing himself, not a vice. Here is one of these tales:

On one warm afternoon the officer in command at the Washington Arsenal observed the chancellor sitting on a broken-down wharf hour after hour, intently watching his float. At last he strolled down from the quarters to inquire, "What luck?"

"None!" replied the chancellor. "I thought I had some bites two or three hours ago, but there is not a fish hereabouts now apparently," etc., etc.

"What is your bait?" asked the son of Mars.

"A plump young frog, hooked through the fleshy part of his leg," etc., etc.

Scarcely had he finished this reply when the questioner

roared with laughter, actually rolling on the grass, and unable to disclose the cause of his merriment. At last he pointed to a log which was partly out of water, and there the chancellor saw *his bait!* froggy having got tired of swimming about, and jumped up on the log to see what the biped at the other end of the line and pole was doing!

When the chancellor was Secretary of the Treasury he was one day importuned by the landlord of a poor clerk, who wished to secure his monthly salary until all arrearages of rent were paid.

"Why has he not paid you?" inquired the chancellor.

"His family have been sick, Mr. Secretary, and he only has a thousand dollars a year, any how."

"Sir!" exclaimed the chancellor, "do you take me, the Secretary of the Treasury, for a miserable constable? No, sir! I never descend to the collection of debts, which is an outrageous custom, although legal! Good-day, sir."

The abashed creditor withdrew, and the clerk was next day promoted to a more lucrative place.

The personal appearance of Chancellor Bibb, aside from his costume, was remarkable, and his great physical vigor of constitution was shown in his erect carriage and firm step after he had become an octogenarian. He was rather above the middle size, and his frame, like his mind, was compact and well knit together. His whole demeanor and appearance proclaimed that he was a *gentleman*, high-toned and courteous; able, yet retiring; a firm friend, a kind husband (he was married thrice), and an affectionate parent. The freedom and the frankness with young people was especially remarkable and pleasing.

The chancellor once delivered a legal opinion of St. Paul. The name of the apostle had been introduced by one of the counsel pleading before him, and the statement made that, with all his learning, St. Paul was long in appreciating the great truths of Christianity. The chancellor interrupting, raised himself up, and standing before the person addressed, as was his habit when excited, said,

"St. Paul was a giant, sir! It took a stroke of lightning to make him understand, but, when he did understand, he talked like thunder!"

THE IMMORALS OF A CULPRIT.

Judge Verplanck, of Buffalo, is widely known throughout Western New York for his habits of unflagging industry, as well as for an appreciation of all sorts of wit. On or off the bench, no one knows better how to enjoy a good thing. A case was before him in which the reputation of one of the parties was involved.

"What is the general character of the defendant?" asked the prosecuting officer.

"Character for what?"

"Why, his morals?"

This particular point was just what the witness was not over-desirous of answering, and knowing the judge quite well, he cast toward him an appealing look, as much as to say, Can't you help me out of this? The judge comprehended the situation, and, with a face of stony gravity, suggested that the answer desired might perhaps be attained by a slight variation of the question. "Suppose you ask him, 'How are his *im*morals?'" The witness looked upon the court, the court dittoed upon the witness, while the latter replied, "Well, judge, I should say that his *im*morals *stand very high!*" The court "noted the exception," while most of the by-standers adjourned to Bloomer's to—talk the thing over leisurely.

ABORTIVE LEGAL EFFORT TO ABOLISH THE FEMININE GENDER.

Judge G——, one of the Supreme Court Justices in the Eighth Judicial District of the State of New York, is no less noted for his keen sense of wit and ready pleasantries than for his profound judicial knowledge, and his impartial conduct on the bench.

On one occasion, on the trial of a cause, when the question arose as to the admission of the wife as a witness where the husband was a party to the action, the judge promptly decided that, under the present rule of practice, no distinction was made as to the admission of witnesses; that the last Legislature had virtually dissolved the marriage relation so far as rules of law practice went. In confirmation of this statement one of the counsel referred to a note in Howard's New York Code of Practice in the Supreme Court, under the act

"*Concerning the Rights and Liabilities of Husband and Wife.*

"*Note.*—There seems to be a slight discrepancy in the *title* of this act as compared with its principal provisions. The more appropriate title would be 'An Act for Divorce between Husband and Wife, *a vinculo matrimonii*, as it respects property, and for the more effectually abolishing the *feminine gender.*'—EDITOR."

Immediately upon the utterance of the last two words the judge replied, "I think the editor is wrong, and, under the sanction of the ermine, I must correct his statement:

"No! the *gender* remains, by a law that's Divine;
'Tis the *wife* that is changed to a mere concubine!'"

For five minutes or more the old court-house rang with the shouts of merriment, in which members of the bar, jurors, suitors, and spectators all heartily untied.

ANECDOTES OF JUDGE PETERS, OF CONNECTICUT.

The late Judge Peters, of Connecticut, was a strong Democrat, and a violent opposer especially of every thing connected with the famous Hartford Convention. Roger Minot Sherman and Calvin Goddard, who had been members of that body, were once talking with Judge P. on the subject, when the latter, half facetiously and half in earnest, said,

"Well, gentlemen, if you had been tried before me for that matter I would have hung you both, not only without law and evidence, but, if need be, against both."

"That," said Sherman, making a low bow, "only proves your honor's remarkable impartiality—that you would decide our case on the same principle that you do the greater part of the cases that come before you."

In his religious views Judge Peters was understood to be a Universalist. On one occasion an offender had been convicted before him of two different crimes, when for the *first* the judge sentenced him to the state prison *for life*, and then for the *second* for *five years more!* As the court was adjourned, Sherman, stepping up to him, said,

"Well, judge, I am happy to see that you are changing your religious views, at least on one important subject."

"How so—how so?" said the judge. "I don't understand you."

"Why," said Sherman, "it is plain, from your sentence, that you believe in punishment *after death.*"

It is but just to the judge, however, to add that he defended his sentence on the ground that the criminal might be pardoned for the first offense, and in that case would be held for the second.

ANECDOTES OF JUDGE JOHN R. BRADY.

Judge J. R. Brady, well known as "the judge who never carries the ermine with him off the bench, and lugs it laboriously around in ordinary life," has plenty of digni-

ty when filling his official position, as more than one lawyer, who for a moment presumed upon outside familiarity to take liberties with the bench, has found to his cost. But there have been instances when, even on the bench, he has been guilty of something very nearly approaching to a joke. One of the drollest of those rare instances, perhaps, was that of the "double lawyer," which the judge was not quite alone in arranging. The court was holding General Term, at which, as is well known, all the judges sit together, and when, for the purposes of the court, no one of the judges ever sits alone. But it so happened one day, when the court had thinned materially, that both his colleagues went for a few moments into Chambers, leaving Judge Brady alone, and of course without any idea of hearing an argument. At this crisis, a certain lawyer, who may be designated as Davy Nathan, arose and commenced making some inquiries as to the intention of the court to hear *his* case. Inquired of as to whether his opponent was present and ready, Davy confessed that he was not, but—

"Then is it your intention to argue both sides yourself?" interrupted the judge, with his face set to the gravity of one of the New Hampshire granite rocks, while it was only to his intimates that the sly twinkle of his eye was apparent.

"Argue both sides, your honor?" returned Davy, with a gravity that was by no means assumed; "I do not know—I had not thought of doing so, but I have no doubt that I could. But," and here Davy hesitated for a moment, "is not such a course a little unusual?"

"Not more unusual," said the judge, with corresponding earnestness, "than for a single judge to *hear* an argument at General Term."

"Very well, then, your honor," replied Davy, "as it will save time, I will adopt your honor's suggestion, and go on."

He did take up his papers and "go on," and though the few remaining lawyers laughed in their sleeves, and the clerks, reporters, and all that class of court *habitues* were convulsed with mirth, not a smile crossed the blandly earnest face of the judge.

"On which side are you going to begin, Mr. Nathan?" inquired the judge.

"Oh, as I am the appellant, I think I will begin on my own," replied Davy, who thereupon opened the chapter of injuries sustained by his client on being mulcted in damages for the sale of a horse under a warranty, when there had been no warranty whatever, before Judge Slider, of the One Hundredth and Seventh District Court. The judge lay back in his chair and listened gravely; some of the others listened not quite so gravely, though Davy never saw any thing out of order. After a time the judge interrupted him:

"Mr. Nathan, hadn't you better give us a little on the other side now?"

"Yes, perhaps I had better, your honor;" whereupon Davy presented the other side, more or less lucidly, for a few moments. Then another suggestion, and another transfer; and then back again, judge and counsel both still the incarnations of gravity, though all other parties had arrived at that state at which an early explosion was inevitable. But the explosion was not reached until Davy came to that point so easily found under such circumstances—the point of wandering and stumbling about under his double load. Then, when the judge, tapping his forehead, as if in a very strong attempt to recollect, sententiously inquired, "Let me see, Mr. Nathan, which side are you on *now?*"—then there certainly *was* an explosion which came very near to the bench, if it did not reach it, and Davy, looking around at the spectators, muttered something about "really finding it a worse job than he thought," dropped his papers, and sat down. He was a little quizzed, possibly, thereafter, as "the lawyer who argued both sides of the case on appeal," and Judge Brady was correspondingly complimented as being "the judge who heard General Term arguments all alone." It would be pleasant to record what eventually became of the horse case, but the records of the court (carefully examined to that end) do not show that the argument so originally begun and so amusingly interrupted has ever yet come to a conclusion.

Judge Brady is not very often "floored" (to use an expressive vulgarism) when on the bench, but there are certain persons who remember to have seen him in that condition. Not many years have elapsed since one morning, during the heat of a trial, a paper, apparently of importance, was handed up to him by an officer, the sender, a lawyer of somewhat run-down condition, waiting anxiously at a little distance for a response, and the paper, when circulated among the members of the bar (as it was the moment after), conveying this somewhat startling legal application to be made to a judge on the bench:

"Thursday morning.

"DEAR JUDGE,—I am busted—dead! Lend me a ten for a few days, and hand it to me in an envelope, so that nobody will know about it. Yours,

"—— ——."

Possibly ex-Excise Commissioner Robert D. Holmes, who was made the first confidant by the bench on that occasion, may remember the incident with some unction; but he will *not* remember, as the relator does not, the handing over of the money.

The greatest charm of one of Judge B.'s best charges lay in the opening sentence. Smith and Jones were fighting (at *nisi prius*) over the value of a certain schooner sold by the one to the other, and used for carrying sand from the Jersey flats. Smith swore that a sounder and more seaworthy vessel had not existed since the days of the Armada—that every spar, timber, and rope was perfect, and that he would have had no hesitation in crossing the Atlantic in her in an equinoctical gale. Jones swore that there was not one timber, spar, or rope but was so rotten as to be picked to pieces with the fingers, and that he would not have crossed the North River in her from Fort Washington to Guttenberg, on a calm day in midsummer, for an interest in Johnstown. When the judge came to charge the jury, his opening sentence was, "Gentlemen of the jury, upon one point I have no occasion to assist your deliberations; if you know any thing in this world, it is the seaworthiness of the boat!" Perhaps they did, though they "smiled audibly," as if they did not; at all events, they disagreed, and the precise money-value of the sand-schooner probably remains undetermined to this day.

Judge Brady was once trying a case in which a party attempted to recover for dry goods sold at auction. The defense was "printer's imperfections on the fabrics sold." The defendant's counsel was a mild and amiable gentleman, under the control, to a greater extent than usual, of his clients. He had asked a number of irrelevant questions (which were not creditable to him as an advocate), and which were duly excluded. A private consultation with his clients ended in his asking another question equally irrelevant with those which had been rejected. It was objected to. The presiding judge said,

"It is certainly irrelevant, Mr. C——," to which the latter answered, looking up at the ceiling of the court-room,

"I knew it was, your honor, but I asked it, sir, to gratify my clients."

The judge, leaning forward, with a gentle but pointed expression of satire, said, in his bland way,

"Mr. C——, during the rest of this trial the court will endeavor to *protect you from your clients.*"

The result was that Mr. C—— was not farther molested by client, court, or jury.

Judge Brady was one day admitting to the duties of citizenship such members of the Milesian and Teutonic persuasions as came armed with the proper documents, and could satisfactorily answer the interrogatories the judge deemed it his duty to propound. One of these was Michael Mahoney, whose face wore a genial smile and his body an old army overcoat. Taking his eye in his hand, and throwing it at the prisoner (to speak metaphorically) full and strong, the judge thus addressed him:

"What's your name?"

"Michael Mahoney, yer hon'r."

"How long have you been in this country?"

"Six years, yer hon'r."

"Never been out of it during that time?"

"Niver a wanst, yer hon'r."

"Sure of it?"

"Bedad you can say that."

Turning to the witness accompanying Michael, and receiving satisfactory replies to the usual questions as to moral character, etc., the judge was on the point of putting his initials to the application, and thus passing it, when Michael interrupted him by asking,

"Judge, what was that ye were after asking about being out of the country?"

"Have you been out of the United States at any time during the last six years?"

"Well, ye'r honor, I may have been out of it *a little*, just wanst."

"When was that?"

"Well" (and he gave a wink at the court), "*that was at the first battle of Bull Run.*"

WIT OF ALEXANDER H. STEPHENS.

The late rebel Vice-President of the late rebel Confederacy was noted for his tact and wit on the stump. During the contest for the Presidency in 1860, Stephens, who supported Bell and Everett, had occasion to address an audience at the same time with Colonel Rance Wright. Wright's turn for speaking came, and, by way of a tale, he said that Mr. Stephens had said he could eat, metaphorically speaking, Ben Hill for breakfast, Rance Wright for dinner, and Bob Trippe for supper. Mr. Stephens being very small of stature, and possessing very little storage-room, of course this brought out a shout. Mr. Stephens rose, and, after denying having made any such statement, said, if he had contemplated such a feast, he surely would have changed the order; he would have taken Ben Hill for breakfast, Bob Trippe for dinner, and, remembering the advice of his mother always to eat a light supper, he would have tipped off with his friend Colonel Wright.

CURIOUS RESEMBLANCE OF A PLAINTIFF TO OTHELLO.

Jefferson Davis, a lawyer of some *little* repute in Mississippi, in a trial for slander in one of the courts of that state, was defending a client who had charged the plaintiff with swindling. The opposing counsel had boasted in his opening speech that the plaintiff had acted entirely under his advice, and in the progress of the cause he introduced in evidence a letter of the plaintiff, in which the phrase was used, "Othello's occupation's gone." Davis, in commenting upon this letter to the jury, said,

"I deny the right of the plaintiff to compare himself to Othello, who was a noble, generous, warm-hearted man—his only fault that he 'loved not wisely, but too well.'

In all these respects the plaintiff is exactly the opposite—a mean-spirited, selfish, avaricious, and treacherous person. But there is, gentlemen, a striking resemblance between the plaintiff and Othello in this—they both had most villainous counsel."

ANECDOTES OF JAMES T. BRADY.

Half the good stories told in this chapter have at various times been attributed to one or the other of the Bradys, each of whom are equally witty and wise. We give below a few of those of undoubted Brady origin:

It is related that Mr. James T. Brady was employed to argue a doubtful case in the Supreme Court of the State of New York while Greene C. Bronson was the chief justice. He felt doubtful as to being able to succeed even in getting the justices to take the case for consideration. The plaintiff had been nonsuited in the former trials of the case for a reason which was apparent—he had "rested" too soon, stopped short in his proof, but whether from necessity or inadvertence was not disclosed by the testimony. Mr. Brady proceeded to state the facts, and, in commenting upon the incidents of the trial, said, "And hereupon the plaintiff rested."

"Rested, sir," said Chief Justice Bronson, who had been grasping the case with avidity, and saw the defect which Mr. Brady apprehended would be fatal, "rested, sir; why did he rest?"

Mr. Brady, with that peculiar involuntary movement or shrug which is often the *avant courier* of a good thing, with great self-possession, but apparently feeling in his neckcloth for the lost Pleiad, said,

"If your honors please, that question has given me much anxiety. I have devoted nearly two weeks to a search for the reason why, at so early and inconvenient a period in this controversy, the plaintiff rested, and I have at last arrived at the conclusion, and it is, in my judgment, the only one that can be sustained on principle and authority, that he must have been very much fatigued!"

It is needless to say that the papers were not taken nor the judgment reserved.

On another occasion Mr. Brady had a case equally defective, and so very lame that he gave his client to understand that it could not be gained. The client insisted on trying it, and Mr. Brady devoted his best talent to making the best show he could. The case was ably put on the other side, and was so plain that the judge, who had made up his mind, rather indicated it by several rulings entirely favorable to the opposite side. Mr. Brady was seeking for an opportunity for covering his retreat from his untenable positions, and on some ruling of the judge highly favorable to his opponent, he blandly inquired,

"May it please your honor, who's engaged on the other side of this case besides the judge?"

Mr. Brady was on another occasion engaged in another and more interesting case, in which the testimony was nicely balanced, and it required an effort to succeed. He was the defendant's counsel, and was addressing the jury with great earnestness. Becoming violent in his tone and gesture, a dog, the fond companion of a juror, and hitherto lying in blissful secrecy and security under the juror's bench, alarmed at the unusual performance, suddenly appeared and barked at the orator. As quick as a flash the speaker turned upon the intruder, and with appropriate gesticulation exclaimed,

> "I am Sir Oracle,
> And when I ope my mouth let no dog bark."

That flight of fancy won the jury and carried the case.

A PROPER COUNTENANCE FOR A JUDGE.

Soon after Judge Busteed's appointment as United States Judge for the State of Alabama, he was conversing with an acquaintance at Mobile about his new and very responsible position. The latter expressed surprise that the judge should have accepted the honor, or consented to go upon the bench under any circumstances—"it would be so difficult for you," said he, jocularly, "to maintain the requisite facial gravity."

"What!" said the judge, assuming an aspect of great severity, "do you mean to say that I do not *look* like the United States Judge of Alabama?"

"Well, judge," was the reply, "I must confess you *have* rather a '*Mobile*' countenance just at this moment, though how it will appear when you visit the other districts I'll not undertake to say."

ANECDOTE OF JUDGE BARNARD.

Judge Barnard, of the Supreme Court of New York, whose rapid way of doing business at Chambers is proverbial, is quick to perceive where a witticism may, without impropriety, be introduced to enliven the proceedings. The writer of this happened to be present one morning when two pillars of the law stood in the presence, each holding some quires of paper facetiously termed "pleadings."

"I ask leave, your honor, to amend so as to insert" so and so.

"And I move to amend," says the other, "by inserting," etc., etc.

This continued for half an hour, when the judge quietly arose, took his hat and cane, and remarked, "Gentlemen, you have each leave, if you wish, to insert *the whole of Webster's Dictionary*. This is my birthday, and I am going home to dinner. Court's adjourned!"

Counsel were disposed to ask for a writ of "No Go" (*ne exeat*); but the judge was off, and we suppose they are now at work on that superior, though somewhat discursive volume.

REMINISCENCE OF GOVERNOR ROBERT P. LETCHER, OF KENTUCKY.

The following interesting and touching reminiscence of Robert P. Letcher is related by a lady:

"When he was Governor of Kentucky I spent a winter at Frankfort, the capital. My father was a member of the Senate, and of the same political party, as well as an old friend of his excellency, so that I became very well acquainted with him during the winter; but the little incident I will relate occurred on the first day I met him:

"The November preceding, a couple of negroes, man and wife, had been tried in the Circuit Court of M—— County for burning down the house of their mistress, a very old lady, who escaped almost by a miracle from perishing in the flames. They were found guilty, and condemned to death. A good many ladies attended the trial, as they often did when it was known that our best lawyers would speak, and I had been one of the number. I heard all the testimony and all the speeches, and came to the decided conclusion that the woman had participated in the crime through fear of her husband. I determined I would try to save her from the gallows. I scarcely knew how to go to work to accomplish my object. All girls of sixteen are keenly alive to ridicule, and I was so much afraid of being laughed at that I kept my intentions to myself. Judge R——, the presiding judge, had postponed passing sentence of death upon the poor creatures until the last day of the term. For many years he had been in the habit of making our house his home while his court was in session. I was a great favorite with him, and when I begged him to give them a 'long day,' he readily granted my request.

"In a few days after we went to Frankfort. I had made up my mind to go directly to Governor Letcher, and ask him to pardon the woman; so, the morning after I reached there, I started out alone, without imparting my plans to my father or elder sister. I knew that the governor transacted business in a room adjoining the office of the secretary of state. With a heart beating loud enough to be heard, I found myself at the door of the room. I dared not give myself time to reflect. I knew, if I hesitated an instant, I would surely *run.* I gave a tremendous rap; it sounded like thunder in my ears, and in a moment I was face to face, for the first time, with Governor Letcher.

"I shall never forget the kind smile and pleasant voice with which he greeted me. 'Come in, my child,' he said, 'and tell me what you want with me; but sit down; you look a little frightened, though I don't think you can be afraid of *me.*' I first told him my name, and who was my father; then I scarcely knew how to begin my petition, but his whole manner and appearance was so *good* that I soon overcame my timidity. I told him the whole story: how the woman's husband had escaped from the county jail a day or two after their sentence had been passed; how she could have done so at the same time if she had been willing to desert her little baby; how young she was, and how — even to a poor slave — how dreadful to die such an awful death, and leave her poor baby forever. I don't remember all I said, but I plead with my whole heart, and became so much excited that I wound up by bursting into tears. Dear old man! I don't think that his eyes were quite dry. 'My dear child,' he said, after a short pause, 'it is very unusual to grant a pardon unless some petition is sent, signed by a sufficient number of respectable citizens, or some written appeal, to place upon record, to show that the executive has not, without good reason, interfered with the execution of the laws of the state. But I will do this: I will grant the woman a reprieve of six weeks,' and, continued he, 'I am sure you know some young gentleman who, for the sake of pleasing you, will draw up a petition and circulate it through your county, and if he can get even twenty names to it you shall have the pardon.' I thanked him over and over again, and he took me with him to the proper office, that I might see for myself that the reprieve was sent off immediately. I am making my story too long, but will close it in as few words as possible. I *did know* the sort of young gentleman he had referred to, and the same mail that carried the reprieve also carried an account of my interview with the governor. In a few days my young friend sent me the result of his labors—a petition more numerously signed than I had dared to hope for. I rushed off with it to his excellency. He seemed almost as delighted as I was, and as he handed me the pardon he placed his hand on my head, and smoothing the curls, that had become rather disordered by my rapid movements, he said to me, 'Remember, L——, that any favor you can ask of old Bob Letcher will be granted as willingly as it would have been to a child of my own, had God seen fit to bless me with one.' Then he added words of praise that I can not place here, but I treasure them still in my heart. I loved him dearly, and will always revere his memory as one of the best men I ever knew."

GENERAL BEN BUTLER'S TACT AS A LAWYER.

One of the very last cases in which that distinguished advocate, Rufus Choate, appeared, was for the prosecution of a railroad for damages in the loss of limb of his client. Associated with him were D—— and L——, two others of the leaders of the Massachusetts bar. The three together made up a trio of legal ability of the very highest order;

while for the defense stood Ben Butler, single-handed, and apparently inattentive to the progress of the trial. He took no notes, but a little occurrence soon brought him to his feet, and proved that he was awake and at his post. A

question had been asked a witness, the answer to which seemed to damage the plaintiff's prospects. One of the trio, in apparently a by-play to his associates, gave a slight groan of incredulity, doubtless intended for effect on the jury. In an instant up sprang the vigilant Ben.

"Stop! stop! stop!" cried he, in his impetuous way, to the witness.

"What is the matter, Mr. Butler?" asks the judge, taken by surprise at the interruption.

"May it please your honor," replies the imperturbable advocate in the blandest of accents, "my brother L—— is taken suddenly ill. Did you not hear him groan just now? The court might like to take a short recess, I thought."

"Proceed with the examination of the witness. Let there be no more interruption," says the judge. But the object of the interruption was accomplished; the effect, or intended effect, of the enemy's gun was neutralized.

Mr. Butler, being for the defense, of course had to address the jury first in the closing arguments. His analysis of the special characteristics of his three opponents was acute and discriminating. To each of them he ascribed the highest of tact and talent in his own department, but to his brother Choate he gave more than common encomium. "He it was," said he, "who is retained in every great case, to lend to it the power of his rare abilities to obtain a verdict. Such, gentlemen of the jury, is the charm of his eloquence, that he has only to wave over you his magic wand, and you are so completely mesmerized by his will that you will say black is white, and white black, if he only says it is so. You are wholly under the bewitching influence of his eloquence, and are led by it whithersoever he chooses to lead you. You start, gentlemen; you brace yourself back with a determined air, as if to say, however it may be with others, you are proof against his blandishments. Ah! gentlemen, little do you know the power of the spell that will soon be upon you. I have myself seen it in so many instances that I speak with confidence and certainty on this point." And so he went on to depict the *Chotean* style of eloquence, with a slight allusion to the famous somnambulist line of defense in the Tyrrell case, till he had succeeded in fortifying the jury against the last words—always the most potent—of the closing argument.

Mr. Choate arose, evidently not in good health, pale and emaciated, the deep lines of his classic face tremulous with emotion, and in his very exordium complained bitterly and earnestly of the injustice done him by the caricature drawn so wantonly and maliciously by the counsel for the defense, asserting over and over again that he was a far different man, and his eloquence—such as he had—far different from that attempted to be fastened on him; that, in short, he was a plain-spoken man, accustomed to use only such common sense as his Maker had given him, and such a presentation of the facts in any case as the testimony warranted. He then proceeded to verify his assertion by a corresponding style of eloquence and argument, entirely unusual with him, and only feebly, for him, put the case to the jury. The damaging effect of Butler's novel tactics was evident from beginning to end, and the jury did not agree upon a verdict, which was equivalent to one for Butler's clients.

EXTEMPORIZING LEGAL AUTHORITIES.

The following true anecdote of the late Mr. J——, one of the most learned and high-minded lawyers of Central New York, shows how necessary is the ability sometimes to *extemporize*, as well as to quote the law pertinent to the case. About twenty years since he was engaged in trying an important case before a country justice of the peace, and had for his antagonist a dogged and determined pettifogger by the name of Briggs, who was considered "great" in justice's courts in general, and in that one in particular, as the justice was a neighbor of his, and had been the opposition candidate for the same office; and as Mr. Briggs was beaten by a very small majority only, the court always seemed to regard him as a man *nearly* capable of holding the office, and one whose opinion, therefore, was entitled to more than ordinary weight. Briggs perceived this confidence, and sometimes endeavored to take advantage of it, and accordingly it was not unusual, when he had a desperate case on hand, to manufacture the law to sustain it, and to quote to the court what the decision of the Supreme Court had been in some case which he would cite, always giving the title of the hypothetical case, and the volume and page where it was reported, and the language used by the court in giving its opinion. This was, of course, all manufactured by Briggs from his fertile and never-failing resources. He tried the same game on the present occasion upon J——. Briggs summed up the case at great length and with considerable ability, and cited at length the case of Frink *vs.* Ferguson, as decided in the Supreme Court, and giving the volume and page, as usual, where the case could be found reported. This was a stumper to J——, who knew that no such decision had ever been made, but who knew also that there was not a law library within twenty miles. The case cited covered the one before the court like a confession of judgment, and how to get rid of its effect was the next question.

The court adjourned for dinner immediately after the conclusion of Briggs's speech, and during the interim the witnesses and such neighbors as had been attracted to the tavern by a lawsuit were busily engaged discussing, as is usual on such occasions, and making bets upon, the probable result of the case.

Upon the reassembling of the court J—— commenced his argument for the plaintiff, and the court-room was more completely packed, if possible, than before dinner. After talking some time about the facts of the case, he approached the law involved in it, and said, while he admired the ability and ingenuity displayed by his opponent, he thought he had not treated the case or the court with that fairness or frankness which should characterize all legal discussions, whose end should always be to discover truth and apply justice. "With the case of Frink *vs.* Ferguson," said he, "upon which my opponent seems to rest his case, and which is perfectly familiar to me, I have no fault to find, as I too rely chiefly upon the same case. I freely admit that the Supreme Court decided that case as stated by my learned opponent, but then my friend ought in honesty to have stated to your honor that the case was afterward *reversed* by the Court for the Correction of Errors," naming the volume and page also where the decision could be found reported, and reading from his brief (which had been prepared during the adjournment) copious extracts from the opinions of the chancellor and several senators, showing the law to be such as fitted the plaintiff's case exactly.

The frank admission of J—— completely nonplused the court, and Briggs too, for that matter, and the result was that judgment was given for the plaintiff for the amount claimed; but a knowledge of the joke having got abroad, Briggs was so annoyed at being "hoist by his own petard" that he soon after removed to Arkansas, where he was afterward appointed judge of the Supreme Court of that state, and was making law there on the breaking out of the rebellion.

AN EFFECTIVE IMPROMPTU.

During the trial of a man named Pugsley in Baltimore for a cruel and outrageous assault upon his daughter—a pretty, gentle girl, just entering womanhood—it was proven that the traverser had seized his daughter in the street by the throat, had dragged her from the protection of persons with whom she was living as a nurse, and having reached his home with his *prisoner*, and regaled himself with a hearty supper, that he had entertained himself for a period of two hours, varied by intermissions for rest and refreshment, by beating his daughter unmercifully with a cart-whip. The defense interposed by his counsel was as extraordinary as the character of the misdemeanor of the accused, and, among other arguments in justification of the father's brutality, it was urged that the daughter was unworthy of belief; that she was habitually disobedient; that the father's "finer feelings" made him solicitous to reform the girl's heart; and that he had only obeyed the spirit of Solomon's maxim, "Not to spare the rod, lest he should spoil the child." As the counsel finished his argument for the defendant, Mr. R. S. Mathews, a member of the bar, handed the following impromptu to Mr. Whitney, the state's attorney, who closed the case for the state by repeating it to the jury with humorous effect:

"His 'finer feelings' made him seek his child,
To train her steps in ways 'uncommon mild;'
And, lest her feet from duty's paths should slip,
He kept her upright by a *drayman's whip.*
The ancient teacher—holy man of God—
Advises 'parents not to spare the rod;'
But in this case the query rises—Whether
Solomon meant *the rod should be of leather?*
If Pugsley's rule the jury should indorse,
His child will fare scarce better than his horse!"

The prisoner was convicted, heavily fined, and imprisoned for three months by Judge Bond, of the Criminal Court.

REMINISCENCES OF JO DAVIESS, OF KENTUCKY.

At the age of twenty-five Jo Daviess had established his reputation as one of the best lawyers and most powerful orators in the Western country. He gained, almost at a single bound, a place that is usually reached only by long and assiduous labor. Nor was this elevation the result of an unhealthy or unnatural precocity, such as is sometimes displayed by men who astonish the world by a splendor of youthful promise which they are unable to realize, and sink into obscurity, or remain throughout life only brilliant school-boys. The height of Daviess's reputation was not at all disproportionate to the capacity of its base, and though it had risen "like an exhalation," it stood the test of time, and only grew higher with each succeeding year of his life.

The incident which gave him his first prominence strongly illustrated not only his ability, but also his benevolence and love of justice. Instead of "riding the circuit," like most of his brethren, it was his custom to shoulder his rifle and range the woods between the different shire towns, and he often appeared in court in his sporting costume, consisting of deer-skin leggins, linsey hunting-shirt, and coon-skin cap. He thus contrived to combine his favorite recreation of hunting with the performance of his professional duties. It was on one of these journeys that the incident alluded to occurred. A poor young fellow had, while wandering through the country, been arrested and taken before a magistrate on a charge of horse-stealing—a charge at that time almost equivalent to a death-warrant. The scene of the trial was one of those log school-houses which we have mentioned, situated in the woods. His honor had taken his seat on the top of a desk, clothed with all the majesty of the law, and prepared, at the proper time, to deliver an impressive address to the convict on the enormity of stealing in general, and of horse-stealing in particular. The small room was filled with an eager crowd, whose feelings, unreservedly expressed, were by no means favorable to the prisoner. The constable having opened the court with much formality, his honor proceeded to read the warrant of arrest, wherein the prisoner was accused of doing so many unheard-of things to John Styles's horse—stealing, abducting, eloigning, and removing—that the feelings of the rustic audience were wrought up to the highest pitch of rage against so hardened an offender. This interval the poor wretch spent in looking pitifully around, to see if he might discover one friendly face amid so many enemies. But the only person who did not seem to display any active hostility was a tall, stalwart backwoodsman, in hunting-shirt and coon-skin cap, who had just entered, and stood leaning on his rifle at the back part of the room, looking on with a sort of indifferent curiosity. He, too, was evidently a stranger to all present. The prosecutor, having announced himself ready, proceeded to the production of his evidence, which was, indeed, overwhelming. The testimony of the last witness especially—a big, double-fisted, loud-voiced bully—was so minute and circumstantial as to admit of no reply. The prisoner was then, as a mere matter of form, asked if he had any testimony to offer or any questions to ask. He made two or three timid efforts to frame some awkward interrogatories by which to break, if possible, the net which he felt to be closing around him, but the loud and facetious replies of the witness completely subdued him, and he was about to give up, and submit to his fate in silence. But just then the tall backwoodsman suddenly set aside his rifle, strode into the presence of the court, and placing himself directly in front of the big witness, asked a few questions in a sharp, peremptory tone, that completely upset that individual's confidence, and at once gave a glimpse of the falsehoods he had been detailing. This unlooked-for change in affairs threw the whole court into a hubbub. The prosecuting attorney hastened to protect his witness; the latter strove to cover his fright and confusion by loud and threatening bluster. At last his honor, who did not like to lose both his chance of sentencing a horse-thief and of making an edifying speech, recovered himself sufficiently to inquire, "I say, stranger, and what mought your name be?" "I am Joseph Hamilton Daviess," replied the stranger. At this announcement the judge instantly subsided, a blank look of dismay usurped the faces of the prosecutor and his witnesses, while one of triumph lit up the dejected countenance of the accused. His innocence was soon clearly proven, and in a short time he left the room not only unconvicted, but cleared of even the suspicion of being a horse-thief—at that time the least tolerated of all criminals. It appeared that this young man was really an honest laborer, who, in trying to make his way on foot to his relations in a distant county, had strayed into the neighborhood, where he was arrested. Daviess refused to receive any part of his little pittance, well content with the reward of his own feelings, and the two trudged off together toward the next town, mutually pleased with each other's company. The client, however, insisted on carrying the gun and accoutrements of his protector. Daviess often declared that he was never better paid in his life than by the simple gratitude of this young stranger.

It may not be generally known that Daviess was the first Western lawyer who ever appeared in the Supreme Court of the United States. He had somehow become interested in a large tract of country lying in the "Green River country," the title of which had long been in litigation, and it was agreed that he was to receive one half of the tract provided he could succeed in establishing the claim.

The fame of his genius and eccentricities had by this time become national; but this was to be his first personal appearance beyond the bounds of his own state, and he seems to have determined that it should be marked both by the most splendid exhibition of his intellectual powers, and by the most glaring display of his eccentricity.

His entrance into the federal capital, as described by an eye-witness of the spectacle, must have been worth beholding. On foot, dressed in an old pair of corduroys, ripped at the ankle for convenience of "rolling up," with a threadbare drab over-coat hanging to his heels, and furnished with innumerable capes of various sizes; with shoes dilapidated, muddy, and destitute of strings or buckles (a constant habit with him), and a hat to match—fancy this stalwart figure, six feet high, stalking solemnly through the street, looking neither to the right nor the left, leading by the bridle a little, black, rough-haired filly, her tail matted into the likeness of a club with cockle-burrs. Over the saddle was hung a small wallet, containing, as afterward appeared, papers, and a provision of *gingerbread* and cheese. Such was the trim in which Joseph Hamilton Daviess presented himself for the first time to the eyes of the denizens of Washington. Few who beheld this strange figure pass by could have imagined that the brain under that "shocking hat" was laboring with thoughts the eloquence and power of which would in a few hours astonish the most learned tribunal of the land.

Putting up his mare at an obscure tavern, the stranger relieved himself of his great-coat, when he appeared in a short gray linsey *roundabout,* into one pocket of which he transferred from his wallet a quantity of bread and cheese, while the other received a bundle of papers, tied with a blue yarn string. Thus equipped, he issued forth into the street again, the observed of all negroes and idle boys. Arriving, as if by chance, in front of the building in which the Supreme Court was holding its sittings, he lounged into the bar and took a seat, not ceasing even in that august presence to regale himself from the store in his roundabout pocket. Unknown to all—taking, as it seemed, no particular notice of any thing (yet in reality, as soon appeared, watching every thing with the eye of a lynx), he passed, as he had done in the street, for some awkward countryman on his first visit to the city.

The case in which he was employed was soon called, and Mr. Taylor, of Virginia, the leading lawyer on the other side, arose to speak. He seemed to be advancing swimmingly in his statement of facts preparatory to beginning his argument, when all at once the stranger ceased eating, listened earnestly for a moment, then tapped him on the back, and very quietly corrected him on some point of his statement. Taylor stopped, turned round, and looked at him an instant without replying, and recommenced his remarks, taking no farther notice of the interruption. Daviess resumed his eating amid the smiles of the bar and audience. In a few minutes he again tapped the speaker and made another correction. This was repeated a third time, when Taylor, becoming irritated at the interruption, begged the court to protect him from the impertinences of "that person." Judge Marshall, always exceedingly lenient, and supposing now that he saw before him some Kentucky backwoodsman come to see the progress of his case, and, if things did not exactly suit him, to take it out of the hands of his attorneys—as lawyers know backwoodsmen will sometimes do—replied that the gentleman was, he supposed, one of the parties to the action; as such he had a right to be heard, and that his corrections seemed very just, though irregularly made. But he advised the stranger to leave his cause in the hands of his counsel, one of whom was present in court. Daviess's colleague had by this time got a hint as to who his strange ally really was, and, to humor the joke, kept silence.

Taylor finished his argument—one of great power and ingenuity—and sat down, not, as may be supposed, in the best of humors. Then, to the amazement of all, the stranger arose, and, throwing aside all oddity of manner, began a speech so clear, so forcible in its compact logic, and so masterly in its exposition of his adversary's weak points, that the gentleman, though well accustomed to the conflicts of the forum, seemed completely paralyzed, and sat like one overwhelmed by some sudden and unavertable calamity. It is said the sweat stood in large drops on his face as he listened to that crushing reply. The man whom he had regarded only as an ignorant or crazy rustic had all at once towered up before him into the proportions of a giant, and it is no wonder if he was confounded by so startling a transformation.

5.

"The Western Bar."

CHAPTER V.

ANECDOTES OF "THE WESTERN BAR."

"The Western Bar" has come to be a distinctive title with the legal profession, and is, indeed, universally used to designate that class of lawyers who are popularly supposed to know more about the practices of Colonel Bowie than of those of Counselor Chitty, and are better versed in "Colt on Revolvers" than "Coke on Common Law." All the peculiar eloquence which is odd and unique in conception and bombastic in style is credited to "the Western bar." Davy Crockett is, in the popular mind, the model "Western" lawyer and orator. All Western lawyers browbeat the jury as well as the witnesses, and all cases end in free fights and bloody noses. Comic annalists have ignorantly attempted to localize this peculiar style, and the popular mind generally believes "the Western bar" to be the bar of the Western and Southwestern States, forgetting all about the existence of that despotic and uncourteous old wretch, Lord Thurlow, and the bombastic, and ignorant, and insulting Jeffreys. So general is the impression that the bar of the Western States is characterized by the ignorance and bombast displayed in the stereotyped stories told of its judges and counselors, that the real characters of such men as Henry Clay, Thomas H. Benton, Sargent S. Prentiss, Tom Corwin, and even Abraham Lincoln, have been misunderstood, and never, perhaps, fully appreciated. The genius which taught them to lower themselves to the intellectual level of their matter-of-fact audiences is frequently mistaken for ignorance. The style of "the Western bar" has been peculiar to all ages and all countries, and the title should henceforth be accepted in a more cosmopolitan and catholic sense. The title, as used in the present instance and in this book, is intended to be taken in its figurative sense. The examples quoted are illustrative of the legal wisdom of all countries, and the stories told are, in many instances, freely acknowledged to be apocryphal.

LEGAL AND POLITICAL QUALIFICATIONS.

About a dozen years ago Governor Y—— and Judge W—— were candidates for Congress in one of the wildest of the Arkansas districts. They were both far-sighted, shrewd politicians—the judge the better lawyer and debater; the governor by far the more winning in his manners, as the sequel will fully establish. One hot day in July, while they were traveling together on the canvass, they came upon a party of twenty men or more, assembled on the road-side for the purpose of having a shooting-match. Thinking it a good time and place for presenting their respective claims, the governor proposed stopping. They halted, and the governor soon made himself at home. He bought a number of chances in the "match," and, being a good marksman, succeeded well, winning quite a quantity of beef, which constituted the prize. The judge had conscientious scruples as to shooting-matches, and did not participate, but stood by conversing with the more sober of the crowd, while his friend, the governor, was in high glee with his companions over their beef. When the beef was given out to the successful shooters, our governor ordered his to be divided among some poor widows, who he ascertained lived in the vicinity, and then asked the b'hoys if they were not "dry." Of course they were, and the governor generously ordered a plentiful supply of the "oh be joyful!" Here again the judge had scruples, and did not participate; but, had it been otherwise, it would have availed nothing. The governor was decidedly *the* man at the shooting-match, while the judge felt himself emphatically in the vocative. Leaving their friends, they proceeded on their way some twelve or fifteen miles, and halted at a camp-ground where the annual camp-meeting was being held. They separated in the crowd, each electioneering with all his might with old and young, friends and strangers—making hay while the sun shone—for there was indeed a fine opening. Toward night the judge began to look round for his distinguished opponent, but could find him nowhere. He waited patiently till evening services began, and concluded he would go to the large shed where the people had assembled for meeting, thinking perhaps he might meet his friend. On going out, what was his astonishment to find the gallant governor, the hero of the shooting-match, in front of the altar, surrounded by ministers and class-leaders, with a hymn-book in his hand, head thrown back, singing as loud as his lungs would permit,

"How firm a foundation, ye saints of the Lord."

"From that moment," said the judge, "I gave up all hopes. I tell you a man that's good for a camp-meeting and a shooting-match can't be beat for Congress; it can't be done, sir!"

And so it proved.

A STUBBORN JURY.

Colonel M——, living in Washington County, Maine, had a great aptitude for serving as a juror. When thus serving, he had a very great anxiety that his opinion should be largely consulted upon a verdict. Some years ago, while upon a case, after many hours' trial to agree, but failing, he marshaled the delinquent jury from the room to their seats in the court, where the impatient crowd awaited the result of the trial.

"Have you agreed upon a verdict?" inquired the clerk.

Colonel M—— arose, turned a withering glance upon his brother jurors, and exclaimed,

"May it please the court, we have not. I have done the best I could do, but here are eleven of the most contrary devils I ever had any dealing with."

COURTESY EXTRAORDINARY TO A CRIMINAL.

The following incident is *said* to have happened in the Recorder's Court in Chicago:

One day a prisoner was on trial for grand larceny, the jury duly impanneled, and the case proceeded with, when the hour of adjournment for dinner arrived, and the court was duly adjourned. The officers who had charge of the prisoner hurried off, with those that were in attendance, to dinner, leaving the prisoner and the clerk (Phil Hoyne) in the court-room. The clerk at the time being busy in making out some subpœnas or other process, the prisoner, after waiting a moment, asked the clerk what he was to do.

"Why, go to dinner, and come back at two o'clock," says the clerk, without looking up from what he was engaged upon. Two o'clock came, and with it the judge, clerk, jurors, and by-standers, all *except the prisoner*.

"Where's the prisoner?" asked the judge.

"In jail," says the officer who had him in charge in the morning; but, upon searching the jail, he was missing. Phil's round face beamed with intelligence about this time, and he stated to Judge Wilson what had taken place, and "supposed the prisoner was still at dinner."

"Yes, I suppose so too," said the judge; "if he is not, you might possibly find him in New York, at the Astor or St. Nicholas, at dinner, about the day after to-morrow. Call the next case, Mr. Clerk; we can't wait for that prisoner."

A POLITE JUDGE AND WILLING CRIMINAL.

Governor Ford, of Illinois, tells a very rich anecdote of one of the early judges of that state, but unhappily the governor does not put upon record the name of the sensitive and considerate magistrate.

At the court over which this judge presided a man by the name of Green was convicted of murder, and the judge was obliged to pass sentence of death upon the culprit. Calling on the prisoner to rise, the judge said to him,

"Mr. Green, the jury say you are guilty of murder, and the law says you are to be hung. I want you, and all your friends down on Indian Creek, to know that it is not I who condemn you; it is the jury and the law. Mr. Green, at what time, sir, would you like to be hung? The law allows you time for preparation."

The prisoner replied, "May it please your honor, I am ready at any time. Those who kill the body have no power to kill the soul. My preparation is made, and you can fix the time to suit yourself; it is all the same to me, sir."

"Mr. Green," returned the judge, "it is a very serious matter to be hung; it can't happen to a man but once in his life, unless the rope should break before his neck is broke, and you had better take all the time you can get. Mr. Clerk, since it makes no difference to Mr. Green when he is hung, just look into the almanac, and see whether this day four weeks comes on Sunday."

The clerk looked as he was directed, and reported that that day four weeks came on Thursday.

"Then," said the judge, "Mr. Green, if you please, you will be hung this day four weeks, at twelve o'clock."

The attorney general, James Turney, Esq., here interposed and said,

"May it please the court, on occasions of this sort it is usual for courts to pronounce a formal sentence, to remind the prisoner of his perilous condition, to reprove him for his guilt, and to warn him against the judgment in the world to come."

"Oh, Mr. Turney," said the judge, "Mr. Green understands the whole matter; he knows he has got to be hung. You understand it, Mr. Green, don't you?"

"Certainly," said the prisoner.

"Mr. Sheriff, adjourn the court."

Four weeks from that day Mr. Green was hung, but not so much to his own satisfaction as his appearance promised on the day of his conviction.

A GIANT DISCOMFITED.

The late talented but eccentric Judge M——, of Mississippi, was making a speech to a large crowd in 1840 in behalf of "Tippecanoe and Tyler too," when the following incident took place, much to the discomfiture of one of the parties:

General L——, a distinguished captain in his day, had made a very violent speech against General Harrison, and had accused him of cowardice in the battle of Tippecanoe —which battle, by-the-way, had given to General Harrison the well-known sobriquet of "Old Tippecanoe." In order to disprove this charge, coming as it did from such high authority, Judge M—— reviewed, in a masterly manner, the plan and order of that famous battle, and showed conclusively that the opinion of the general was entirely unfounded. He took particular pains to paint to the eye of his vast audience where General Harrison stood, what were his movements, and what his orders; at what point stood the gallant Daviess, and where he received his death-wound; at what point the enemy made their most deadly attack, and how and where they were repulsed; at what point the clarion voice of the general gave confidence to the troops, and caused them to regain their confidence in the deadly fight. After dwelling upon all the stirring incidents of the battle, and depicting the glories of the triumphant victory, he asked the audience, in a high and indignant key, "if there was a man in the sound of his voice who, after hearing this vindication of General Harrison, could for one moment believe that the noble old hero of Tippecanoe acted cowardly on that glorious occasion? I repeat," said the judge, "is there a man in this vast crowd who has the hardihood, after all I have said, to declare that General Harrison, the renowned warrior and statesman, was a coward in the battle of Tippecanoe?"

A voice from the outskirts of the crowd cried, in thunder tones, "I say it!"

"Who are you?" said the judge. "Stand up, and let me see you. I wish to let the crowd see what sort of a man you are!"

The crowd around the person who had thus created a sensation so thrilling literally pushed him up, so that all could see him. While standing upon the bench opposite the judge he proved to be almost a giant in size, fully equal to the judge, who, like Saul, was a head and shoulders taller than his tribe. The judge gazed upon the bold intruder with magnificent disdain. It seemed as though he was trying to blast him with a look, the crowd meantime looking on with intense interest, and wondering how it would end.

"Are you the man," said the judge, "who says General Harrison acted cowardly at the battle of Tippecanoe?"

"I am!" said the man, in tones both loud and bold.

"Upon what grounds do you have the brazen impudence to make the charge?" said the judge, in a higher and loftier key.

"Because I was there and saw him," said the man.

The judge looked at him with scorn, and cried, "Do *you* say you were at the battle of Tippecanoe?"

"I do!" said the man.

The judge raised himself on tip-toe, elevated both arms above his head, and thundered forth in the voice of Stentor, "You're a liar! for if you had been there *I'd have seen you!*"

The big fellow dropped from the bench on which he was standing as suddenly as though he had been shot through the heart. The vast crowd yelled with delight at his discomfiture. The bold assertion of the judge overthrew the slanderer, and the people rejoiced. He not only made the Goliah of the base falsehood believe that he had been in the battle, but the crowd too, when nothing was farther from the truth. He knew the intruder was gasing, and he went a stone's throw beyond him, and beat him at his own game.

HARD OF COMPREHENSION.

Judge G——, of Georgia, was very Democratic, both in politics and religion, and especially so in the latter. Several years ago he was in attendance on the Superior Court. The Presbyterians of the place, headed by their zealous and energetic minister, were at that time actively engaged in an effort to build a new house of worship. The Rev. Mr. Collins was zealously enlisted in the good cause, and never let an opportunity slip without presenting his subscription-list to all whom he might meet. One day, when court adjourned, as the judge was passing out of the court-house door, the reverend gentleman touched him on the shoulder and asked him to step aside with him a moment, when the following colloquy took place:

"This is Judge G——, I believe?" said Mr. Collins.

"It is," said the judge.

"We are engaged," said Mr. C., "in endeavoring to build us a new house of worship. Perhaps this (handing the judge his subscription-list) will inform you of my object better than I can tell you."

Here the judge looked very professional, took out his spectacles, examined the heading of the list very critically, and for a moment seemed engaged in profound thought; then turning to the expectant parson, the judge, with a sly twinkle of the eye and the blandest smile imaginable, remarked, "*that will bind them*, sir—that will bind them; no doubt about it—that will bind them."

This took the reverend gentleman a little aback. But rallying again, he renewed the attack in the following style:

"But, judge, you don't understand me; I want you to help us. We are going to raise—"

"Ah!" said the judge, "you are going to have a raising—a house-raising, are you? Well, just let me know when it is, and I will send up three or four hands with pleasure."

Here Mr. C.'s countenance exhibited a good deal of disgust, and he appeared to be perfectly bewildered at what seemed the judge's stupidity. "Why," said he, "judge, it's a brick house we want."

"A brick house, is it?" said the judge; "a brick house? Won't a log house do as well? Several years ago we built a log house in our community for religious purposes—some cut the logs—some hewed them—some split the boards—some raised the house—and some covered it—and the Lord has never made any complaint against it yet. If you build a log house, and the Lord complains, I'll head your subscription-list for a brick one."

The parson gave in and left.

CITING EXTRAORDINARY AUTHORITIES.

Judge Williamson, or "Three-legged Willie," as he was familiarly called, was one of the early judges of Texas. In his court a lawyer by the name of Charlton started a point of law, and the court refused to admit the counsel's statement as sufficient proof.

"Your law, sir," said the judge; "give us the book and page, sir."

"This is my law, sir," said Charlton, pulling out a pistol, "and this, sir, is my book," drawing a bowie-knife, "and that is the page," pointing the pistol toward the court.

"Your law is not good, sir," said the unruffled judge; "the proper authority is *Colt on Revolvers*," and he brought a six-shooter instantly to bear on the head of the counsel, who *dodged* the point of the argument and turned to the jury.

On another occasion this same judge concluded the trial of a man for murder by sentencing him to be hung that very day. A petition was immediately signed by the bar, jury, and people, praying that longer time might be granted the poor prisoner.

The judge replied to the petition "that the man had been found guilty, the jail was very unsafe, and besides, it was so very uncomfortable that he did not think any man ought to be required to stay in it any longer than was necessary."

The man was hung!

TEST OF INTELLIGENCE IN WESTERN WITNESSES AND LAWYERS.

"William, look up. Tell us, William, who made you. Do you know?"

William, who was considered a fool, screwed up his face, and looked thoughtful and somewhat bewildered, slowly answered,

"Moses, I sposes."

"That will do," said Counselor Gray, addressing the court; "the witness says he supposes Moses made him. That certainly is an intelligent answer—more than I supposed him capable of giving, for it shows that he has some faint idea of Scripture; but I must submit that it is not sufficient to entitle him to be sworn in as a witness capable of giving evidence."

"Mr. Judge," said the opposing lawyer, "may I ax the counsel a question?"

"Certainly," said the judge.

"Wal, then, Mr. Gray, who d'ye spose made you?"

"Aaron, I spose," said Counselor Gray, imitating the witness.

After the mirth had somewhat subsided, the questioner drawled out,

"We do read in the good book that Aaron once made a calf, but who'd a thought the darned critter had got in here?"

The judge ordered the man to be sworn.

DRY HUMOR OF A MISSISSIPPI LAWYER.

The following incident happened some years ago in the Federal Court at Jackson, Mississippi:

Judge T—— was celebrated for his dry and caustic humor. He was the softest talking man in the world, and the meekest in appearance, but he had the courage and the voice of a lion. On the trial of a case before Judges M'K—— and G——, Judge T—— was the plaintiff's counsel. The suit was brought on a note for one thousand dollars, to which an offset of three hundred dollars for the value of a horse was pleaded. The jury allowed the offset. When the verdict was read, Judge T—— arose, and in his fullest, softest manner, addressed the court as follows:

"May it please your honors, I gave the plaintiff a receipt for a note of one thousand dollars, and he expected me to obtain a judgment for that amount and the interest, and I apprehend that when my client comes to settle with me I may have difficulty with him."

Judge M'K——. "The verdict will protect you from liability."

T——. "But, if your honors please, the plaintiff said nothing to me about a horse being in this case; and as he is a very honest though strict man, he must have forgotten about the horse—or there may be some mistake about it. I wish something to appear on the record to show how it happened that a verdict could be rendered for a less amount than the demand of the plaintiff."

Judge. "The court can see no farther action which it can take in the premises, but allows counsel to make any suggestion which may occur to him."

T——. "I humbly and sincerely thank your honor, and will suggest that Mr. George W. M——, the clerk of this court, is very skillful in the use of his pen and pencil, and eminently skillful in drawing the pictures of horses and other animals, and I request the court to direct said M—— to draw the picture of a horse as near like the one described by the witnesses as he can, and attach the same to the declaration in this suit, where it will stand as a perpetual memorial of this transaction, and will remind the plaintiff of that part of it which he seems to have overlooked or forgotten."

BLACKSTONE IN THE SHADE.

A young lawyer in Arkansas was arguing a case before a judge whose self-conceit was in inverse proportion to his knowledge of the law. The counsel offered to quote Blackstone, and proceeded to read from him, when the court ordered him to desist, adding, "It is presumed, sir, that this court knows the law, and it will not be dictated to with impunity. If such an infringment be made again on the dignity of this court, it will immediately order the offender to jail."

The lawyer quietly replied,

"If it please your honor, I was just reading this to show what a great fool Blackstone was."

MAKING THINGS EQUAL.

Judge Dooly, of Georgia, was a man of undoubted bravery as well as waggery. Once on a time he had the misfortune to offend Judge White, who wore one cork leg, and challenged Judge Dooly to mortal combat.

The two judges met on the field at the hour appointed, but Dooly was alone. White sent to ask where his second was. To this Judge Dooly replied, "He has gone to the woods for a bit of a hollow tree to put one of my legs in, that we may be even."

The answer was too much for his opponent; he turned on the only heel he had, and left the field.

JUSTICE IN THE WEST.

The following, told by a member of the Western Bar, is designed to show how they suffer from the combined miseries of an elective judiciary, and the payment of the officers thereof by the fees which they make. He says,

"We have a court in this county called the 'Law Commissioners;' it is a Court of Record, the judge appointing his own clerk, and receiving certain fees prescribed by statute. Of course, the larger business done the more fees made. Among other powers exercised by this court is that of naturalizing foreigners. The judge is in the habit of stopping the trial of causes, and, indeed, any other business of the court, in order to make a citizen, and thereby earn a fee. A short time since, while one of our lawyers was arguing a cause, he was stopped by the judge, who wished to grant the final paper of naturalization. The counsel immediately addressed the court as follows: 'Judge, you will only make a dollar by naturalizing that man, and I will give you a dollar and a quarter if you postpone him and listen to me.' Whereupon the judge smiled very amiably, and did as he was desired."

AN AGGRAVATED OFFENSE.

Old Judge Cole, of Texas, was characterized by his attachment to that seductive beverage called "peach and honey," and by his hatred of whisky and whisky-drinkers. While holding a court at Austin, two men were brought up on a charge of a drunken affray. It was a plain case; the row had occurred in the public street, in open day, and there were fifty witnesses to the whole transaction. So the two delinquents pleaded guilty, by the advice of their counsel, and threw themselves on the mercy of the court. They were then brought up for sentence separately.

"You are guilty of an affray," growled the judge.

"Yes, your honor," whined the offender, thoroughly frightened.

"Drunk, I suppose," grunted the judge.

"Yes, your honor," murmured the prisoner, with some faint hope that having been drunk would mitigate the punishment.

"Drunk on rye whisky, too, I'll warrant," roared the judge, in a voice of thunder.

"Yes, your honor, drunk on rye whisky."

"Mr. Clerk, record a fine of fifty dollars against this man," cried the judge, "and send him to jail for sixty days. I shall fine the next one who is guilty under such aggravating circumstances a hundred dollars, and send him to jail for six months."

This was poor comfort for the unfortunate fellow who was waiting his turn, and now came forward with fear and trembling. As he passed along by his lawyer, that thoughtful gentleman whispered in his ear,

"When the judge asks you what you got drunk on, tell him on *peach and honey!*"

He took his stand.

"You, too, are up here for an affray," growled the old judge, gnashing his teeth as if he would like to bite the culprit at the bar.

"Yes, your honor."

"Drunk, too, I suppose?"

"Yes, your honor — sorry to say it — drunk — very drunk."

"Drunk on rye whisky, too, I suppose?"

"Oh no, your honor; I never drink whisky; I got drunk on peach and honey."

The judge's features relaxed in an instant. Leaning forward and raising his spectacles, he contemplated the offender with interest, and then, with something like tenderness, said,

"Ah! sir; peach and honey, eh! That's a gentlemanly drink, sir. The court sympathizes with you, sir, and does not regard your offense as *very serious.* Mr. Clerk," he continued, in a softening tone, "enter a fine of one dollar against this gentleman, and discharge him on payment of costs."

WHAT AN OATH OF ALLEGIANCE IS.

A young man came from South Carolina and placed himself under the tuition of Judge J——, of Marietta, Georgia, expecting to be admitted in a few months to all the rights and privileges of a full-fledged attorney at law. Occasionally he would call on his neighbor who occupied the adjoining office, and expatiate freely on his progress in Blackstone, and his expectations at the approaching examination. Upon one of these occasions his friend proposed to examine him a little (though no lawyer) by asking a few questions which might suggest themselves to his mind in looking over the book he had been reading. Accordingly his friend took the book, and, turning back a few pages, asked the young man,

"Can you tell me what an oath of allegiance is?"

"An oath of allegiance?" said he; "yes, I reckon"—running his finger through his hair and trying to look very wise—"an oath of *allegiance* is—when a man takes an oath and swears what he *alleges* is true!"

His friend did not proceed any farther with the examination, but advised the would-be lawyer to drop Blackstone and take up Webster for a while.

During the progress of the late rebellion, Southern law-students probably arrived at more definite conceptions of the "oath of allegiance" than when the hero of this anecdote gave his luminous definition.

A PERPLEXING CASE.

Hon. James H. Knowlton, one of our most eminent Western advocates, met with the following perplexing adventure in his early practice in Wisconsin:

A stranger came into his office and abruptly informed him that his wife had deserted him, and wished to have her replevined at once. Knowlton told him that remedy would not meet his case exactly, and went on to inform him that, if he would be patient until the desertion had continued one year, he could obtain a divorce. The stranger said that he did not know as he wanted a divorce; what he most feared was that his wife would run him in debt all over the country.

"In that case," said Knowlton, "you had better post her."

What his client understood him by posting remains a mystery to this day. He said, in a meditative way, that he didn't know where she had gone, and besides, that she was fully as strong as he was, and he didn't believe he could post her, even if he knew where to find her.

Knowlton hastened to inform him that by posting his wife he meant putting a notice in the newspaper, saying, "Whereas, my wife Helen has left my bed and board without any just—"

"But that ain't true," interrupted the client, "that ain't true. She didn't leave my bed—she took it away with her."

LEGISLATIVE INTELLECTS.

One of the State Legislatures has won a distinction for an average of intellectual weakness which will render it memorable for many years to come.

"I rise for information," said one of the dullest of the members.

"I am very glad to hear it," said one who was leaning over the bar, "for no man wants it more than yourself."

Another member rose to speak on the bill to abolish capital punishment, and commenced by saying,

"Mr. Speaker, the generality of mankind in general are disposed to exercise oppression on the generality of mankind in general."

"You had better stop," said one who was sitting near enough to pull him by the coat-tail, "you had better stop; you are coming out of the same hole you went in at."

MISTAKEN IDENTITY.

A distinguished gentleman, ex-governor of an Atlantic state, was employed for the defense on a trial for murder. The governor found it necessary, in the course of his speech, to comment with some severity on the testimony of a witness for the prosecution. In the midst of a most searching and logical sentence, wherein he was convincing the jury that the witness had sworn to more than the truth, he was interrupted by a juryman—a tall, lank fellow, evidently from the backwoods—who, rising, addressed the governor:

"See here, Mr. Lawyer, I don't want you to go on that way abusing me; I won't stand it; I'll break up the court if you do; I didn't come here to be abused."

"My dear sir," replied the governor, in his politest manner, "I was alluding to the witness, not to you; my remarks were not intended to apply to any of the jurors."

"Well, then," said the juror, "just quit a *pint*ing your finger at me when you talk that way." His honor smiled audibly, for the first time in his life, as he sat on the bench.

AN UNHEALTHY SOIL.

Colonel Aaron Finch was a distinguished Democratic politician in Indiana. He had some thoughts of emigrating to Arkansas, and, meeting a gentleman from that part of the country, asked him what were the inducements to remove to that state. Particularly he inquired about the soil. The gentleman informed him that the land was good, but in some parts very sandy. Colonel Finch then asked about the politics of Arkansas, and the prospects of a stranger getting ahead.

"Very good," was the reply. "The Democratic party is strongly in the majority, but, to succeed, a man must load himself down with revolvers and bowie-knives, and fight his way through."

"Oh, well," said the colonel, "on the whole, from what you say, I think Arkansas wouldn't suit me. I rather think the soil is a *little too sandy!*"

A QUACK WITNESS.

Hon. David Paul Brown, of the Philadelphia bar, relates the following good story in a late work of his:

A quack had instituted a suit for medical services against one of his neighbors, and the suit being brought for the use of another, became himself the witness. A Mr. Williams, who was employed to defend the suit, and to expose the quackery and worthlessness of the services rendered, subjected the doctor to the following cross-examination:

"Did you treat the patient according to the most approved rules of surgery?" asked the counsel.

"By all means—certainly I did," replied the witness.

"Did you decapitate him?" inquired the counsel.

"Undoubtedly I did; that was a matter of course," answered the doctor's witness.

"Did you perform the Cæsarean operation upon him?" asked the counsel.

"Why, of course," answered the witness; "his condition required it, and it was attended with very great success."

"Did you, then," still farther queried the counsel, "subject his person to autopsy?"

"Certainly," replied the witness; "that was the very last remedy I adopted."

"Well, then, doctor," said the counsel, "as you first cut off the defendant's head, then dissected him, and he still survives it, I have no more to ask; and if your claim will survive it, quackery deserves to be immortal."

THE GOOSE A NATIONAL BIRD.

While Judge Thacher was a member of the House of Representatives of the United States, a bill was reported on the subject of American coins, which made provision that one side of them should bear the impression of an *eagle*. Mr. Thacher moved an amendment that the word *eagle* should be stricken out wherever it occurred in the bill, and the word *goose* be substituted. He rose to support the amendment, and with great gravity stated that the eagle was an emblem of royalty, and had always been so considered.

"It is a royal bird, Mr. Speaker, and the idea that it should be impressed upon our coinage is inexpressibly shocking to my republican feelings. Sir, it would be grossly inconsistent with our national character. But the goose, sir, is a republican bird—the fit emblem of republicanism. Ever since I became acquainted with classic lore, sir, I have remembered, with ever new satisfaction, that it was the cackling of a flock of these republicans which saved the greatest city in the world, and always since I have felt disposed to greet every goose I have seen as a brother republican. These reasons, sir, upon which I could enlarge very much, are, in my view, conclusive in favor of the amendment proposed, and I hope our dollars will bear the impression of a goose, and the goslings may be put on the ten-cent pieces."

When the amendment was proposed, every countenance was relaxed into a smile. As Mr. Thacher proceeded to state his reasons, there was a universal peal of laughter loud and long. Unhappily, the member who reported the bill—and who must certainly have been a goose himself—thought that all the laugh was *at* him. The next day he sent a friend to Mr. Thacher with a challenge. When the message was delivered, and the reason of it told, Mr. Thacher replied,

"Tell him I won't fight."

"But, Mr. Thacher, what will the world say? They may call you a coward."

"A coward!" said Mr. Thacher; "why, so I am, as the world goes, and he knows that very well, or he would never have challenged me. Tell him that I have a wife and children who have a deep interest in my life, and I can not put it to such danger without their consent. I will write to them, and if they give their permission I will accept his challenge. But no," he added, "you need not say that. Tell him to mark out a figure of my size on some wall, and then go off to the honorable distance and fire at it; if he hits within the mark, I will acknowledge that he would have hit me had I been there."

The gentleman laughed, returned to the challenger, and advised him to let Mr. Thacher alone, for he believed that if they should fight, and Thacher were killed, he would, in some way or other, contrive to get a laugh upon his opponent that he would never get over. The point of honor was abandoned.

NOT A QUACK JUDGE.

During a protracted trial, which elicited a good deal of feeling, Mr. R——, one of the counsel engaged (somewhat intoxicated), in response to an ungenerous allusion of the "opposite counsel" to his condition, caught up an inkstand and hurled it at the opposer's head. The court immediately committed the belligerent Blackstone for a contempt, and imposed a fine of twenty-five dollars.

Mr. R—— (in explanation). "If the court please, I confess myself guilty of a gross breach of decorum, but I hope—"

The Judge (interrupting). "Thus far, sir, the court agrees with you cheerfully; but your remorse comes too late, for you stand convicted of a contempt of court."

Mr. R—— (meekly). "I hope the court will spare me the disgrace of a fine, for I was under the influence of—"

The Judge (impetuously). "Sit down, sir; you are already fined."

Mr. R—— (persistingly). "I was, as I said, under the influence of strong drink, and I think that circum—"

The Judge (indignantly). "Sit *down*, sir. Does the counsel consider this court a mere *quack doctor* who does not know what ails a lawyer without *seeing his tongue?*"

The convulsion of laughter which followed convinced the judge that he had been indulging in repartee.

A MATTER-OF-FACT ARGUMENT.

One of the most amusing scenes in the Legislature of Pennsylvania occurred on a motion to remove the capital of the state from Harrisburg to Philadelphia. A matter-of-fact member from the rural districts, who had heard of the great facility with which brick houses are moved from one part of a city to another, and who had not the least idea that any thing but moving the State-house was in contemplation, rose and said,

"Mr. Speaker, I have no objection to the motion, but I don't see how on airth you are going to git it over the river."

A LEGISLATIVE WIT.

One of the members of the Lower House of the Legislature of the State of New York rejoiced in the name of Bloss. He had the honor of representing the County of Monroe, and, if his sagacity as a legislator did not win for him the respect of his associates, his eccentricities often ministered to their entertainment. Many a good story is told of the shrewd replies with which Mr. Bloss electrified the House, but we recall nothing better than his thrust into the member from one of our own up-town wards, an inflated fellow, whose windy speeches at the primary meetings and the oyster-cellars had won for him a reputation as an orator, and procured his election to the Assembly, where he was bound to be distinguished as the most eloquent man in Albany. So he was in his own opinion, and he lost no opportunity to submit his oratorical powers to public observation. Literally, he sought to ventilate every subject that came before the House. One day, in the midst of a windy harangue, that had become intolerable for its length and emptiness, he stopped to take a drink of water. Bloss sprang to his feet and cried,

"Mr. Speaker, I call the gentleman from New York to order!"

The whole Assembly was startled and stilled; the member from New York stood aghast, with the glass in his hand, while the Speaker said,

"The gentleman from Monroe will please to state his point of order."

To which Mr. Bloss, with great gravity, replied,

"I submit, sir, that it is not in order for a *wind*-mill to go by *water!*"

It was a shot between wind and water. The ventose orator was confounded, and put himself and his glass down together.

A DISTINCTION WITH A DIFFERENCE.

If General Barnes was not possessed of very superior legal attainments, yet, as a lawyer, he had the happy faculty of impressing his clients that justice and law were with them in all cases. We have a handsome illustration of this talent of the general:

A rough countryman walked into the office of General Barnes one day, and began his application,

"General Barnes, I have come to get your advice in a case that is giving me some trouble."

"Well, what is the matter?"

"Suppose now," said the client, "that a man had a fine spring of water on his land, and his neighbor living below him were to build a dam across a creek running through both their farms, and it was to back the water up into the other man's spring, what ought to be done?"

"Sue him, sir, sue him, by all means," said the general,

who always became excited in proportion to the aggravation of his client's wrongs. "You can recover heavy damages, sir. It is a most flagrant injury he has done you, sir, and the law will make him pay well for it, sir. Just give me the case, and I'll bring the money from him; and if he hasn't a good deal of property, it will break him up, sir."

"But stop, general," cried the terrified applicant for legal advice, "it's me that built the dam, and it's neighbor Jones that owns the spring, and *he's* threatening to sue *me!*"

The keen lawyer hesitated but a moment before he tacked ship and kept on,

"Ah! Well, sir, you say you built a dam across that creek. What sort of a dam was that, sir?"

"It was a mill-dam."

"A mill-dam for grinding grain, was it?"

"Yes, it was just that."

"And it is a good neighborhood mill, is it?"

"So it is, sir; you may well say so."

"And all your neighbors bring their grain there to be ground, do they?"

"Yes, sir, all but Jones."

"Then it's a great public convenience, is it not?"

"To be sure it is. I would not have built it but for that. It's so far to any other mill, sir."

"And now," said the old lawyer, "you tell me that this man Jones is complaining just because the water from your dam happens to back up into his little spring, and he is threatening to sue you. Well, all I have to say is, let him sue, and he'll rue the day he ever thought of it, as sure as my name is Barnes."

A WESTERN JUDGE'S IDEA OF DOING HIS DUTY.

Judge D—— was fond of card-playing, and occasionally indulged in the amusement. During the period he occupied a seat on the bench the Legislature of Georgia passed very stringent laws to prevent gambling, and made it imperative on the judges to charge the grand juries, at the opening of each session of the court, to present all who were known as gamblers, etc. The judge had conformed to the requirements of the law, but none were presented, and gambling seemed to flourish as it ever had. On an occasion when the judge was on his circuit, and after his usual charge to the grand jury, and, as usual, no notice taken of the charge, Judge D—— ascertained there was a faro-bank in successful operation in the very precincts of the court. The judge thought he would indulge his propensity for play, and visited the bank. He played, and was very successful, as was his wont; he won all the money, and broke up the establishment. After he had pocketed his winnings and was about retiring, he perceived several of the grand jury in the room, who had likewise been engaged in the game. Judge D—— observed to them,

Gentlemen of the grand jury, the law requires me to do all in my power to suppress the vice of gambling. I have charged the grand juries upon the subject time after time without any good effect. It was time for me to act, and see if I could not enforce the law. I have done so; and the most effectual way of doing it is to break the bank, which I have done to-night. I do not think these fellows will trouble the public for some time to come, and the law in me is vindicated. Gentlemen, I bid you good-night."

FALSE SPELLING IN PROPER NAMES.

Many years ago, when Florida was still a Territory, justice was administered there by one Judge Douglas, more noted for his claiming descent from the great Scot than for his judicial ability. On one occasion, when holding court at Tallahassee, a man by the name of Whiteman was arraigned for horse-stealing. Mr. Wescott, afterward United States senator, counsel for the prisoner, moved for the discharge of his client on account of the false spelling of Whiteman's name in the indictment. The judge overruled the motion, remarking that general reputation as to a man's name is all that is necessary in an indictment for a criminal offense, and that the addition or omission of a letter makes no difference.

"For instance," illustrated the judge, "if you were arraigned before this court, Mr. Wescott, for murder, do you suppose because your name might happen to be spelled Waistcot, or Waistcoat, or Westcoot, instead of Wescott, you would escape punishment? No, sir; you should be hung, sir—you should be hung, sir!"

This was an illustration but little relished by Wescott, who, in reply, admitted that, for all he knew, *Whit*man, who was here indicted, might have stolen the horse, as charged in the indictment, but it was unfair, he thought, to make his innocent client, *White*man, suffer for *Whit*man's offense.

"As for the right of the community to make names by which men are to be known in law, or to change the orthography of a name, it can not be maintained," said Wescott. "For instance, your honor's name is Douglas, and I believe you are very careful about the orthography—D-o-u-g-l-*a-s;* yet, if the right of the community to alter names or their orthography be granted, I believe nine tenths of the population of this Territory would come into court and swear that your honor's name should be spelled —D-o-u-g-l-*ass*."

"Mr. Clerk," roared the irate judge, "enter a fine of fifty dollars against Mr. Wescott for contempt of court!"

A WESTERN JUDGE'S CHARGE.

The following is a charge given to a grand jury by a Western judge. He was dwelling upon the offenses in the penal code to which the attention of the jury should be directed, and, after dwelling on the crime of perjury, he proceeded, in the next place, to say, "Then, gentlemen, thar's subornation of perjury, which is likewise forbid by the law, and which I reckon is one of the meanest crimes that men get to do fur money. It's when a feller's too smart or too scary to swar to a lie hisself, and so gits another man to do it fur him—one of yer mean, dirty, snivelin', little-minded fellers! Why, a whole regiment of sich souls could hold a jubilee in the middle of a mustard-seed, and never hear of one another!"

ADJOURNING COURT TO SEE THE ELEPHANT.

During a session of the Circuit Court at ——, Kentucky, Judge M—— presiding, an important case, involving much money and interest, was called for trial. An eminent attorney conducting the defense in the case was not ready for trial, and having no legal excuse for delay, suggested to the court that his client and witnesses had gone to see an elephant swim the river. The judge remarked that he knew a large circus company was to perform in town that day, and asked if they intended to make their elephant swim the river. Having received an affirmative answer, the judge said he did not blame witnesses for leaving court to see a sight of such uncommon interest, and he did not intend to let the opportunity slip to see it himself. Whereupon he ordered the sheriff to adjourn the court until the next morning, in order that every person might see the elephant swim the river. The attorney, in the mean time, applied himself to hunting up his witnesses, and next morning appeared ready for trial. The judge waited upon the river-bank for hours, smoking his pipe, but no crowd collected, and no elephant appeared!

The judge was said to be so cautious in dealing rigid justice that he often took the will of the house upon knotty cases, and entered judgment by a vote of majority. Two attorneys, Lindsay and Harlan, had plead a cause before him, and a judgment was given in favor of the latter's client, when Lindsay remonstrated, to the judge's surprise, who silenced him by saying that he had given two decisions in his favor that day, and only one to Harlan—*that he was quite too hard to satisfy.*

At a term of the Circuit Court held for Grant County, at Williamstown, Kentucky, Judge M—— presiding, the case of a young man who had been indicted for grand larceny was called for trial. The attorney and witnesses for the Commonwealth were ready, and the prisoner was ordered to be brought into court. As soon as the prisoner entered the room the judge fixed his eyes upon him, and regarding him for some time very intently, then turned to the crowded throng, and addressed them as follows:

"Gentlemen, I do not believe that any man who dresses so decently, and looks as handsomely as this man does, could ever be guilty of stealing. He looks like an honest man; and, notwithstanding this 'indictment,' I believe he is one. All of you who are in favor of his going quits hold up your hands!"

The hands having been shown, the judge turned to the

prisoner, and remarked, "There, go now; you are unanimously discharged!"

ELECTIONEERING TACTICS.

It has been the custom, time out of mind, for opposing candidates for office in the Western States to canvass their district in company, and to discuss together their issues before the people. In the rich regions the candidates discuss principles; but in the poorer regions, among the more ignorant mountaineers, they take other means of convincing or persuading the people. On one occasion two very distinguished lawyers as opposing candidates offered themselves for Congress from the same district in Kentucky—W. W. Southgate, Whig, and John W. Tibbatts, Democrat. Of course they canvassed together. Both were talented, accomplished, and witty, and both knew well how to please the people. Personally they were friends and relatives. In the intelligent districts they battled like intellectual giants; in the poor regions they fired wit at each other, and made the people laugh. In one of these places they had been peculiarly happy in their remarks, and the people greatly enjoyed it. When they left sentiment was about equally divided, and the even cry of "Hurrah, Southgate!" "Hurrah, Tibbatts!" was shouted from the harmonious throats of even parties. Both candidates mounted their horses, and left together for the next appointment; but the people, determined to have a good time, remained to finish the enjoyment with a dance. As the opposing aspirants slowly left the scene of mirth, each longed for the finishing touch in moulding political sentiment, and each distrusted the other. When they had gone a mile, Tibbatts discovered that he had left something at the meeting, and asking Southgate to wait for him, rode back. Southgate, distrusting him, waited a while, and then also returned, where his suspicions were verified; for there he found Tibbatts playing the fiddle, and the people dancing. Sentiment was all on one side; it was all "Hurrah for Tibbatts!" He had carried the day. (Both played with equal skill, but Tibbatts only left-handed.) Southgate, mortified at his loss, determined to regain his position. Making his acknowledgments, he told the people that, with their leave, he would play a second to his brother Tibbatts's delightful music; and with a bow he played his best, and soon divided again the people. Throwing aside his violin, he remarked he hated fiddling, but by their leave he would join in the dance. In that he had no equal, and soon brought the unanimous "hurrahs" for Southgate. He had triumphed, and Tibbatts was vanquished.

Before filling their next appointment Southgate was taken sick, and Tibbatts, after waiting two weeks, continued his canvass alone. When recovered, Southgate followed. He found his rival had stolen the hearts of the people, and it was an uphill business with poor Southgate. In one place, like that mentioned, Tibbatts had pleased them so well—telling stories and jokes, and playing for them—that they utterly refused to hear Southgate. They said Tibbatts was the man for them, that they wanted no better, and Southgate had better go home; they wouldn't vote for him, etc. He told them that Tibbatts was a dear friend and relative of his, and a noble fellow—no better man was to be found (Southgate seems like an honest fellow, said they; let us hear him). "And, fellow-citizens," said Southgate, "if I can't go to Congress without abusing my dear friend Tibbatts, I'll stay at home forever." (Hurrah for Southgate! Good! He ought to go to Congress too.) "Why, fellow-citizens! he is the most talented man in Kentucky, and for accomplishments he hasn't his equal in the world!" (We know; we heard him; he played for us. Hurrah for Tibbatts!) "But here, my friends, is one thing I can not approve of in my dear brother: he plays better left-handed than most musicians with their right; but if you only heard him right-handed, he would bend the trees with his sweet tones. What I blame in him is, that when he is among nice people whom he likes he plays right-handed; but when he is among ignorant people for whom he has no regard, whom he thinks jackasses, he says any thing is good enough for them, and so he plays for them left-handed!" (What! Why, he played left-handed here! Does he mean to insinuate we are ignorant jackasses? D—n Tibbatts; away with him! Southgate is my man! Hurrah for Southgate, etc.) When the election came Tibbatts got but sixteen votes in that precinct.

SENTENCED TO THE LEGISLATURE.

A few years since one Lindsey was arraigned before one of the Illinois circuit courts, Judge Davis presiding, to answer an indictment for highway robbery, to which charge, there being conclusive testimony against him, he plead "Guilty." The crime was a very bold and atrocious act, denoting great skill in that kind of "rough gambling," as well as a very abandoned and wicked heart. At the close of the term Lindsey was brought up to receive his sentence, when Judge Davis, who is a great admirer of honest industry, as well as an inordinate hater of such "laripins" as Lindsey, who subsist by thieving, proceeded to pass the sentence of the law upon him. His honor commenced by reminding the prisoner that he was yet a young man, possessed with a more than ordinary share of natural endowments, sufficient, if well applied, to place him in the foremost ranks of honorable society. He next informed him that, by his own plea, he was guilty of robbing—in open day, and almost in the presence of the whole community—an old and helpless man of his hard-earned money—a crime recognized by the law of the land as of the most abandoned and wicked character. In rehearsing this scathing prelude to the sentence of the law, the judge, as is usual in such cases, got himself very much warmed up, so that when he came to close his remarks with the sentence, he found our state institutions somewhat mixed up in his mind, for, said he,

"Lindsey, I shall sentence you to *seven years in the Illinois Legislature!*"

"The penitentiary, your honor," suggested the prosecuting attorney, who was standing by.

The judge accepted the correction of the prosecutor, muttering at the same time something about the "slight difference" that existed. A titter ran around the bar, when the matter was dropped for the time; but Judge Davis frequently hears of his accommodating sentence upon Lindsey.

ONE MAN PLAINTIFF, WITNESS, LAWYER, AND JUDGE.

A certain nameless city in the West had an eccentric Scotch mayor, who earnestly desired to further public interests, but chose a way peculiarly his own. Among other ordinances passed at his instance was one which provided that the mayor might bring an action in his own name, and recover damages for any breach of the laws of the town. At the same time was passed an ordinance making it penal to tear up the sidewalks or pavements and to dig holes in the streets. By law the mayor was given the same power in actions, criminal and civil, as a justice of the peace, and it was of course contemplated that if the mayor sued in his own name he would bring his suit, not in his own court, but before a justice of the peace. But one John Peters having, in violation of the town ordinance, dug a hole in the street, the mayor proceeded to punish him, and, thinking it safer, brought the suit in his own name, in his own mayor's court. The mayor also proceeded to view the premises, and satisfy himself of the facts. When the day of trial came, quite a crowd gathered, for it was doubted whether even the mayor could properly bring an action in his own name as plaintiff, and try the cause himself. When the hour of trial came, however, the mayor, nothing abashed, took his seat, and the defendant appeared in due form. The case was called for trial, and the defendant denied the charge. Thereupon the mayor arose with great dignity, and stated, as a witness, in the presence of the crowd, the facts, and proved the defendant's guilt, and estimating the public damages at ten dollars. The mayor then proceeded, and, as a lawyer, argued the case to the crowd, and expatiated upon the impropriety of allowing such an offense to go unpunished. He then took his seat with much decorum, and, as a judge, entered up a judgment in his own form against the transgressing defendant for the ten dollars damages which he had previously estimated as a witness. This is the only instance on record where the same man was plaintiff, witness, lawyer, and judge.

A QUEER CASE OF CONFLICTING AUTHORITY.

The "free and easy" relations of bench and bar are set forth by the following incident, which actually occurred in a Western town:

Judge Nelson was holding court; there was a case being tried wherein T. R. More, Esq., who was mayor of the city as well as lawyer, was counsel for one of the parties. When the evidence was all in, and the respective counsel had argued the case to the jury, More supposed he "had a sure thing of it" for his client with the jury. But, to his astonishment, when the judge came to charge the jury, he charged square against his client. Whereupon More arose and said,

"Your honor, I object to your charge."

The judge turned indignantly and said,

"Sit down, Mr. More!"

More responded, "I sha'n't do it, sir!"

The judge then turned to the sheriff and said,

"Mr. Sheriff, arrest Mr. More for contempt of court!"

Mr. More retorted by saying, "Mr. Sheriff, *as mayor of this city*, I command you to stay where you are!" and, turning to the judge, he continued, "Judge, if you don't behave yourself and keep quiet, I will have you arrested!"

At this stage of the proceedings the judge ordered the sheriff to adjourn court till two o'clock P.M., and at the opening of court in the afternoon the case went to the jury without any farther charge.

AN IMPUDENT ATTORNEY.

There once resided in the county of L——, in Eastern Mississippi, a young lawyer, whom we will designate as B—— H——, who was remarkable for nothing except his insolence to the court and his diminutiveness in size, being just five feet and one inch. At a recent term of the Circuit Court for said county, Judge W—— presiding, the court, for some discourtesy on the part of B—— H——, imposed a fine of ten dollars on him, which had been made the judgment of the court, but remained unpaid; the judge, proceeding with the business of the term, called the next case in its order—John C. Patterson *vs.* Robert Blakeney, E. and C. for plaintiff, and "W." for defense.

Judge W——. "You perceive, gentlemen, that I was

counsel for the defendant before I was elected to the office of judge, and am therefore incompetent to preside in this trial. The cause must be continued unless the parties can agree to try it before some member of the bar, to be selected by themselves." (The statute authorized parties to appoint a special judge to try cases where the judge presiding is interested.)

After a short consultation, E——, one of the counsel for plaintiff, addressed the court: "If your honor pleases, the parties have agreed to call B—— H—— to the bench, to preside on the trial of this cause."

Judge W——. "Very well."

He retired from the bench, and B—— H—— took the seat with an air of dignity which could find no parallel in the history of jurisprudence.

B—— H—— (presiding). "Mr. Sheriff, let us have order in court. *Mr. Clerk, remit that fine that Judge W—— imposed on me this morning!*"

The clerk, believing it to be his duty to obey all orders from the bench, promptly entered the order setting the judgment for the fine aside, greatly to the amusement of the bar and the discomfiture of Judge W——. The joke was so good that Judge W—— let the last order remain undisturbed.

A WESTERN BULL.

Mr. W——, an attorney in one of the central counties of Pennsylvania, many years ago, when that part of the state was "backwoods," was a genuine Irishman, possessed of little learning, professional, scientific, or literary, and always went at business in a manner peculiarly his own. On one occasion, when the courts were in session in his county, a client of his had been induced to execute a judgment bond, by some trick or fraud, for which he had received no consideration; and, on reflection, having become alarmed, applied to Mr. W—— for advice. Mr. W—— examined the records, and finding that no judgment had been entered on the bond, suspected that the party to whom the bond had been given would not enter judgment until the court had risen and the judge gone to another county, when he might enter judgment, issue execution, make the money, and pocket it before the defendant could obtain any relief. Mr. W—— determined to head the villain, and accordingly prepared a motion, and an affidavit of the facts to support it, and coming into the court in a great hurry, said,

"May it plase yer honors, I jest want to move the co-r-r-rt to strike off a judgment that hasn't been entered at all, at all."

The judge pleasantly said, "I think you are a little too premature, Mr. W——. Hadn't you better wait till the judgment is entered?"

"And may it plase the co-r-r-rt," said W——, "I'm jest fearing they'll never enter it, and that's why I want it struck off!"

EFFECTIVE WESTERN ORATORY.

Some of the most effective, if not the most brilliant specimens of oratory in the world are to be found among the Western stump speakers. They excel particularly in a style not set down in the books, which may be termed "the inference." Can any thing be more to the purpose than the following passages?

"Gentlemen, I have heard of some persons who hold to the opinion that just at the precise moment one human being dies another is born, and that the just-departed soul enters and animates the new-born babe. Now I have made particular and extensive inquiries concerning my opponent there, and I find that for some time previous to his nativity *nobody died!*"

"Colonel Skinner, of Texas," who was going it on "a high figure" before the right kind of audience, thus settled a long-disputed fact in history and "elevated" himself.

"Feller-citizens," said he, with a very knowing look, "I was at the battle where Tecumsey was killed—*I* was! I commanded a regiment there—*I* did! I'm not gwine to say who *did* kill Tecumsey—*I* won't! But this much I will say, Tecumsey was killed by one of *my* pistols; and, gentlemen, I leave it to your knowledge of human nature if a man would be very *apt* to lend out his pistol on an occasion of that sort."

The following is in another, but not less effective style, nor of less frequent occurrence in the West. Judge Williams, of Iowa, like a good many other old Iowan politicians, "crossed the plains" and settled in Oregon. During the Territorial pupilage of Oregon he worthily served as chief justice. Just before the Territory was admitted as a state, at the last sitting of the court in Portland, after the last case on the docket had been disposed of, and there was nothing to do but adjourn, a loquacious member of the bar suggested to his associates that it was incumbent on them to return thanks to the court for its services, and professed himself willing to act as spokesman. Accordingly, just prior to adjournment, "he took the floor," and held it quite a while too, pouring out his adulations to the court until he had thought of every thing he could say, when, after suggesting to the court the fact that if it had any remarks to offer the Bar would be pleased to hear them, to the great relief of all he took his seat. The court arose to its feet, seized its hat in its hand, and with a comical smile said, in effect, "Gentlemen, the remarks which I am assured the Bar would be most pleased to hear would be an invitation to the nearest grocery to take a drink. Come on, boys!" The judge led the way, the profession followed close at his heels, and the loquacious lawyer scarcely recovered his equilibrium in time to bring up the rear.

A similar instance of "highfalutin" oratory not less handsomely rebuked is told as follows:

Judge G—— was a justice of the Supreme Court in the western part of the State of New York a short time before the rebellion broke out, but while the distant mutterings of its thunders could be heard. The judge was as renowned for his solid learning and patriotism as he was for a certain quaintness of expression, that ofttimes produced a laugh in court, to the great surprise of the judge. One day a feigned issue in a divorce suit, involving abandonment and desertion on the part of the guilty party, was on trial at the circuit, and the counsel for the plaintiff, who sometimes indulged in "spread eagles," was in the very climax of his rhapsody, when, turning for a moment from the jury, whom he was addressing, to the court, he said,

"What would your honor do, I would like to know, if a portion of the states of this glorious Union should 'shoot madly from their spheres,' and attempt the destruction of the nation?"

"What would I dew?" asked the judge; "why, I'd try and *shute* them back."

PUTTING AN EARTHQUAKE TO GOOD USE.

Counselor G——, a leading lawyer of a Southwestern city, and whose eloquence is only exceeded by a love of the ardent, was one day arguing a case before a jury, and was descanting in his most lofty strain upon the enormous frauds which were being committed upon his client by the other side, when suddenly the court-house was rocked like a cradle by the terrible throes of an earthquake. Every sound was hushed and every breath suspended, and as the fearful vibrations ceased every cheek was blanched and every body trembled. But the counselor, though livid as a corpse, was quick to gain his presence of mind, and the very air was made to ring again with his clear, loud voice as he cried, "Yes, gentlemen, the very earth trembles with the enormity of their frauds!" G—— got the verdict.

LEGAL DECISION FROM HEAVEN.

California furnishes, among its other curiosities, the most remarkable legal decision on record.

During a season of avalanches, the ranch of one Tom Rust slid down from the mountain-side and pretty nearly covered a ranch belonging to Dick Sides. Some of the boys in the town of Carson persuaded Sides to bring suit in a referee's court for the recovery of his ranch, which Mr. S. did, alleging that Rust now claimed the surface of the ground as his own, although he freely admitted that the ranch underneath it belonged to Sides, who, it grieved him to reflect, would probably never see his property again. The court-room was crowded. The judge-referee presided with a grave dignity in keeping with his lofty position; the sheriff guarded the sacred precinct of the court from disturbance and indecorum with exaggerated vigilance. The witnesses were examined, and all the evidence of any value went in favor of Sides. His counsel, General Bunker, made a ponderous speech of two hours in length; the opposing counsel replied, and the case went to the judge. He said:

"Gentlemen, I have listened with profound interest to the arguments of the counsel in this important case, and while I admit that the reasonings of the distinguished gentleman who appeared for the plaintiff were almost resistless, and that all the law and evidence adduced are in favor of his client, yet considerations of a more sacred and exalted nature than these compel me to decide for the defendant, and to decree that the property remain in his possession. The Almighty created the earth and all that is in it, and who shall presume to dictate to Him the disposition of His handiwork? If He saw that defendant's ranch was too high up on the hill, and chose, in His infinite wisdom, to move it down to a more eligible location, albeit to the detriment of the plaintiff and his ranch, it is meet that we bow in humble submission to His will, without inquiring into His motives or questioning His authority. My verdict therefore is, gentlemen, that the plaintiff Sides has lost his ranch by the dispensation of God."

The crowd of spectators, defying the sheriff, shook the house with laughter. Bunker asked to appeal the case. The great judge frowned upon him with severe dignity for a moment, and then replied solemnly that there was no appeal from the decision of the Lord.

AN ATTORNEY BY PRESUMPTION.

At the bar of one of the counties of Maine a person never admitted to practice had, by a sort of common consent, been permitted to do business as an attorney. He rejoiced in the sobriquet of Judge Bones. "Once on a time," Colonel H——, a splendid specimen of a man, and one of the best common lawyers in the state, made a motion for the disposition of a case. But Bones resisted the motion. Colonel H——, knowing that the disposition he desired was in accordance with the wishes of the parties, pressed the motion, and finally demanded the written authority of

Bones to appear in the case, and remarked that "it did not appear that he was an attorney of the court."

"The *presumption* is, your honor," replied Judge B——, "that I *am*, till the contrary appears."

Colonel H—— turned away, tearing off with his teeth a huge piece of paper, and muttered, in a voice audible all over the court-room, "It's the greatest piece of *presumption* I ever heard of, though!"

The joke was of course repeated, and it nettled Bones very much whenever he heard the word mentioned, and any thing said about "members of the bar" or "lawyers" he took in high dudgeon. Especially was this so when he was slightly "elevated" by practice at another bar. Soon after the occurrence above mentioned he was trying a case in a justice court with a lawyer named Wood. The latter, in his argument, stated that he would risk his reputation as a lawyer upon the correctness of a certain proposition. Judge Bones, who had been half snoozing, and was in a condition in which he heard double as well as saw double, caught the word "lawyer," and instantly fired up, taking it to be an invidious allusion to himself. With a look of intense scorn he commenced his reply, "May it please the court, the gentleman says he states the law as a lawyer. He a lawyer—*a lawyer!* Fling a handful of hops into Moosehead Lake, and call it *beer!*"

DRAWING ONE'S OWN INFERENCES AND JUDGMENT.

Squire Joshua Williams was the first justice of the peace at the county seat of Carroll County, Mississippi, when the Choctaw nation became an integral portion of the State of Mississippi, after the treaty of Dancing Rabbit Creek in 1833. He was a plain, blunt man, without education, who had squatted near the centre of the county, and was therefore elected a "justice," to settle the innumerable difficulties growing out of the location of roads, erection of mills, the establishment of ferries, etc. The county lines were scarcely defined before Mr. S——, a lawyer from Tennessee, and Mr. K——, a lawyer from Kentucky, settled at the courthouse, and were engaged in all the suits in this important court. The squire, without any pretension to learning, much less a knowledge of the law, generally rendered very prompt decisions from the bench. At intervals the records were made up by the assistance of some friend who could "read and write." A case of considerable consequence, which had involved much discussion between the lawyers, was concluded by the summing up facts by Mr. S——, in an ingenious and imposing manner, "*leaving the court to draw its own inferences.*" This was the *last say*, and the case seemed hopeless to Mr. K——, who sat near the squire, who hesitated for a moment, seemed confused, and, turning to Mr. K——, said, "As you are pert with a pen, will you be good enough to draw up the *inferences* in the case?" Mr. K—— reached to the docket and entered a judgment for *his* client, which was immediately signed by the squire, and the court was adjourned. The squire was not thereafter troubled to draw his "own *inferences.*"

A DECIDED COURT OF ERRORS.

In a small town in Northern Indiana, an attorney by the name of H—— was arguing a question before Judge C——, after the court had plainly intimated its view of the matter. H—— persisted in his remarks, and the judge, who was in a hurry at the time, said,

"The court has made up its mind on that subject; if you don't think it is right, you can take it up to the Court of Errors and have the decision reversed."

"If this is not a Court of Errors," was the reply, "I would like to know where you would find it!"

CHARACTERISTIC WESTERN DECLARATION AND PLEA.

Some years since, previous to the adoption of the Code in Kentucky, the following declaration and plea were filed in the Whitely Circuit Court. The plaintiff, Goins, didn't like it to go out that any man could abuse him so badly as the plea set up that the defendants had, and dismissed his suit:

State of Kentucky. Whitely Circuit Court. } Canada Goins, plaintiff, by his attorney, complains of Thomas R. Harmon and Cornelius Finlay, defendants, of a plea of trespass *vi et armis*.

For that the said defendants, on the day of , 18—, at the state and circuit aforesaid, with force and arms, assaulted the said plaintiff (to wit), and then and there seized and laid hold of the plaintiff, and with great force and violence pulled, shook, and dragged about the said plaintiff, and gave and struck the said plaintiff a great many violent blows and strokes on divers parts of his body, and then and there, with great force and violence, knocked, cast, and threw him, the said plaintiff, down and upon the ground, and then and there violently kicked the said plaintiff, and gave and struck him a great many other blows, and other wrongs did to the said plaintiff then and there did against the peace and dignity of the Commonwealth of Kentucky, and to the damage of the said plaintiff two thousand dollars —and therefore he brings his suit.

Thomas Harmon *vs.* Canada Goins. } And the defendant comes and acknowledges the force and injury complained of in plaintiff's declaration in said action sworn because he says that he did draw back his fist and hit plaintiff at the but of the ear, and knock him heels over head, and as he arose he gave him a tremendous kick, and turned him about three times over, and as the plaintiff arose the second time he arose a-running, and defendant after him, and as the plaintiff run he hallooed murder every jump for about two hundred yards, when defendant, being faster on foot than the plaintiff, caught him again, and did then and there cuff, flog, castigate, and whip the said plaintiff until he begged and plead with him, and said, in a pitiful and plaintive tone, Don't, Tom! don't Tom! and promised the defendant, if he would let him alone, he would always behave himself well, and love this defendant; and after the matter was all over he came to defendant in cool blood and agreed with defendant that if defendant would never whip him any more that he would not sue this defendant for the above thrashing, which defendant agreed to, and has not whipped him since, which agreement this defendant relies on as a bar to this action; and this, and no other, is the trespass complained of in the plaintiff's declaration, and this he is ready to verify.

TESTIMONY, NOT ARGUMENT, WANTED.

Soon after Judge H——, of Northwestern Indiana, commenced the practice of law, he was engaged in trying a small matter of accounts before a justice of the peace, another young lawyer being employed on the other side. There was not much to be said, it is true; and about the time they got through with the testimony, Judge H—— noticed the justice figuring on a piece of paper and writing in the docket. As soon as the last witness was through he got up to argue his side of the case. The court, who was of a thirsty temperament, got up, and as he left the bench, said coolly, "Young men, you can go on with your arguments;

I will be in pretty soon. The judgment is fifty dollars!" They didn't proceed.

SENSIBLE ADVICE.

The late J—— M—— was for many years the leader of the bar in New Hampshire, and one of the most estimable of men. Between Mr. M—— and Judge C—— a feeling of intimacy existed that seemed to justify in each a joke at the expense of the other. Among the cases to be tried in the court over which Judge C—— presided was one for theft. On being called, the prisoner, aware that the proof was too positive to admit of any doubt of conviction, and intending to plead guilty and throw himself upon the mercy of the court, appeared without counsel. In such cases it was customary for the judge to appoint counsel, always selecting from the younger members of the bar. Here was an opportunity too good to be lost for Judge C—— to wipe off at least one of the scores of jokes standing to his debit in his account with Mr. M——. So, quite deliberately, the judge appointed him to defend the prisoner. Mr. M—— thanked the judge for the compliment and promptly accepted the appointment, remarking that as the case was new to him he should like a few minutes' private conversation with his client. "Certainly," replied the judge, immediately directing the sheriff to conduct Mr. M—— and the prisoner to a private room. On leaving, the judge, with a peculiar smile which Mr. M—— well understood, expressed the hope that he would give his friend some good advice. Locking the door of the room to which the sheriff had conducted them, Mr. M—— asked the prisoner if he was guilty. "Guilty," was the frank reply. "Do you see the woods yonder?" "Yes." "Well, beyond them is a small brook, the dividing line between the two counties; once over that brook you are out of the jurisdiction of this court; and if you are as guilty as you say you are, I advise you to lose no time in passing that line." No sooner said than done: out of the open window he jumped, and run for dear life. The court, getting impatient, sent the sheriff for them. Returning without the prisoner, the judge asked Mr. M—— where he was. "May it please your honor," he replied, "as we were leaving this room for a private consultation, you kindly expressed the hope that I would give my friend the prisoner some good advice; and learning from him that he was guilty, and acting in accordance with your suggestion, I advised him to cut and run, and the last I saw of him he was streaking it for the adjoining county as though the very evil one was after him." The judge concluded that he had not made much progress in squaring accounts.

"DOING WELL" IN THE ILLINOIS SENSE.

There were few abler lawyers in the State of Illinois during the past quarter of a century than the late Judge Purple, of Peoria. He was the author of several important law-books, and by his entire devotion to his profession had attained a merited celebrity both as an advocate and a jurist.

Some years since, Judge P., when in the city of Washington, met with a gentleman from Boston, who, upon learning that the judge was from Illinois, made particular inquiry as to the success of a young sprig of the law, by the name of B——, who had emigrated "West" some five years before. "He is doing well," promptly replied the judge. "He *is;* well, I am glad to hear it—glad to hear it, indeed," continued his friend. "You think he has a good practice, do you, judge?" "Don't know any thing about his practice," replied Purple; "but he is doing well —succeeding finely." "Making money, then, is he?" persisted Boston. "I tell you I don't know any thing about his business," said Purple. "Well," said the Boston man, "you seem to think B—— is doing well, and yet you know nothing about his practice or business; what do you mean?" "I mean just this," said Purple; "that any man who practices law in Illinois five years and keeps out of the penitentiary is doing well, whether he has much practice or not!"

6.

Miscellaneous Legal Witticisms.

CHAPTER VI.

MISCELLANEOUS LEGAL EPIGRAMS, PUNS, AND POEMS.

DEFINITION OF A LAWYER.

In one of the old English comedies is introduced the character of a learned and jocose pedant, Sir Andrew All-realize, who is compiling a dictionary of the English tongue, for which he claims both learning and humor. He defines therein a lawyer to be "a man who lives by litigation, declaration, replication, consultation, cross-examination, botheration, damnation (of others), and who, on the day of trial, proposes arbitration, keeps his fee, and returns his brief.".

Ben Jonson, in his *Volpone, or the Fox*, with more wit, and perhaps not less truth, speaks of a lawyer as one with

> " So wise, so grave, of so perplexed a tongue,
> And loud withal, that would not wag, nor scarce
> Lie still without a fee."

Another poet, turning his attention to the law itself, has defined it as follows:

> "Law is like longitude, 'about,'
> Never completely yet found out,
> Though practiced notwithstanding.
> 'Tis like the Fatalist's strange creed,
> Which justifies a wicked deed
> While sternly reprimanding."

THE IDENTITY OF DUCKS.

At a term of the Court of Sessions a man was brought up by a farmer accused of stealing some ducks.

"How do you know they are your ducks?" asked the defendant's counsel.

"Oh! I should know them *any* where," replied the farmer; and he went on to describe their different peculiarities.

"Why," said the prisoner's counsel, "those ducks can't be such a rare breed; I have some very like them in my own yard."

"That's not unlikely, sir," replied the farmer; "they are not the *only* ducks I have had stolen lately."

"Call the *next* witness," quickly exclaimed the disconcerted lawyer.

A CUTE LAWYER.

A gentleman, dying, left all his estate to a monastery, on condition that on the return of his only son, who was then abroad, the worthy fathers should give him "whatever they should choose." When the son came home he went to the monastery, and received but a small share, the monks choosing to keep the greater part for themselves. A barrister to whom he applied, on mention of the case, advised him to sue the monastery, and promised to gain his cause. The gentleman followed his advice.

"The testator," said the ingenious barrister, "has left his son that share of the estate which the monks should choose; these are the express words of his will. Now it is plain what part they have chosen by what they keep for themselves. My client, then, stands upon the words of the will. 'Let me have,' says he, 'that part they have chosen, and I am satisfied,'" and he gained the suit.

SPEAKING LONGER THAN HE PLEASED.

A lawyer having wearied the court by a long and dull argument, the judge suggested the expediency of his bringing it to a close.

"I shall speak as long as I please," he replied, angrily.

"You have spoken longer than you pleased already," answered the judge.

GRAND JURISPRUDENCE.

The grand jury in the Criminal Court of Baltimore City had quite a dispute with Judge Bond, and a good deal of bickering among themselves. They were finally reminded by the judge that it was highly improper for them to publicly disclose what had transpired in their room, and requested them to retire. Whereupon a witty lawyer remarked, "The whole proceeding was what might be properly classed as a racy specimen of *grand jury's prudence*" (jurisprudence).

A QUICK-WITTED WITNESS.

A lawyer, who prided himself upon his skill in cross-examining a witness, had once an odd-looking genius upon whom to operate.

"You say, sir, that the prisoner is a thief?"

"Yes, sir, because she confessed it."

"And you also swear that she bound shoes for you subsequent to the confession?"

"I do, sir."

"Then," giving a sagacious look to the court, "are we to understand that you employ dishonest persons to work for you, even after their rascalities are known?"

"Of course; how else, pray, could I get assistance from a lawyer?"

The witness was peremptorily ordered to "stand down."

A LEGAL JOKE FOR THE REVENUE OFFICERS.

A plaintiff sued before a Wisconsin justice for damages caused by the bite of defendant's dog; and on the trial, being examined on his own behalf, under the statute, he was asked "how much he was damaged by the dog." Objection being made by defendant's counsel, the esquire, who was a Hibernian, said he would put the question himself, which he did thus:

"This is the question. What would ye tak to be bit by the same dog agin?"

Exemplary damages were recovered.

THE GRIEF-STRICKEN CRIER.

A judge did once his tipstaff call,
And say, "Sir, I desire
You go forthwith and search the hall,
And bring me in the crier."

"And search in vain, my lord, I may,"
The tipstaff gravely said;
"The crier can not cry to-day,
Because his wife is dead."

HIRSUTE WIT.

Two lawyers in a country court—one of whom had gray hair, and the other, though just as old a man as his learned friend, had hair which looked suspiciously black—had some altercation about a question of practice, in which the gentleman with the dark hair remarked to his opponent,

"A person at your time of life, sir," looking at the barrister's gray head, "ought to have long enough experience to know what is customary in such cases."

"Yes, sir," was the reply, "you may stare at my gray hair if you like. My hair will be gray as long as I live, and yours will be black as long as you dye."

A TIGHT CASE.

"Come here, my lad," said an attorney to a lad about nine years old. "A case is between the devil and the people; which do you think will be most likely to gain the action?" The boy replied,

"I guess it will be a tight squeeze: the people have the money, but the devil has the lawyers."

A GAME WITH COURT CARDS.

Several years ago the Circuit Court was in session at ——, Wisconsin, Judge —— presiding. A man was on trial for some violation of the law to suppress gambling. Mr. K—— was defending him. The witness upon the stand talked glibly of "*checking*," "*passing*," "*going blind*," etc. The defendant's counsel seemed to understand the terms without difficulty. The judge, who enjoyed a joke, said to him,

"Mr. K——, you seem to understand the witness; will you explain the terms used by him?" A scarcely suppressed laugh ran through the court-room. But K—— was equal to the emergency; he walked deliberately up to the judge's bench, and reaching out his hand in the most innocent manner in the world, answered,

"Certainly, sir, certainly, if your honor will be kind enough to lend me your *deck*."

LEGAL DEFINITIONS.

For pay, to prove an honest man's a thief,
For pay, to break the widow's heart with grief,
To stifle truth, for lies to gain belief—
That's a brief!

Ten thousand words, when ten would serve the need,
Ten thousand meanings, discord meant to breed,
Where none can understand, and few can read—
That's a deed!

JUSTICE IN NEW YORK.

The following witty epigram was written on a wall of the City Hall in New York, the dome of which is graced by a figure of justice:

"The lawyers all, both great and small,
Come here to cheat the people;
For be it known that justice's flown,
And perches on the steeple."

AN IRISHMAN'S IDEA OF DUELING.

A famous duelist challenged an Irish barrister for some remark made by the barrister while the duelist was giving his testimony on the stand in some important case. The barrister knew precisely as much about fighting as a fancy boxer about Milton's "Paradise Lost." His friends told him, however, that there was no way to avoid the scrape, and it was certainly expected of him either to fight or apologize. This settled the point, for the proud little Hibernian, though he would rather eat than fight, still infinitely preferred being shot to making an apology. So the two duelists, with their seconds, etc., were soon upon the battle-ground. The challenger was notorious as a great pistol-shot, and had fought some half dozen duels before, in one of which he was so badly wounded as to be left a cripple for life. When other preliminaries were arranged, he requested, through his second, one favor from his adversary, which was permission to stand up against a mile-stone that was on the chosen ground. He sought no advantage, but wished to lean upon the stone, being too lame to stand without support. His request was at once granted, and just as the word was about to be given, the lawyer issued the mandate to stay proceedings, as he had also a request to make. In the gravest manner in the world, he solicited permission to lean against *the next mile-stone*, and the joke was so good that the challenger took his revenge out in a hearty roar of laughter, withdrawing his deadly defiance, and declaring that he could never shoot a man of such excellent humor.

A LEGAL DECLARATION OF LOVE.

Fee simple and a simple fee,
  And all the fees in tail,
Are nothing when compared to thee,
  Thou best of fees—female!

AN AMPLE APOLOGY.

A lawyer of fluid tendencies was discussing some nice point of law, and, getting out of patience at the inability of the court to take his own view of it, said the intellect of the court was so dark a flash of lightning could not penetrate it. The judge, being a new-comer, and not knowing the peculiarities and failings of the man, imposed a severe punishment on him for contempt of court. Some of the lawyer's friends stated the case to his honor, and the punishment was remitted on the condition that he should publicly apologize to the court. He was accordingly brought up the following morning, and made amends by saying,

"I regret very much that I said, in the heat of the moment, that the intellect of the court was so dark lightning could not penetrate it. I guess it could; *it is a very penetrating thing.*"

A POETICAL WILL.

The following will was duly proved in the Prerogative Court of Canterbury, England:

"What I am going to bequeath,
When this frail part submits to death—
But still I hope the spark divine,
With its congenial stars will shine—
My good executors, fulfill;
And pay ye fairly my last will,
With first and second codicil.
And first I give to dear Lord Hinton,
At Twyford school now, not at Winton,
One hundred guineas and a ring,
Or some such memorandum thing.
And truly much I should have blundered
Had I not given another hundred
To dear Earl Paulett's second son,
Who dearly loves a little fun.
Unto my nephew, Stephen Langdon,
Of whom none says he ere has wrong done—
The civil law he loves to hash—
I give two hundred pounds in cash.
One hundred pounds to my niece Tudor
(With luring eyes one Clark did view her);
And to her children, just among 'em,
A hundred more; and, not to wrong 'em,
In equal share I freely give it,
Not doubting but they will receive it.
To Betsy Mudford and Mary Lee,
If they with Mrs. Mudford be,

Because they round the year did dwell
In Davies Street, and served full well;
The first ten pounds, the other twenty,
And, girls, I hope that will content ye.
In seventeen hundred and sixty-nine,
This with my hand I write and sign,
The sixteenth day of fair October,
In merry mood, but sound and sober.
Past my threescore and fifteenth year,
With spirits gay and conscience clear;
Joyous and frolicsome, though old,
And, like this day, serene, but cold.
To foes well-wishing, and to friends most kind,
In perfect charity with all mankind.
For what remains, I must desire
To use the words of Matthew Prior:
'Let this my will be well obeyed,
And farewell all; I'm not afraid;
For what avails a struggling sigh,
When soon or later all must die?'

"M. Darley."

PAID FOR HOLDING HIS TONGUE.

A young pert, prating lawyer one day boasted to the facetious Costello that he had received five-and-twenty guineas for speaking in a certain cause.

"And I," said Costello, who was to have been a witness in the case, "received *double* that sum for *holding* my tongue."

OVERSHOOTING THE MARK.

Some years since the case of a sister of a man deceased against the administrators came up in one of the New York Circuit Courts. The plaintiff brought suit for twenty-six hundred dollars, amount claimed for thirteen years' services, during which time she had attended to and taken care of her brother, who had died without rewarding her pecuniarily for her really invaluable devotion.

There being a great number of cases in court, by consent of counsel the matter was submitted to three referees, who, after hearing the arguments *pro* and *con*, were to decide whether the bill should be allowed or not. At the appointed time the room was crowded with spectators, and no little interest was manifested in the result. The counsel for the plaintiff, a sedate and solemn man, concluded that the best way to secure his ends was by adopting the *pathetic*. Accordingly he began:

"Gentlemen, for thirteen long years did my client devote herself to her unfortunate brother. With an affection such as only a sister can feel did she minister to his every want. Patiently, faithfully she toiled, never complaining, never unwilling, never murmuring; and never was she rewarded, except in that inward consciousness of having done a noble and self-sacrificing deed. Yes, gentlemen, for thirteen long years she toiled and labored, and during that time she never received enough to *buy her a pair of pantaloons!*"

The perfect simplicity of this forgetfulness of his client's sex was so apparent, and the mistake so natural, the flight from the pathetic to the broad ridiculous was so sudden and complete, that the effect can scarcely be imagined.

A JUDGE WHO WAS NEVER JUST BEFORE.

Mr. Justice Page was renowned for his ferocity on the bench. While going to circuit, a facetious lawyer, named Crowe, was asked if "the judge was not just behind."

"I don't know," said Crowe, "but if he is, I am sure he was never just before."

AN ABLE EXAMINATION.

The late Governor Mattox, of Vermont, was chairman of a committee appointed to examine candidates for admission to the bar of Caledonia County, Vermont, and reported that one of them was not qualified for admission, for he had answered but one question right which had been asked him.

"And what was that question, Brother Mattox?" inquired the presiding judge.

"We asked him, your honor, what a freehold estate is, and he answered *he didn't know!*"

RETAINED FOR THE SNAKE.

Colonel T——, at present occupying a high federal office in California, found himself some time since in Yreka, a mining town in the north of California. An immensely heavy losing at "poker" one night left him without money to pay his bills or get away, and he remained in bed late in great disgust. During the morning a man came to the landlord of the hotel, and told him he needed a first-rate lawyer to conduct an important case for him. The landlord told him that a celebrated San Francisco lawyer was up stairs, and showed him up to Colonel T——, who listened with great eagerness to the man's story. His case was this: A neighbor had a pet rattlesnake which had escaped from his cage and bitten the complainant's horse. The horse died, and he wanted to prosecute for damages, and a first-class lawyer to bring suit.

"How much was your horse worth?" asked Colonel T——.

"Five dollars," was the reply.

"I am very sorry," said Colonel T——, "that I can't serve you. *I am retained for the snake!*"

HONEST LAWYERS A SCARCE COMMODITY.

Quite a number of persons were chatting before the court-house door in the town of Anderson while waiting for court to be called, and among other subjects discussed the character of a lawyer named *Scarce*, deceased a short time before. There was a general agreement that he had been an honest man. A young and talented lawyer, named B——, was striding importantly up and down, and in a pause in the conversation stopped and said, grandiloquently, "An honest man's a noble work of God, but an honest *lawyer's* the *noblest* work of God!" An old backwoodsman, a suitor in the crowd, instantly and eagerly said,

"It's the *skeercest* work of God!"

A JURY OF HIS PEERS.

Parsons, a lawyer in Chicago, was trying a case before a jury, being counsel for the prisoner. The judge was very hard on him, and the jury brought in a verdict of guilty. Parsons moved for a new trial. The judge denied his motion, and remarked,

"The court and the jury think the prisoner a knave and a fool."

Instantly the counsel replied,

"The prisoner wishes me to say he is perfectly satisfied —he has been tried by a court and jury of his peers!"

NO REFLECTIONS ON WASHINGTON PERMITTED.

Some years since Seth P. Johnson was elected a member of the —— Legislature from one of the Western counties. Desiring to make a favorable impression, he prepared himself with great care for his first speech. He commenced:

"Mr. Speaker, when I reflect on the character of General Washington—" and came to a sudden stop. Again he commenced, "Mr. Speaker, when I reflect on the character of General Washington—" and again stopped. He essayed a third time, and got no farther, when a fellow-member brought him and the House both down by suggesting whether it was in order for a member of the House to be making *reflections* on the character of General Washington!

MANNERS NEEDED MENDING.

An American advocate, to "the manor born," but who had in him several drops of the blood which flowed through the veins of a son of the Emerald Isle, was once cross-examining in the Court of Common Pleas of New York an Irishman, who was trying to shield himself from the scrutiny of his tormentor by endeavoring to get the advocate excited, and in his answers to a number of questions used the latter's name with the prefix of an O, to which it was not entitled; for example: "Yes, Misther O'B.," "Not at all, Mr. O'B." Mr. O'B. tried to stop this by saying to the witness,

"You need not call me 'Mr. O'B.' Since I came to this country I've mended my name by dropping the O."

"Have ye, now?" said Pat, in response; and, with the same sarcastic grin, "'Pon me sowl, it's a pity ye didn't mend your manners at the same time!"

A JUSTICE IN A BAD BOX.

Mr. Justice Mullen, of the Supreme Court of New York, is distinguished for great simplicity of manner and superior ability as a judge. The exigencies of judicial business frequently demand his presence in this district. On a recent visit he brought with him a valuable silver tea-pot needing a little repair, and requiring nicer manipulation than was obtainable at his rural residence. On leaving the St. Nicholas Hotel, where he was stopping, he did precisely as he would have done at home—took the pot in his hand to carry to the silversmith. On coming out of the door, however, he thought he would slip it under his over-coat, which he did, but did it just at the moment a detective happened to be passing, who noticed the movement, and thought he would "pipe" the old gent. After doing this for a few rods, and noticing that the party frequently cast furtive glances at different objects, he became satisfied that that pot must have been purloined from the hotel. He therefore quietly tapped the judge on the shoulder, and said,

"I want you!"

"For what, sir?"

"Oh, you know! Just you come along with me!"

"Come with you? What do you mean?"—slightly indignant.

"Oh, no use to try that on me; you come quietly to the station-house, that's all! That tea-pot under your coat—you understand?"

"Why" (assuming a more decided tone), "that's my tea-pot."

"Oh, certainly! by all means! of course, it's your tea-pot; 'twon't do, though; that dodge is played out; come along, and don't bother!"

Here the judge stopped and said,

"Sir, I am Justice Mullen, of the Supreme Court. I don't know you, nor what you mean, and do not wish to be annoyed."

"You Justice Mullen! Oh, certainly! no doubt about that! of course you're Justice Mullen! Justices of the

Supreme Court are always going down Broadway with silver tea-pots under their coats—always doing that sort of thing! But that cock won't fight; so come along, or I'll make short work with you."

"Look here, sir!" said the judge, "here is an establishment (pointing to the store in front of which they stood), the proprietor of which will at once identify me, and stop this farce."

"All right; go in!"

In they walked, but, unfortunately, the proprietor was out. Detective, becoming impatient, said,

"Do any of you know this fellow?"

Not being recognized by any of the clerical force, the officer, thinking there had been too much "talkee, talkee" already, insisted upon a prompt compliance with his requisition. His honor saw the ridiculous predicament in which he was placed, and at once proposed to return to the hotel, where his identity could be promptly established. Detective, sure he had "nipped" an old and adroit offender, and thinking it might perhaps be well to restore the tea-pot to the owners, and then have his light-fingered friend committed, acquiesced, and accompanied the "hotel thief" to the St. Nicholas. The sequel can be better imagined than written. A cheaper-looking, cheaper-feeling individual than the "expert" it would be difficult to find. He is familiarly alluded to as "Justice Mullen," but he don't like it much.

"A GOOD MORAL CHARACTER."

Michael Muldoon was a tall, slim Irishman, with eyes full of humor, and manners of the strictly private and confidential kind. In his interviews with one he desired to be in such close communion that the words he used would fall sooner upon your lips thán ears. 'Twas a way he had, but it was an objectionable way. He came into the Court of Common Pleas of New York one morning with a crowd of other men, as a witness for his friend, Thomas O'Flaherty, who desired to become a citizen of the United States. He answered the questions put to him by the presiding judge, but ever and anon endeavoring to get closer and closer to his interrogator, and in his efforts leaning over the rail which kept him from the sacred precincts of the bench until he ceased to be upright. At length he was asked, "Is Thomas O'Flaherty a man of good moral character?" Drawing himself up to his full height (six feet at least), stepping back from the rail as he did so, and looking both astonished and indignant, responded,

"Do you mane to ax me if me friend Tom is a man of good karacther?"

"I do," said the judge.

"Well, then," said he, "av ye do, and it's jokin' I think ye are, I'll tell ye all about it. He plays upon the fiddle; he reads the Bible; he doesn't whip the ould woman, an' he takes a dhrop of whisky now and thin. Will that plaze ye?"

The success of this defense of his friend was satisfactory to all parties concerned, and another defender of the Union walked gallantly away.

A NOVEL PLEA.

Judge Ingraham, one of the justices of the Supreme Court, was presiding in the Court of Oyer and Terminer in the city of New York, when a prisoner was arraigned for stealing a quantity of flannel, which was alleged to be worth forty-five dollars, and the offense charged was therefore grand larceny. The prisoner listened attentively to the reading of the indictment, and when asked, as usual, whether he was guilty or not guilty, said,

"Not guilty—the flannel wasn't worth half so much!"

He evidently knew the difference between grand larceny and the state prison, and petit larceny with a short residence on Blackwell's Island.

A KIND-HEARTED JUDGE SOLD.

The Honorable Richard Riker, who, as recorder, presided many years in the General Sessions of New York, was loved and respected by all who knew him. He was a kind-hearted gentleman who leaned ever to the side of mercy, and saved many a trembling criminal from a life of infamy by treating him generously, and counseling a better course of conduct. On one occasion a young negro was placed at the bar to be sentenced. He was not more than nineteen years old, and the recorder, influenced by his youth, and assuming that he was a novice in crime, after commenting on the offense, and kindly to the prisoner of its consequences upon the threshold of manhood, concluded by saying, "On account of your youth, and in the agreeable hope that you will never commit another offense, I sentence you to confinement in the Penitentiary for thirty days."

The "dark-eyed one," looking up at the recorder with a cheerful face, but with manners very much "devil may care," exclaimed, leaving the dock as he did so,

"Is dat all for dis nigga, massa! Dat's only a breakfast spell! I gets de dinner de next time, I supposin'—dat's so; yah, yah!" and he left the court amid laughter which could not be instantly repressed. He was known afterward as the Epicurean colored bredren of many spells!

DID NOT WANT A TRIAL.

Harry Vandevoort, the amiable, competent, and gentlemanly clerk of the Court of Sessions of New York, has heard many striking Hibernicisms, one of which he tells in this wise:

An Irishman, who had doubtless been "blue-mouldin' for want of a baten," and could not resist the temptation to have a little exercise, was arraigned for an assault and battery. He listened with apparently rapt attention to the reading of the indictment. When that ceremony had ended, Mr. Vandevoort asked him, in accordance with the form then in use,

"Do you demand a trial on this indictment?"

Pat, putting his hand to his ear, and leaning forward in seeming utter ignorance of what had been asked him, said,

"What's that?"

Mr. Vandevoort, a little dashed by the manner of the man, repeated the question, and the response was,

"The divil a thrial I want. Ye need not give yourself the throuble of thryin' me. You may as well save the expinse of that, and put me down innocent. Contint am I to lave this wid me blessin' on ye; indade, I'm anxious, for me boss is waitin' for me beyant. Oh no, no, the divil a thrial I want at all, at all!"

All this was said so rapidly that Mr. Vandevoort could not interpose to stop it, and the prisoner having, as he supposed, settled the business, attempted to leave the court, but was of course prevented. Mr. Vandevoort, when the mirth subsided which Pat had occasioned, changed the question, and asked him,

"Are you guilty or not guilty?"

"What's that?" said he, again leaning forward with his hand to his ear, as if he had not heard the question.

"Are you guilty or not guilty?" said Mr. V.
The answer came at once,
"Arrah, how the divil can I tell till *I hear the evidence!*"

JUSTICE NOT TO BE HAD.

"Do you think I shall have justice done me?" said a culprit to his counsel, a shrewd Kentucky lawyer of the best class in that "eloquent state."

"I am a little afraid that you *won't*," replied the other; "I see two men on the jury who are opposed to hanging."

CELTIC WIT.

An Irish counselor having lost his cause, which had been tried by three judges, one of whom was esteemed a very able lawyer, though the other two were indifferent, some of the other barristers were merry on the occasion.

"Well, now," said he, "who could help it, when there are a hundred judges on the bench?"

"A hundred!" said a by-stander; "there were but three."

"By St. Patrick!" replied he, "there were one and two ciphers."

A HANGING VERDICT.

A jury in Alabama was impanneled in the case of a Mr. Johnson, charged with killing his wife. The evidence was positive and conclusive, leaving not a doubt of his speedy conviction. To the amazement of all, the jury, after a short absence, returned a verdict, "Guilty of horse-stealing!" The judge, astonished, asked an explanation, stating that the indictment was not for horse-stealing, but manslaughter. The foreman, with his hand upon a huge law-book, and with an amazingly dignified air, informed the court that "it was not a case of *man*slaughter, but *woman*slaughter, for which the law made no provision; but, being satisfied the man deserved to be hung, they had brought in a verdict of horse-stealing, *which, in that county*, would be sure to *swing him!*"

A JUDGE TAKEN ABACK.

Judge Benjamin Tappan, at one time United States senator from Ohio, was remarkable for two piercing eyes, whose line of vision crossed so closely above the bridge of the owner's nose that each appeared to be endeavoring to surmount that obstacle to have a combat with the other. The judge was holding court in one of the newly-organized counties of the state in which there was not, as yet, any jail, except a log stable fitted up for that purpose. During the sessions of the court "a green un from the country" sat with eyes and mouth wide open, listening intently to the proceedings. At length two of the attorneys got into a personal altercation, at which the judge reproved them sharply, at the same time giving them such a look as no one with ordinary optics could command. This was decidedly a rich scene for "green un," who instantly shouted, "That's right! give it to um, *gimlet eyes!*" A burst of laughter succeeded, and the judge, not yet perceiving who it was that had so offended the dignity of the court, looking out on the crowd, called out, "Who was that?" At which the same voice, in an effeminate, drawling tone, responded,

"It was this 'ere, old hoss."

"Sheriff," exclaimed the judge, "take that horse and put him in *the stable*."

A PROFESSIONAL OPINION.

There was, some years ago, in the eastern part of the Empire State, a very pompous gentleman of the legal profession, who somewhat resembled necessity in that he knew no law, but whose huge body and conceited manners made him the butt of his professional brethren. At the same bar practiced a keen, active, energetic little lawyer, almost a dwarf in stature, but intellectually very much the superior of his ponderous friend. It happened, during one of the sessions of the court, a heavy rain fell, and one morning the wide street which separated the court-house and tavern was ankle deep with water.

"B——, my dear little fellow," said the gigantic W——, "you never can get across the street in this flood; you will certainly drown. I shall have to take you across on my back."

"You would have more law on your back than you ever had in your head," was the ready retort.

LEGAL CONUNDRUM.

Why is a lawsuit like a wood-saw?

Because whichever way it goes, down comes the *dust.*

A LEGAL LECTURE TO A CRIMINAL.

The county courts of Virginia, composed of justices of the peace who never studied law, furnish many amusing incidents. Five honest farmers in the county of M—— were convened as an examining court, to determine by the evidence whether a mere boy, who was arrested upon a grave charge of felony, should be "sent on" to the Circuit Court for trial. The evidence furnished the court by the prosecuting attorney was very conclusive against the prisoner. The justices heard the evidence, and then held a consultation how they would dispose of the case. After some time the court determined that, as the prisoner was quite young and might reform, they would, through the oldest member of the court, give the young man a severe lecture, and then discharge him. Accordingly, old Squire H——, who talked through his nose, arose, and, looking fiercely at the prisoner, ordered him to stand up, and then commenced his lecture:

"Young man, it's awful—awful, I say!" and then, remembering the points of the evidence, his indignation reached the highest point as he exclaimed, in thunder tones, "*Clear out of my sight, you ornary scamp!*"

Thus closed the lecture, amid roars of laughter from the spectators.

CONTINUANCE ON THE GROUND OF SURPRISE.

In a murder trial in the District Court at Austin, on Reese River, a dog was annoying the attendants within the bar by prying his nose every where, and getting between the legs of the persons present. The judge nodded to the sheriff, who in an instant snatched the dog by the throat and jerked him out of the window. The shock of the seizure by the sheriff was so great that the cur did not have time to yelp, whereupon a wag at the bar whispered loud enough to be heard, "That dog should have moved for a continuance upon the ground of surprise!" The seriousness of the murder trial was interrupted by quite a titter around the bar.

PLEADING GUILTY FOR A CLIENT.

A number of gamblers were indicted before the Circuit Court held in B—— for indulging in certain practices contrary to the statute in such cases made and provided. The delinquents, finding that the prosecuting attorney had "a sure thing on them," concluded not to come before the court in person, but retained Mr. H—— to appear for them, plead guilty, and pay the fine. Accordingly, when the case was called, Mr. H—— rose, and the following colloquy ensued:

Mr. H——. "I appear for the defendants, and plead guilty."

Judge (entering on the docket). Mr. H—— appears, pleads guilty, and is fined—"

Mr. H——. "But, your honor, I have not yet received the money for the fine. I expect it to-morrow."

Judge. "It makes no difference, sir. You are fined, and *stand committed to jail* until it is paid."

H——'s blank look, as he drew out his private pocket-book, and muttered, "You won't catch me again in this way," was slightly amusing.

ALLEGATION AND ALLIGATOR.

When Minnesota was a Territory, Squire F—— acted as justice of the peace in the town of H——. He was more noted for his frankness, and the pointed manner in which he expressed his opinions, than for his choice selection of words. One day, when a suit was on trial before him, the counsel for the defendant claimed that the allegations contained in the plaintiff's complaint were false, and moved to have them stricken out. Squire F—— patiently heard the counsel for the plaintiff in support of his complaint and in opposition to the motion, and the counsel for the defendant in reply. He then gave his decision in the following language:

"It is the opinion of this court that the allegations in the plaintiff's complaint are false, and" (pointing to the plaintiff's counsel) "that that are *alligator* knew it when he made them!"

A LAW REPORT IN RHYME.

Two cousins claimed an account, each against the other, and litigated very spiritedly. The case was reported as "Owen Kerr *vs.* Owen Kerr." While this trial was in progress, a prominent member of the bar, possessing a decided poetical turn of mind, composed the following lines on the true merits of the case, which are too good to be lost, though not legitimately belonging to the regular "law report:"

OWEN KERR *vs.* OWEN KERR.

If the strife in this case is extremely perverse,
'Tis because 'tis between a couple of "Kerrs."
Each Owen is Owen—but here lies the bother—
To determine which Owen is owin' the other.
Each Owen swears Owen to Owen is owin',
And each alike certain, dog-matic, and knowin',
But 'tis hoped that the jury will not be deterred
From finding which "Kerr" the true debt has incurred;
Thus settling which Owen by *owin'* has failed,
And that justice 'twixt curs has not been *cur*-tailed.

A JOB-LIKE JUDGE.

The most extraordinary instance of patience on record in modern times is that of an Illinois judge, who listened silently for two days while a couple of wordy attorneys contended about the construction of an act of the Legislature, and then ended the controversy by quietly remarking, "Gentlemen, the law is repealed."

LAWYERS DEFINED TO BE GENTLEMEN.

An old English law-book defines a gentleman as follows: "Whosoever studieth the laws of the realm, who studieth in the universities, who professeth the liberal sciences, and (to be short) who can live idly, and without manual labor, and well bear the port, charge, and countenance of a gentleman, he shall be called 'master,' and taken for a gentleman."

WIT IN THE JURY-BOX.

When the late Judge Wells, of Boston, was living, and presiding in the Court of Common Pleas, an action was brought to recover the price of some *felloes* and *tires* to wheels furnished by the plaintiff. The counsel in the case were Messrs. Maine and Morris, and they proved to be so tedious that court and jury got out of all patience, and the foreman perpetrated the following *impromptu:*

> "Morris and Maine, two lawyers shrewd
> (Though they themselves may like the sport),
> Talking of *felloes* and of *tires*,
> *Tire* all the *fellows* in court."

That foreman has, since that day, been the well-known editor of one of the Boston daily papers.

At a court in Texas, the Hon. Judge Devine presiding, the jury in a criminal case failed to agree, and, as is usual in such cases, the court attempted to coerce a verdict, which elicited from the foreman, J. R. Sweet, the following impromptu lines addressed to his honor:

"Dear Judge *Divine*, do send us wine,
Or something good to eat;
For 'tis plain to see we can't agree—
Your obedient servant, SWEET."

The judge dismissed the jury.

A PUNNING JUDGE.

The late Judge Peters has left behind him a countless host of well-remembered puns. Some few of the rarest are worth relating:

A gentleman presenting his only son to the notice of the judge, said,

"He is my all."

The boy was a long, thin, whey-faced stripling, and the judge said to the father,

"Your awl, and your last too, I suppose, but I can't call him a strapping fellow."

When on the District Court bench he observed to Judge Washington that one of his witnesses had a vegetable head.

"How so?" was the inquiry.

"He has carroty hair, reddish cheeks, a turn-up nose, and a sage look."

"HOLY PICTURES."

Judge G——, of the Sixth Judicial District of New York, was holding a circuit in Norwich, Chenango County, and, as the duties of the term had been somewhat arduous, the judge, whose nature was not the mildest, had become somewhat irritable, and he desired to dispatch as soon as possible the business before him. Among the last causes was one brought by an old Irishman for recovery on a trunk which had been lost on the railroad between Norwich and Binghamton. The old man took the stand as a witness, and the judge interrogated him as to the contents of the trunk.

"Now, sir," said the judge, abruptly, "what was in the trunk?"

"Well," replied the ancient Hibernian, in an accent modified by long residence in this country, "there were some clothes and some holy pictures."

"Holy pictures! holy pictures!" exclaimed the judge; "what do you mean by holy pictures?"

"Well, first there was a picture of Father Mathew, who introduced temperance into Ireland; perhaps your honor's heard o' him?"

"Yes, yes; go on!"

"And then there was a picture of the blessed St. Patrick, who banished snakes from Ireland; perhaps your honor's heard o' him?"

"Yes, yes; what else?"

"Well, then," said the old man, fixing his eyes on the judge, "there was a picture of our blessed Lord, who came on earth to save men from their sins; perhaps your honor's heard o' him!"

The effect on the hearers may be easily imagined.

"A PROPER SUBJECT OF CONTEMPT."

Many of the old residents of Illinois will remember Knowlton, now dead, a lawyer of considerable celebrity. He was wont to say that he was never "taken down" but once. It happened in this wise: He had a suit before a magistrate in his county, who was a shoemaker, and dispensed justice from his *bench* with a dignity worthy of a higher place. Knowlton called at the shop a little before the hour fixed for the trial of the case to have a friendly chat, and while there he yielded to temptation, and perpetrated some joke upon the old fellow, as he had often done before. He was astounded when Crispin, laying aside his lapstone and adjusting his spectacles, remarked that he was about to enter up a fine of five dollars against him for contempt of court. Knowlton remonstrated—court was not in session—the fine was absurd. But the worthy justice of the peace in a very impressive manner said to him,

"Mr. Knowlton, you will understand that this court is a proper *subject of contempt* at all times."

Knowlton paid his fine; and that decision, as applied to justices' courts, continues to be good law in Illinois to this day.

A LAWYER'S RETAINING FEE.

Mr. Burchard, the revival preacher, went about the villages to enlist the wealthy and influential to attend his preaching in order to give some eclat to his meetings. In the course of his perambulations one day he fell in with Bob S——, an attorney of some reputation, and very famous for his wit and his readiness at repartee.

"Good-morning, Mr. S——," said the "evangelist;" "understanding that you are one of the leading men of the town, and a lawyer of high standing, I have called upon you in hopes to engage you on the Lord's side."

"Thank you," replied Bob, with an air of great sobriety, and with the most professional manner possible; "I thank you; I should be most happy to be employed on that side of the case, if I could do so conscientiously with my engagements; but you must go to some other counsel, as I have a standing retainer from the opposite party."

The itinerant was amazed, piqued, and nonplused, and departed without attempting to suppress his laughter.

FANCY FOR ANKLES.

A Massachusetts judge on circuit, as he rode to the door of an inn, saw the landlady's daughter jump over the fence.

"Do that again, Sallie, and I'll marry you."

The girl again leaped the fence. The judge was as good as his word, and a year from that day married the light-heeled Sallie.

GIVING THE PRECISE WORDS.

A witness was examined before a judge in a case, who required him to repeat the *precise* words spoken. The witness hesitated till he riveted the attention of the entire court upon him; then, fixing his eyes earnestly on the judge, began:

"May it please your honor, you lie and steal, and get your living by stealing!"

The face of the judge reddened, and he immediately said,

"Turn to the *jury*, sir."

NO DESIRE TO CATCH HER.

Charles Chapman, a witty lawyer of Hartford, was once called out of town to act in a case in which a lady was the principal witness. Her husband was present—a diminutive, meek, forbearing sort of man—who, in the language of Mr. Chapman, "looked like a rooster just fished out of a swill-barrel," while the lady was a large, portly woman, evidently the "better horse." She balked on the cross-examination, and the lawyer was pressing the question with his usual urgency, when she broke out, with vindictive fire flashing from her eyes, "Mr. Chapman, you needn't think you can catch me, if you try all day!"

Putting on his most quizzical expression, Mr. Chapman replied,

"Madam, I haven't the slightest desire to *catch* you, and your husband looks to me as if he was sorry *he* had."

The husband faintly smiled assent.

LEGAL BULLS.

Judge Brackenridge used to relate the following:

"I once had a Virginia lawyer object to an expression in one of the acts of the Assembly of Pennsylvania, which read, 'That the State-house yard in the city of Philadelphia should be surrounded by a brick wall, and remain *an open inclosure* forever.'

"But I put him down by citing one of the acts of the Legislature of his own state, which is entitled, 'A supplement to an act entitled an act making it penal to alter the mark of an unmarked hog.'"

NOVEL FEES.

Judge Ochiltree, of Texas, once defended a criminal for stealing a pistol, having been assigned to that duty by the court. He made an eloquent appeal in behalf of the prisoner, and convinced the court and jury of his entire innocence. He was accordingly acquitted. Taking his deliverer aside, the man said, "I have no money to pay you, but you shall have the pistol," and handed it to the lawyer.

It seems the same judge got another tool in the same way. He was successful in defending a prisoner, who asked him afterward what was his fee. The judge said an X would be enough. The fellow brought him a beautiful *axe*, actually understanding his counsel to name that article as his charge. The judge took it and *axed* no questions.

but told the story often of the heaviest fee he ever got in his life.

JUDICIAL DISPATCH.

In Columbia County, Ohio, the Common Pleas Court was composed of a president-judge, who was a lawyer by profession, and three associate justices who were not lawyers. At a term of the court, when several important criminal causes had been tried, and the prisoners were awaiting sentence, when several motions for new trials were pending, and the decisions on demurrers in a number of civil suits which had been ably argued were also expected, the president-judge on the last day of the term happened to be absent. The court-room was crowded with the friends of the prisoners, counsel, and anxious litigants, to listen to the judicial determinations. After a short pause, the Dutch associate drew forward his chair. Said he,

"Misther Clark, de motions for new trial ish all overruled, and the demurrers ish all sustained. De prisoners ish all sentenced to penitentiary for dree years. Make de endries vorthwith, for in one hour dis court vill pe on a steampoat."

Several of the sovereigns went to the penitentiary *vorthwith* accordingly.

A NOVEL PLEA AND PRAYER.

Judge R—— relates the following incident as occurring in his practice:

He was trying a petty case, in which one of the parties was not able to pay counsel fees, and undertook to plead his own cause. But he found, in the course of the trial, that the keen and adroit attorney who managed the case for the other party was too much for him in legal strategy, evidently making the worse appear the better cause. The poor man, Mr. A——, was in a state of mind bordering upon desperation when the opposing counsel closed his plea, and the case was about to be submitted to the justice for decision. "May it please your honor," said the man, "may I pray?" The judge was taken somewhat by surprise, and could only say that he saw no objection. Whereupon Mr. A—— went down upon his knees, and made a fervent prayer, in which he laid the merits of his case before the Lord in a very clear and methodical statement of all the particulars, pleading that right and justice might prevail. "O Lord, thou knowest that this lawyer has misrepresented the facts, and thou knowest that it is so and so"—to the end of the chapter. Arguments which he could not present in logical array to the understanding of men, he had no difficulty in addressing to the Lord, being evidently better versed in praying than pettifogging. When he rose from his knees, Esquire W——, the opposing counsel, very much exasperated by the turn which the case had taken, said, "Mr. Justice, does not the closing argument belong to me?" To which the judge replied, "You can close with prayer, if you please." Esquire W—— was in the habit of praying at home, but, not seeing the propriety of connecting his prayer with his practice, wisely forbore, leaving poor Mr. A—— to win his case, as he did, by this novel mode of presenting it.

BULLYING WITNESSES AS AN ART.

Many attorneys in all courts frequently owe their success and notoriety to their art in "bullying" witnesses on the opposite side of the cases in which they are engaged; but occasionally they "wake up the wrong passenger."

There was a horse case in the justice's court of N—— one day, in which a "bullying counsel" named Wayke happened to be engaged. A slow and easy witness had been called to the stand by the plaintiff, who, in a plain, straightforward manner, made the other side of the case look rather blue. The plaintiff's attorney being through, Wayke commenced a regular cross-examination, which was cut short in this manner:

"Well, what do you know about a horse—are you a *horse doctor?*" said he, in his peculiar contemptuous and overbearing manner.

"No, I don't pretend to be a horse doctor, but I know a good deal of the nature of the beast."

"That means to say that you know a horse from a jackass when you see them," said Wayke, in the same style, looking very knowingly at the court, and glancing rather triumphantly around the crowd of spectators with a telegraphic expression which said, "Now I've got him on the hip."

The intended victim, gazing intently at his legal tormentor, drawled out,

"Oh ye-as—just so—for instance, *I'd never take you for a horse!*"

A THOUGHTFUL WITNESS.

In one of the county courts of Northern New York, a witness in a case of an assault was asked by the junior counsel, "How far were you, sir, from the parties when the alleged assault took place?"

"*Four feet five inches and a half,*" was the answer promptly given.

"Ah!" fiercely demanded the lawyer, "how came you to be so very exact in all this?"

"Because," said the witness, very coolly, "I expected that some confounded fool would as likely as not ask me, and so I went and measured it."

THREE DECIDED CASES OF "CONTEMPTS OF COURT."

One of the members of the bar in the city of Buffalo, while arguing an appeal at the General Term of the Supreme Court at which the three judges of that district were sitting, was greatly irritated by the frequent expression of dissent made by the court to his propositions of law. Pausing abruptly at length, in the midst of his argument, he exclaimed, with marked emphasis,

"I will, perhaps, be excusable in remarking that this court strongly reminds me of a Demerara team."

"And what kind of a team may that be, Mr. ——?" asked the presiding justice.

"It is said to be composed," was the reply, "of *two mules and a jackass!*"

The consequences of the comparison are not reported.

A recorder of the city last mentioned, since deceased, was noted for his love of order in court, the strict observance of which was always insisted on. Upon one occasion a well-known lawyer appeared in the bar in a condition which conclusively showed that he had lately partaken by far too deeply of the cup which cheers *and* inebriates. As a consequence, the court was several times interrupted by as many maudlin witticisms as vagaries of speech from the counselor spoken of. The recorder had already once requested the gentleman to observe silence; and when another breach of decorum was perpetrated, he said,

"This must be suffered no longer. If Mr. —— has any friends in court, I advise his instant removal, otherwise I shall instantly commit him for contempt."

This was an intimation not to be disregarded; and, in pursuance of it, several persons present took the threatened "object of contempt" by the arm and moved him forcibly to the door. Struggling to free himself as he was forced out, the latter sent a farewell shot toward the bench after this fashion:

"Commit me, judge—*me?* If you do, it will be the confounded est *error you* ever committed!"

The last relates to a justice's court, also of the city of Buffalo. Becoming vexed at a functionary who there presided, a lawyer took occasion to remark that this court was the "greatest legal anomaly" he was acquainted with.

"You will not repeat that remark," the justice observed; "it is extremely offensive."

"I am of opinion," rejoined the audacious pettifogger, "that the court does not understand the meaning of the word."

"Perfectly, sir, perfectly!" was the indignant response. "You mean to intimate that *the court doesn't know beans!*"

SETTING HENS AND LAYING LAWYERS.

Judge R——, who presided in the county court of a certain county in the State of New York, was fond of indulging himself occasionally in a joke at the expense of Counselor B——, a practicing attorney in the same court with whom he was intimate, and for whom he had a high regard. On a certain occasion, when pleading a cause at the bar, Mr. B—— observed that he would conclude his remarks on the following day, unless the court would consent to *set* late enough for him to finish them that evening.

"*Sit*, sir," said the judge, "not *set;* hens set."

"I stand corrected, sir," said the counselor, bowing.

Not long after, while giving an opinion, the judge remarked that, under such and such circumstances, an action would not *lay*.

"*Lie*, may it please your honor," said the counselor, "not *lay*; hens lay."

A debate once took place among the members of a court of another state as to how long they should *set* to dispose of the business before them. *Three weeks* were at last determined on.

"Why, in the name of wonder," inquired a wag at the bar, "do they not set four weeks, like other geese?"

INDEX.

THE END.

VALUABLE STANDARD WORKS

FOR PUBLIC AND PRIVATE LIBRARIES,

PUBLISHED BY HARPER & BROTHERS, NEW YORK.

For a full List of Books suitable for Presentation, see HARPER & BROTHERS' TRADE-LIST *and* CATALOGUE, *which may be had gratuitously on application to the Publishers personally, or by letter enclosing Five Cents.*

HARPER & BROTHERS *will send any of the following works by Mail, postage prepaid, to any part of the United States, on receipt of the Price.*

NAPOLEON'S LIFE OF CÆSAR. The History of Julius Cæsar. By His Imperial Majesty NAPOLEON III. Volumes I. and II. now ready. Library Edition, 8vo, Cloth, $3 50 per volume; Half Calf, $5 75 per volume.
Maps to Vols. I. and II. sold separately. Price $1 50 *each,* NET.

MOTLEY'S DUTCH REPUBLIC. The Rise of the Dutch Republic. A History. By JOHN LOTHROP MOTLEY, LL.D., D.C.L. With a Portrait of William of Orange. 3 vols., 8vo, Cloth, $9 00; Sheep, $10 50; Half Calf, $15 75.

MOTLEY'S UNITED NETHERLANDS. History of the United Netherlands: from the Death of William the Silent to the Synod of Dort. With a full View of the English-Dutch Struggle against Spain, and of the Origin and Destruction of the Spanish Armada. By JOHN LOTHROP MOTLEY, LL.D., D.C.L., Author of "The Rise of the Dutch Republic." 2 vols., 8vo, Cloth $6 00; Sheep, $7 00; Half Calf, $10 50.

WOOD'S HOMES WITHOUT HANDS. Homes Without Hands: Being a Description of the Habitations of Animals, classed according to their Principle of Construction. By J. G. WOOD, M.A., F.L.S., Author of "Illustrated Natural History." With about 140 Illustrations, engraved by G. Pearson, from Original Designs made by F. W. Keyl and E. A. Smith, under the Author's Superintendence. 8vo, Cloth, Beveled Edges, $4 50; Full Morocco, $8 00.

ALCOCK'S JAPAN. The Capital of the Tycoon: A Narrative of a Three Years' Residence in Japan. By Sir RUTHERFORD ALCOCK, K.C.B., Her Majesty's Envoy Extraordinary and Minister Plenipotentiary in Japan. With Maps and Engravings. 2 vols., 12mo, Cloth, $3 50.

ALFORD'S GREEK TESTAMENT. The Greek Testament: with a critically-revised Text; a Digest of Various Readings; Marginal References to Verbal and Idiomatic Usage; Prolegomena; and a Critical and Exegetical Commentary. For the Use of Theological Students and Ministers. By HENRY ALFORD, D.D., Dean of Canterbury. Vol. I., containing the Four Gospels. 944 pages, 8vo, Cloth, $6 00; Sheep, $6 50; Half Calf, $8 25.

ALISON'S HISTORY OF EUROPE. FIRST SERIES: From the Commencement of the French Revolution, in 1789, to the Restoration of the Bourbons, in 1815. [In addition to the Notes on Chapter LXXVI., which correct the errors of the original work concerning the United States, a copious Analytical Index has been appended to this American edition.] SECOND SERIES: From the Fall of Napoleon, in 1815, to the Accession of Louis Napoleon, in 1852. 8 vols., 8vo, Cloth, $16 00; Half Calf, $34 00.

BARTH'S NORTH AND CENTRAL AFRICA. Travels and Discoveries in North and Central Africa: Being a Journal of an Expedition undertaken under the Auspices of H.B.M.'s Government, in the Years 1849-1855. By HENRY BARTH, Ph.D., D.C.L. Illustrated. Complete in 3 vols., 8vo, Cloth, $12 00; Half Calf, $18 75.

BEECHER'S AUTOBIOGRAPHY, &c. Autobiography, Correspondence, &c., of Lyman Beecher, D.D. Edited by his Son, CHARLES BEECHER. With Three Steel Portraits and Engravings on Wood. In 2 vols., 12mo, Cloth, $5 00; Half Calf, $8 50.

BRODHEAD'S HISTORY OF NEW YORK. History of the State of New York. By JOHN ROMEYN BRODHEAD. First Period, 1609-1664. 8vo, Cloth, $3 00.

BURNS'S LIFE AND WORKS. The Life and Works of Robert Burns. Edited by ROBERT CHAMBERS. 4 vols., 12mo, Cloth, $6 00.

CARLYLE'S FREDERICK THE GREAT. History of Friedrich II., called Frederick the Great. By THOMAS CARLYLE. Portraits, Maps, Plans, &c. 6 vols., 12mo, Cloth, $12 00; Half Calf, $22 50.

CARLYLE'S FRENCH REVOLUTION. History of the French Revolution. Newly Revised by the Author, with Index, &c. 2 vols., 12mo, Cloth, $3 50.

CARLYLE'S OLIVER CROMWELL. Letters and Speeches of Oliver Cromwell. With Elucidations and Connecting Narrative. 2 vols., 12mo, Cloth, $3 50.

CHALMERS'S POSTHUMOUS WORKS. The Posthumous Works of Dr. Chalmers. Edited by his Son-in-Law, Rev. WILLIAM HANNA, LL.D. Complete in 9 vols., 12mo, Cloth, 13 50; Half Calf, $29 25.

JOHNSON'S COMPLETE WORKS. The Works of Samuel Johnson, LL.D. With an Essay on his Life and Genius, by ARTHUR MURPHY, Esq. Portrait of Johnson. 2 vols., 8vo, Cloth, $4 00.

CLAYTON'S QUEENS OF SONG. Queens of Song: Being Memoirs of some of the most celebrated Female Vocalists who have performed on the Lyric Stage from the Earliest Days of Opera to the Present Time. To which is added a Chronological List of all the Operas that have been performed in Europe. By ELLEN CREATHORNE CLAYTON. With Portraits. 8vo, Cloth, $3 00; Half Calf, $5 25.

COLERIDGE'S COMPLETE WORKS. The Complete Works of Samuel Taylor Coleridge. With an Introductory Essay upon his Philosophical and Theological Opinions. Edited by Professor SHEDD. Complete in 7 vols. With a fine Portrait. Small 8vo, Cloth, $10 50; Half Calf, $22 75.

CURTIS'S HISTORY OF THE CONSTITUTION. History of the Origin, Formation, and Adoption of the Constitution of the United States. By GEORGE TICKNOR CURTIS. Complete in two large and handsome Octavo Volumes. Cloth, $6 00; Sheep, $7 00; Half Calf, $10 50.

DAVIS'S CARTHAGE. Carthage and her Remains: Being an Account of the Excavations and Researches on the Site of the Phœnician Metropolis in Africa and other Adjacent Places. Conducted under the Auspices of Her Majesty's Government. By Dr. DAVIS, F.R.G.S. Profusely Illustrated with Maps, Woodcuts, Chromo-Lithographs, &c. 8vo, Cloth, $4 00.

DOOLITTLE'S CHINA. Social Life of the Chinese: With some Account of their Religious, Governmental, Educational, and Business Customs and Opinions. With special but not exclusive Reference to Fuhchau. By Rev. JUSTUS DOOLITTLE, Fourteen Years Member of the Fuhchau Mission of the American Board. Illustrated with more than 150 characteristic Engravings on Wood. 2 vols., 12mo, Cloth, $5 00; Half Calf, $8 50.

DRAPER'S AMERICAN CIVIL POLICY. Thoughts on the Future Civil Policy of America. By JOHN W. DRAPER, M.D., LL.D., Professor of Chemistry and Physiology in the University of New York, Author of a "Treatise on Human Physiology," and a "History of the Intellectual Development of Europe." Crown 8vo, Cloth, $2 50.

DRAPER'S INTELLECTUAL DEVELOPMENT OF EUROPE. A History of the Intellectual Development of Europe. By JOHN W. DRAPER, M.D., LL.D., Professor of Chemistry and Physiology in the University of New York. 8vo, Cloth, $5; Half Calf, $7 25.

MISS EDGEWORTH'S NOVELS. With Engravings. 10 vols., 12mo, Cloth, $15 00; Half Calf, $32 50.

GIBBON'S ROME. History of the Decline and Fall of the Roman Empire. By EDWARD GIBBON. With Notes by Rev. H. H. MILMAN and M. GUIZOT. A new cheap Edition. To which is added a Complete Index of the whole Work, and a Portrait of the Author. 6 vols., 12mo (uniform with Hume), Cloth, $9 00; Half Calf, $19 50.

GROTE'S HISTORY OF GREECE. 12 vols., 12mo, Cloth, $18 00; Half Calf, $39 00.

MRS. HALE'S WOMAN'S RECORD. Woman's Record; or, Biographical Sketches of all Distinguished Women, from the Creation to the Present Time. Arranged in Four Eras, with Selections from Female Writers of each Era. By Mrs. SARAH JOSEPHA HALE. Illustrated with more than 200 Portraits, 8vo, Cloth, $5 00.

HALL'S ARCTIC RESEARCHES. Arctic Researches and Life Among the Esquimaux: Being the Narrative of an Expedition in Search of Sir John Franklin, in the Years 1860, 1861, and 1862. By CHARLES FRANCIS HALL. With Maps and 100 Illustrations. The Illustrations are from Original Drawings by Charles Parsons, Henry L. Stephens, Solomon Eyting, W. S. L. Jewett, and Granville Perkins, after Sketches by Captain Hall. A new Edition. 8vo, Cloth, Beveled Edges, $5 00; Half Calf, $7 25.

HALLAM'S CONSTITUTIONAL HISTORY OF ENGLAND, from the Accession of Henry VII. to the Death of George II. 8vo, Cloth, $2 00.

HALLAM'S LITERATURE. Introduction to the Literature of Europe during the Fifteenth, Sixteenth, and Seventeenth Centuries. By HENRY HALLAM. 2 vols., 8vo, Cloth, $4 00.

HALLAM'S MIDDLE AGES. State of Europe during the Middle Ages. By HENRY HALLAM. 8vo, Cloth, $2 00.

HARPER'S NEW CLASSICAL LIBRARY. Literal Translations.
The following volumes are now ready. Portraits. 12mo, Cloth, $1 50 each.

CÆSAR.
VIRGIL.
SALLUST.
HORACE.
CICERO'S ORATIONS.
CICERO'S OFFICES, &C.
CICERO ON ORATORY AND ORATORS.
TACITUS. 2 vols.
TERENCE.
SOPHOCLES.
JUVENAL.
XENOPHON.
HOMER'S ILIAD.
HOMER'S ODYSSEY.
HERODOTUS.
DEMOSTHENES.
THUCYDIDES.
ÆSCHYLUS.
EURIPIDES. 2 vols.

HARPER'S PICTORIAL HISTORY OF THE REBELLION. Harper's Pictorial History of the Great Rebellion in the United States. Vol. I. now ready. More than 500 Illustrations. 4to, $6 00. Vol. II. is now being Published in Numbers.

HILDRETH'S HISTORY OF THE UNITED STATES. *First Series:* From the First Settlement of the Country to the Adoption of the Federal Constitution. *Second Series:* From the Adoption of the Federal Constitution to the End of the Sixteenth Congress. 6 vols., 8vo, Cloth, $18 00; Half Calf, $31 50.

HUME'S HISTORY OF ENGLAND. History of England, from the Invasion of Julius Cæsar to the Abdication of James II., 1688. By DAVID HUME. A New Edition, with the Author's last Corrections and Improvements. To which is prefixed a short Account of his Life, written by Himself. With a Portrait of the Author. 6 Vols., 12mo, Cloth, $9 00; Half Calf, $19 50.

JAY'S WORKS. Complete Works of Rev. William Jay: comprising his Sermons, Family Discourses, Morning and Evening Exercises for every Day in the Year, Family Prayers, &c. Author's enlarged Edition, revised. 3 vols., 8vo, Cloth, $6 00; Half Calf, $12 75.

KINGLAKE'S CRIMEAN WAR. The Invasion of the Crimea: Its Origin, and an Account of its Progress down to the Death of Lord Raglan. By ALEXANDER WILLIAM KINGLAKE. With Maps and Plans. 2 Volumes. Vol. I. Maps. 12mo, Cloth, $2 00.

LAMB'S COMPLETE WORKS. The Works of Charles Lamb. Comprising his Letters, Poems, Essays of Elia, Essays upon Shakspeare, Hogarth, &c., and a Sketch of his Life, with the Final Memorials, by T. NOON TALFOURD. Portrait. 2 vols., 12mo, Cloth, $3 00.

DR. LIVINGSTONE'S SOUTH AFRICA. Missionary Travels and Researches in South Africa; including a Sketch of Sixteen Years' Residence in the Interior of Africa, and a Journey from the Cape of Good Hope to Loando on the West Coast; thence across the Continent, down the River Zambesi, to the Eastern Ocean. By DAVID LIVINGSTONE, LL.D., D.C.L. With Portrait, Maps by Arrowsmith, and numerous Illustrations. 8vo, Cloth, $4 50; Half Calf, $6 75.

LIVINGSTONE'S ZAMBESI. Narrative of an Expedition to the Zambesi and its Tributaries; and of the Discovery of the Lakes Shirwa and Nyassa. 1858–1864. By DAVID and CHARLES LIVINGSTONE. With Map and Illustrations. 8vo, Cloth, $5 00; Half Calf, $7 25. [*Uniform with Livingstone's "South Africa."*]

LOSSING'S FIELD-BOOK OF THE REVOLUTION. Pictorial Field-Book of the Revolution; or, Illustrations by Pen and Pencil of the History, Biography, Scenery, Relics, and Traditions of the War for Independence. By BENSON J. LOSSING. 2 vols., 8vo, Cloth, $14 00; Sheep, $15 00; Half Calf, $18 00; Full Turkey Morocco, $22 00.

MACAULAY'S HISTORY OF ENGLAND. The History of England from the Accession of James II. By THOMAS BABINGTON MACAULAY. With an original Portrait of the Author. 5 vols., 8vo, Cloth, $10 00; Half Calf, $21 25; 12mo, Cloth, $7 50; Half Calf, $16 25.

MARCY'S ARMY LIFE ON THE BORDER. Thirty Years of Army Life on the Border. Comprising Descriptions of the Indian Nomads of the Plains; Explorations of New Territory; a Trip across the Rocky Mountains in the Winter; Descriptions of the Habits of Different Animals found in the West, and the Methods of Hunting them; with Incidents in the Life of Different Frontier Men, &c., &c. By Brevet Brig.-General R. B. MARCY, U.S.A., Author of "The Prairie Traveller." With numerous Illustrations. 8vo, Cloth, Beveled Edges, $3 00.

BANCROFT'S MISCELLANIES. Literary and Historical Miscellanies. By GEORGE BANCROFT. 8vo, Cloth, $3 00.

BOSWELL'S JOHNSON. The Life of Samuel Johnson, LL.D. Including a Journey to the Hebrides. By JAMES BOSWELL, Esq. A New Edition, with numerous Additions and Notes, by JOHN WILSON CROKER, LL.D., F.R.S. Portrait of Boswell. 2 vols., 8vo, Cloth, $4 00.

DR. OLIN'S LIFE AND LETTERS. 2 vols., 12mo, Cloth, $3 00.

DR. OLIN'S TRAVELS. Travels in Egypt, Arabia Petræa, and the Holy Land. Engravings. 2 vols., 8vo, Cloth, $3 00.

DR. OLIN'S WORKS. The Works of Stephen Olin, D.D., late President of the Wesleyan University. 2 vols., 12mo, Cloth, $3 00.

LAURENCE OLIPHANT'S CHINA AND JAPAN. Narrative of the Earl of Elgin's Mission to China and Japan, in the Years 1857, '58, '59. By LAURENCE OLIPHANT, Private Secretary to Lord Elgin. Illustrations. 8vo, Cloth, $3 50.

MRS. OLIPHANT'S LIFE OF EDWARD IRVING. The Life of Edward Irving, Minister of the National Scotch Church, London. Illustrated by his Journals and Correspondence. By Mrs. OLIPHANT. Portrait. 8vo, Cloth, $3 50.

PAGE'S LA PLATA. La Plata: The Argentine Confederation and Paraguay. Being a Narrative of the Exploration of the Tributaries of the River La Plata and Adjacent Countries, during the Years 1853, '54, '55, and '56, under the orders of the United States Government. By THOMAS J. PAGE, U.S.N., Commander of the Expedition. With Map and numerous Engravings. 8vo, Cloth, $5 00; Half Calf, $7 25.

SHAKSPEARE. The Dramatic Works of William Shakspeare, with the Corrections and Illustrations of Dr. JOHNSON, G. STEEVENS, and others. Revised by ISAAC REED. Engravings. 6 vols., Royal 12mo, Cloth, $9 00; Half Calf, $19 50.

THE POETS OF THE NINETEENTH CENTURY. Selected and Edited by the Rev. ROBERT ARIS WILLMOTT. With English and American Additions, arranged by EVERT A. DUYCKINCK, Editor of "Cyclopædia of American Literature." Comprising Selections from the greatest Authors of the Age. Superbly Illustrated with 132 Engravings from Designs by the most Eminent Artists. In elegant Small 4to form, printed on Superfine Tinted Paper, richly bound in extra Cloth beveled, gilt edges, $6 00; Half Calf, $6 00; Full Turkey Morocco, $10 00.

PRIME'S COINS, MEDALS, AND SEALS. Coins, Medals, and Seals, Ancient and Modern. Illustrated and Described. With a Sketch of the History of Coins and Coinage, Instructions for Young Collectors, Tables of Comparative Rarity, Price-Lists of English and American Coins, Medals, and Tokens, &c., &c. Edited by W. C. PRIME, Author of "Boat Life in Egypt and Nubia," "Tent Life in the Holy Land," &c., &c. 8vo, Cloth, $3 50.

RUSSELL'S MODERN EUROPE. History of Modern Europe, with a View of the Progress of Society, from the Rise of Modern Kingdoms to the Peace of Paris in 1763. By W. RUSSELL. With a Continuance of the History, by WM. JONES. Engravings. 3 vols., 8vo, Cloth, $6 00.

SPEKE'S AFRICA. Journal of the Discovery of the Source of the Nile. By Captain JOHN HANNING SPEKE, Captain H. M. Indian Army, Fellow and Gold Medalist of the Royal Geographical Society, Hon. Corresponding Member and Gold Medalist of the French Geographical Society, &c. With Maps and Portraits and numerous Illustrations, chiefly from Drawings by Captain GRANT. 8vo, Cloth, uniform with Livingstone, Barth, Burton, &c., $4 00; Half Calf, $6 25.

SPRING'S SERMONS. Pulpit Ministrations; or, Sabbath Readings. A Series of Discourses on Christian Doctrine and Duty. By Rev. GARDINER SPRING, D.D., Pastor of the Brick Presbyterian Church in the City of New York. Portrait on Steel. 2 vols., 8vo, Cloth, $6 00.

MISS STRICKLAND'S QUEENS OF SCOTLAND. Lives of the Queens of Scotland and English Princesses connected with the regal Succession of Great Britain. By AGNES STRICKLAND. 8 vols. 12mo, Cloth, $12 00; Half Calf, $26 00.

WILKINSON'S ANCIENT EGYPTIANS. A Popular Account of their Manners and Customs, condensed from his larger Work, with some new Matter. Illustrated with 500 Woodcuts. 2 vols., 12mo, Cloth, $3 50; Half Calf, $7 00.

ADDISON'S COMPLETE WORKS. The Works of Joseph Addison, embracing the whole of the "Spectator." Complete in 3 vols., 8vo, Cloth, $6 00; Half Calf, $12 75.

TICKNOR'S HISTORY OF SPANISH LITERATURE. With Criticisms on the particular Works, and Biographical Notices of prominent Writers. 3 vols., 8vo, Cloth, $5 00.

THE STUDENT'S HISTORIES.

France. Engravings. 12mo, Cloth, $2 00.

Gibbon. Engravings. 12mo, Cloth, $2 00.

Greece. Engravings. 12mo, Cloth, $2 00.

The same, abridged. Engravings. 16mo, Cloth, $1 00.

Hume. Engravings. 12mo, Cloth, $2 00.

Rome. By Liddell. Engravings. 12mo, Cloth, $2 00.

Smaller History of Rome. Engravings. 16mo, Cloth, $1 00.

THOMSON'S LAND AND THE BOOK; or, Biblical Illustrations drawn from the Manners and Customs, the Scenes and the Scenery of the Holy Land. By W. M. THOMSON, D.D., Twenty-five Years a Missionary of the A.B.C.F.M. in Syria and Palestine. With two elaborate Maps of Palestine, an accurate Plan of Jerusalem, and *several Hundred Engravings*, representing the Scenery, Topography, and Productions of the Holy Land, and the Costumes, Manners, and Habits of the People. 2 elegant Large 12mo Volumes, Cloth, $5 00; Half Calf, $8 50.

VÁMBÉRY'S CENTRAL ASIA. Travels in Central Asia. Being the Account of a Journey from Teheran across the Turkoman Desert, on the Eastern Shore of the Caspian, to Khiva, Bokhara, and Samarcand, performed in the Year 1863. By ARMINIUS VÁMBÉRY, Member of the Hungarian Academy of Pesth, by whom he was sent on this Scientific Mission. With Map and Woodcuts. 8vo, Cloth, $4 50; Half Calf, $6 75.

ABBOTT'S HISTORY OF THE FRENCH REVOLUTION. The French Revolution of 1789, as viewed in the Light of Republican Institutions. By JOHN S. C. ABBOTT. With 100 Engravings. 8vo, Cloth, $5 00; Half Calf, $7 25.

ABBOTT'S NAPOLEON BONAPARTE. The History of Napoleon Bonaparte. By JOHN S. C. ABBOTT. With Maps, Woodcuts, and Portraits on Steel. 2 vols., 8vo, Cloth, $10 00; Half Calf, $14 50.

ABBOTT'S NAPOLEON AT ST. HELENA; or, Interesting Anecdotes and Remarkable Conversations of the Emperor during the Five and a Half Years of his Captivity. Collected from the Memorials of Las Casas, O'Meara, Montholon, Antommarchi, and others. By JOHN S. C. ABBOTT. With Illustrations. 8vo, Cloth, $5 00; Half Calf, $7 25.

www.ingramcontent.com/pod-product-compliance
Lightning Source LLC
LaVergne TN
LVHW010138110826
845151LV00002B/380

* 9 7 8 1 4 2 5 5 3 9 0 1 6 *